The Secret Escort

© Alan Zoltie 2021. All Rights Reserved.
Alan Zoltie Publishing inc.
ISBN: 978-1-7374122-1-2

All women should be treated with the respect that all men know they command

Mans natural desire to succeed is greatly surpassed by his desire to destroy everything that is naturally successful.

Prologue

I like to fuck, in fact it became a hobby for me when I was in my late 20's, but that's not the point, the point is, I love sex. Sex is wonderful, it is also scary, crappy, mundane, and more often than not, messy. Overall, my feelings towards sex have kind of numbed over the years, mainly because of the number of cocks I've had inside my pussy. I've seen, fucked and swallowed, small cocks, large cocks, wide cocks and also thin cocks. I have been with white men, black men, brown men and yellow men, along with men who are mixed race and men who have no race, and believe me if there's a cock I haven't seen, albeit shape or size or color, then I beg you to show it to me. I've loved fucking men, lots of men, and sometimes women, since I was 13 years of age. In the beginning it was just a rite of passage, but now, some 40 years on, it's more a passage of rights, a means to an end, a way to survive and purely, other than the odd occasion, a business that I run between my legs instead of at an office. My home is my sanctuary and my clients are the life blood of how I live and choose to spend my time. I am an E$cort by profession, and have been for the past 20 plus years. I am now 57 but just quite how I became an E$cort is really the most incredible, unbelievable story I'm about to tell you, none of it made up, all of it true and completely accurate, with names, dates and places all changed, just to protect those with whom I have had the pleasure, although it's not been pleasurable all of the time, of fucking for those past 20 odd years. My life today is simple. I don't need a lot, and I don't require a lot to survive. I have made great decisions and some very poor ones, since I left high school at 18 and went straight into community college here in Orange Country California, to further my education. I wasn't admitted to any well-known university, and community college was all I could afford. My life though has been interesting, and governed by chance more than by design.

I feel that by relating this story to you, especially young women who are out there, confused and lost in their grasp of exactly what to do with their lives, my experiences will shed some light on what not to do should your choices become desperate, which mine did, although that's a tale for later on in this book. My whole experience of life being an E$cort has led me into places that I rarely, if ever would have ventured. I sometimes think that my life has been wasted, yet there are other times where I believe that I am here for a certain purpose, and that purpose is to pleasure and heal men who are broken or lost. Men who need comfort, men who are just lonely, or indeed, men who are hornier than fuck and don't have the outlet for a release, and are encamped either in a broken marriage or relationship that just isn't working. No matter how they feel, what they do, no matter what they look like or how large or small their cock is, I am there. I have been there, for all who choose to pay, pay my small sum, my fee, my cost of living, to fuck me and to obtain relief from all of the pent-up energy that's inside them, sperm build up that needs to flow freely into this world or just extinguish memories of their last relationship, and, whatever they want, I try to provide, and provide with a smile.

I have been asked so many times, why I do what I do? My answer is always the same. I started out in this profession by accident, and I never left. At times the money was good, at times it was great, but believe me, there have been more bad times than good times, more debt than profit and more grief and stress than happiness. Now, that's not to say I haven't had a blast, of course I have. I have seen and done things that other people only dream of. I have had my fair share of success and sometimes of love too, but in general, my life has been mundane to the extent of being sad, other than on those occasions I mentioned above, and they are few and far between. I'm not looking for sympathy or solace from anyone out there, I am just stating the facts as I feel them.

My family, well, that's another story completely. I have two sisters and a half-brother. My oldest sister knows what I do, but chooses to ignore it, for what reason, I have no idea. Probably embarrassment or jealousy, or both. My other two siblings, and my mother, have no idea. Thank goodness! My father is dead, and my step father is no longer with my mother, so all in all, just like most people on this planet, my family is dysfunctional and self-centered, without being overbearing and demanding. My mother and I still chat every day, but she thinks I work in a different industry, nothing to do with the sex industry. If only she knew! She'd probably die of a heart attack or just die of embarrassment, whichever one got to her first. I love my mother, who doesn't, but our relationship has been strained for many years, probably since she found a letter I wrote to the second guy I fucked when I was about 14 years old, promising him I'd suck his cock and swallow his whole load, while hanging on to his balls and singing. At one point in time, she and my step dad, threw me out the house we all lived in and made me go to live with my older sister, and all because they knew I was out every night fucking boys that they never liked. Again, all for the sake of growing up and becoming a woman, in my humble opinion.

I sat down before I wrote this book and at the request of more than just one person in my life, decided to try and calculate just how many cocks I've fucked in my 57 years on this earth. The total, although staggering to many of you reading this, wasn't too staggering to me. It was around 9,500, which is probably 2000 or 3000 less than I'd imagined. In any event, this book will unravel and divulge many of these 'cock' stories, some funny, some not so funny and some just mind-blowing, for you hopefully not to judge, but to understand the life of an E$cort, here in Orange County California, where everything seems fake, including all the orgasms!

Enjoy.

Blondie

Boyfriends

Believe it or not, I DO have a boyfriend, or at least I did at the time I began writing this book. In fact, over the years working as an E$cort, I've had several. You may ask, 'how's that possible when all I do is fuck strange men?' Why would anyone want to be my boyfriend knowing that I fuck for a living? It's a very valid point, but in truth, this current one in particular, and we will call him Moses, just for laughs, even though he does look like that biblical character depicted in so many portraits, has no fucking clue that I am an E$cort. None whatsoever!

    Moses and I met a long time ago. I used to attend ice hockey games, and he would be there, as part of the Anaheim Ducks cheering squad, a small group of self-named, highly motivated, semi-drunk individuals, who attend Duck games to shout and scream and blow off steam. Only Moses never cheered for anything other than weed, (marijuana), he loves the stuff. He and I became friends, sharing war stories from previous seasons when we both used to attend games as kids and then adults. Moses, when he was 20, got a job as an usher at the Ducks stadium. I didn't know this until one night I showed up and there he was, all uniformed up, showing me to my seat. After that happened, Moses decided that he'd get me tickets for every game, free of charge, as long as I provided a never-ending supply of weed, something I had unlimited access to. This went on for a couple of years, until one night, about 18 months ago, around January of 2018, we decided to become more than just friends, and after yet another Ducks defeat, I took him home and fucked him. It was sooooooooo good! We just fucked all night, about 8 to 9 hours of continual penetration, something I had never done before, nor will I ever do again. The following day, I felt violated, but in a strange, good way, I felt calm, satisfied and incredibly in love. Moses has exceeded all expectations, being possibly THE best kisser, I'd ever met, by a mile. His lips, when they touch mine, just work undeniable magic with my vaginal juices, bringing me from dry to very wet, in a fraction of a second. No idea why or how this works, because it's never quite happened like this before, and as I told you, I have fucked thousands of guys. Anyway, the purpose of telling you this story, and I know you really want to hear all my perverted sex experiences too, is to tell you what happened last night when we were at my home, waiting to leave to go to see a movie. Oh, before I tell you the dirty facts, please note that under normal conditions, even with Moses, I always use lube before penetration, because after having so many cocks inside my very tight vagina, (yes, even after 10,000 cocks, it's very tight), it's kind of easier to use lube for granting men access inside my tight pussy, all of whom are desperate to just fuck me into submission, and not make love or any semblance of love, and for the most part, are useless at sex and unwilling to go through any form of foreplay to turn me on and make me wet. It's usually just 'get it in and cum', then leave. Such is the nature of the E$corting life. Last night for example, I saw this regular client, Bill, and all Bill does is massage my tits, stick two fingers in my cunt and get on top of me with his soft cock. I then have to rub that cock vigorously up and down, trying to make it hard, before he attempts to put it inside me and cum in 20 seconds. We go through the same process once a month, and have done for some years now. Bill has ED, and erection issues have always been his problem, but oh no, he always shows up expecting me to do all the work to arouse that short stubby cock of his, and then once he's done, he basically gets off me, takes the condom to the bathroom, flushes it and leaves, without even a simple thank you or wow, you are the best BLONDIE!! Not that I expect any of my guys to be so polite, but once in a while, it would be nice.

Which brings me back to my afternoon session today with Moses. We were about to leave my home, the car was ready, I was ready and the movie was starting in 30 minutes, and suddenly, as I was walking downstairs to retrieve my car keys, Moses grabbed me from behind, one hand on each tit, turned me around, pulled up my dress as he lay down flat on the stairs and begged me to fuck him. I love this kind of spontaneity, especially with Moses, but even though we've been fucking for over a year, and Moses really makes me wetter than most men can make me feel, we still use lube, just to be safe and to protect my tiny V. Of course, Moses has no idea I am an E$cort and no idea why I really need the lube, but his fascination with my pussy and my pussy's willingness to get wet, still don't erase the fact we need lube. He's kind of well-endowed and as I mentioned, I am kind of tight. With Moses on the ground, half way up the stairs and bent over two or three steps, and me on top of him, legs spread, all I could hear was his huge booming voice," get the lube!" I didn't know what to do, I was stuck between just trying to fit him in and fuck him and laughing until I peed, or killing the moment and running upstairs to my bedroom to find the lube. Without warning, my mind focused back to my date with Bill, from the night before, and within that split second my pussy dried up! She just froze, instantly, with thoughts of Bill and his soft cock running circles around my psyche and playing tricks with my natural sex-drive. I decided there and then, I needed the lube. I ran upstairs, found the jar, ran back down again, applied the lube, fucked Moses and then went to see the movie. We missed the previews, but who cares, the sex was worth it. You probably want to know what Moses thinks I do for a living? Really, he has no idea that I'm an E$cort. He just hasn't got a clue. When I first met him and we began our friendship, long before we were intimate, I told him I was a trust fund baby, living well within my means. He accepted that, just like I accept that I need to fuck guys to make a good living, but Moses, if he ever found out what my real profession was, would dump me in a heartbeat and run. I know this for certain, because of conversations we've had, unrelated to me, but related to my chosen profession, and he has a real aversion to anything connected with the sex industry. I go daily from mercy fuck with my clients, to super great fuck with Moses and believe me, that's the hardest thing on the planet to adjust mentally to. I never believed I would meet a 'Moses', ever. I always thought I'd be limited to client fucking, but hey, things change and miracles happen.

Boyfriends have come and they have gone. Beginning at 13 when I fucked Nigel Bruce, only because I thought I needed to. I'd been on vacation with the family, can't recall where we were, but somewhere like San Diego or Oceanside and I'd come back home to find out that Nigel, the boy I'd kissed when we were 12-years-old behind the bike racks at middle school, was now kissing Haley, my supposed best friend in life. Not only that, I was secretly informed that Nigel and Haley had been 'doing it' and Haley was no longer a virgin. With that in mind, I decided to 'go for it' myself. Why should Haley have all the fun? I took Nigel home one afternoon, on a hot August day in 1977, about a week after school had resumed, got naked in my bedroom, opened my legs and told Nigel in no uncertain terms that if he wanted to keep me as his girlfriend, he needed to do it to me there and then and he needed to do it to me better than he'd done it to Haley. It lasted about 15 seconds, and Nigel, now spent, cleaned up, walked out and was never to be seen again. Typical teenager, running away and bragging to the whole world that he'd 'done it' with me, and that I was no longer a virgin, I was just a slut. It took me a while to get over that. Everywhere I went at school, fingers were pointing. "It's her, yes her" "She's the slut" and so on and so forth. It just rubbed off on me and I carried on, head held high, pretending not to notice. I did, however, receive so many new proposals from boys I never knew existed. They chatted me up on the premise that if I'd fucked Nigel, I'd fuck them too, which, by the way, I never did, well, not all of them. Eddie, another nice-looking guy, or so I thought at the time, came on strong to me and about 4 months after losing my virginity to Nigel. Eddie and I became an item, and I became known as the 'school bike', the girl everyone took out for a ride! Again, at first, that bothered me, but then, as things subsided and my relationship with Eddie grew, tongues stopped wagging and my female friends began to listen to me when I told them that sex was overrated and that they should just get down and dirty and get it out the way. Being a virgin forever was a waste of time, in my humble opinion. And why wouldn't I say that? I was being fucked by a boy, yes, a boy, not a man, who could cum 5 or 6 times inside me in the space of 40 minutes, without too much effort, and I was happy to expose the fact that it was sort of enjoyable. Enjoyable, other than the mess that sex created on my nice clean bedsheets. I wasn't on birth control but I did have this spray filled with spermicide, which, back then, was an alternative contraception method easily hidden from my parents. I am not sure who put me on to this particular method of contraception, but unprotected sex was the order of the day, not only for me, but eventually for all of my friends who'd begun following me into the unspoken world of debauchery and orgasm. My parents, and my friends' parents, knew nothing about our exploits, well, that was until my mother discovered the spermicide can, nestled in the bottom drawer of my closet. When that happened, all Hell broke loose. My mother had remarried by then, and my step-dad wasn't really interested in my sex life, but my mother? Well, you'd have thought she'd lost her own virginity by the way she went off on me the day she found that can. "You whore, you fucking whore", the profanities came spewing from her mouth. I swore to God, right to her face, that the can belonged to my bestie, Sheila Ferguson and that it wasn't mine. My mother didn't believe me, and our relationship descended into a chaotic mix of hallway sex for the next two years. What's hallway sex I hear you ask? That term not only applied to me and my mother, it also applies to all married couples, or those who have been married for 5 years or more. You pass each other in the hallway and one says FUCK YOU, and the other says, NO FUCK YOU! That was my mother and I. No matter who my boyfriend was, no matter how nice he was or how accommodating towards her he became, she hated all of them, and there were many, believe me. As I said, I loved sex, I loved the feeling when a man came inside me, and so I went out and I fucked a lot. Fucking a lot is something that's been prevalent in my life ever since. I thought I was good at sex, if indeed there is a way to be good at it. Since I fucked my third boyfriend Jim and he'd told me exactly that, "you're great at this babe", I believed him, but who really knew if it was me or Jim who was good at it?

    I kept a diary, something I've done all my life, and thank God I did, because some of the things that have happened to me, which you're going to read about, have been worthy, or either cringe worthy, of publication in a novel. My love life has been my WHOLE life. Does that make sense? Everything in my life has been centered around sex for the most part. There was a time when I had a 9 to 5 job, which again, I'll relate to you, but my life has been sex, sex and more sex.

    In this book I am going to tell you more stories about fucking than about love, so look out, here they come.

My Diary

I began keeping a diary almost as soon as I could write or indeed comprehend what was going on around me. My mother and father used to fight with one another, and I think around the age of 3, after they'd moved me and my sister from Detroit to Orange County, the fighting became a daily ritual. At first, I thought it was all my fault, and then, as I grew used to the temper tantrums both my parents were guilty of, I came to terms with the fact that they just didn't get along. I had friends when I was 3, and we all got along, and I knew in my own self what 'getting along' with someone really meant. My parents should never have married and I found out in my later years that they believed the same thing too. When divorce finally arrived, not only was there a certain amount of peace that arrived in my young life, but gratitude too, gratitude to God that I no longer needed to listen to the abuse each parent threw at the other. I started with my diary around that same time, writing seriously, as best as my skill level would allow, the events of each day. It mattered not if they were good, or bad thoughts or experiences, they were all duly noted with vigor and pride. I have kept every diary I've ever written, and at one time, to my determent, my mother actually took a peek inside one of the volumes which lay quite open and unprotected in my bedroom. She just wanted to make sure I wasn't fucking Dave from Huntington Beach, who, by the way, I was. After she'd read this, she had a complete meltdown. Reading some of my accounts of him penetrating me in different holes and in different locations had pushed her over the top. That nearly ruined our relationship for good, but I am glad to say, we mended that broken fence, although it did take many years. My diary to me, is sacred, but I'm going to share some of it with you, especially the early years, because right now, those years, seem so far away and so irrelevant, even though they shaped my life into what I have become, an E$cort.

As I write this, I remember some of the crazy things I used to do with all of the 'lovers' I had at the time, things that have continued to creep into my repertoire even today. A few nights ago, I was with an old client, when I say old, I mean he's been with me for over 15 years. He's married of course, and Asian, not that it makes any difference, and he expects a lot and so he pays a lot. Our average dates are about three hours long for which I receive about $1000 in cash. Sometimes he stays an hour, and I only make $400. I would like to preface this story by going back to my diary. When I opened it up recently, after having not read it for over 25 years, I was caught off guard by just how 'mental' I really was and by all the crazy things I used to do, but then I stopped, and I thought about these past situations a little more and realized, things for me haven't changed. I am still fucking on chairs, on kitchen counters, in cars and often, although not as often as I like, on sandy beaches. I love the feel of the sand on my ass when a guy is inside my pussy banging away. It's just so erotic. The grains of sand become like a vibrator inside my ass crack as the guy thrusts inside my pussy, double the pleasure and double strength orgasms. Without doubt though, I love to fuck in cars more than I like to fuck anywhere else. In the E$corting business, a 'car date' is normally shorter than an 'in call' date, and performed in remote places, obviously, to avoid detection by either the public or law enforcement. I've met ladies who will only perform car dates, one after another after another, to make as much as possible in as short a time as they can. It's just like a cash register for them!

Anyway, my situation in my new home in Orange County, a home that I share with two guys, one gay and one just weird, although I have known both for many years and have never had many issues with either, up until now, has become very strange indeed. The weird guy is complaining constantly about the amount of rent he has to pay, even though we discussed this before we all moved in together, and although not there very often, this week he decided to bring home a house guest, a very beautiful young lady who, he either is, or he isn't fucking. One way or another, I don't really care, it's the fact that suddenly my apartment has gone from having me and one other, my gay friend, and sometimes weird Sam, that's what I will call him, to having me, my gay buddy and weird Sam plus 1. It has cramped my style beyond repair. I can no longer invite who I want to do what I want when I want, and basically, any guy, old or new client, who wants to fuck me in my bed, can now only fuck me in my car or his. My options have become extremely limited, and it's driving me nuts. When I looked in my old diaries, I see I used to have those same issues back then with my parents and siblings, and now, I realize that my problems have followed me for 25 years or more, and at the age of 57, you'd think I'd have outgrown these problems, but oh no, not me. I have inherited everyone else's problems and now not only do I have my own issues, I have to carry my roommates' issues too! Mr. Wong, my Asian client, made the appointment for our usual fucking session, only this time, I couldn't screw him in my own bed because of the room-mate issues. 'What should I tell him?', I asked myself. Well, me being me, and honestly, I have learned over the years how to improvise impeccably, had to come up with an excuse and do it rapidly while the texts were flying back and forth arranging the times and place for our date. Mr. Wong is expectant and horny and Mr. Wong wants to come over within the hour and me, well, I just want the $1000.

My thoughts eased back to my early days and my diary. I remembered one night, I was living in Huntington beach at my sister's place, my parents having thrown me out because of what they'd suspected I was doing in their home, fucking anyone I could whenever I could, and at the time, I was dating this guy, Dave. He lived next door to my sister, a real hunk of a man. I was 15 and he was 20. When we first hooked up our biggest issue was trying to find someplace private to fuck twice or three times a day. He lived with someone, his best buddy Bob, I think, and I was at my sister's place, and so the back seat of his car, a very nice Toyota Corolla, parked in whatever remote place we could find, became our sex haven. I'll tell you more about that later on, but in the meantime, Mr. Wong, remember him, my horny client, was becoming impatient with my lack of response to his texts, and I had to think fast.

Text conversation

Mr. W. "I want to see you in 2 hours. I need to lick you all over. Stick my tongue in your pussy and make you cum. Make the bed. I am soooo horny"

Me "Honey, I am so bored of fucking you in my bed, why don't we try something different?"

Mr. W "Oh now you make hard and harder"

Me "I will swallow you whole if you take me in your car and go down on me!"

Mr. W. "On my way. My erection (which by the way, because of his Asian background, always came out as election when he said it to me in person, so when he typed it, I always spoke it just like him and chuckled), wait for nobody!"

Me "I hope it waits for me honey."

Mr. W. "You too funny"

End of texting.

Problem resolved, and weird roommate with gorgeous woman in his room, saved from the fake screaming and yelling match that normally took place when Mr. W stuck his tongue and then his dick in my vagina. A girl has to act, and I am incredibly good at 'faking it' and I am loud too. Loud enough that Pavarotti would face serious competition if he were still alive! I sing when I cum, often beautiful notes, at least I think they are beautiful, although when I cum I am kind of preoccupied by feelings, but I scream when I fake it and it sounds like a Night in Jail instead of a Nightingale. Honestly, I am terrible at faking it, but for $1000 I will do almost anything, even taking lessons on how to fake it, if that makes the client experience even better.

Mr. W was on his way. My weirdo roommate wasn't going anywhere, and my choice of locations where to park Mr. W's car were limited to either the back end of my complex, or a 35 min drive to a remote beach I know in OC. Mr. W's determination to be satisfied probably won the day, and therefore, the rear end of my complex was the safer quieter and quicker option.

And with that thought, a decision was made, at least by me. No sooner did that decision become final, than my phone rang again and Mr. W. had announced his arrival in my parking lot. Time to become a performer.

Remember, I have known this man for many years, and the routine has always been the same, as it is with most of my clients. Park up outside in the visitor's spaces, text me to tell me you are there, and then I will come out, hug you and bring you inside for a good fucking. Simple and easy and normally drama free. This was going to be different though. The text came through from Mr. W. telling me he was at the front of my building. I was wearing a short dress, no bra of course, and yes, I do think I have amazing tits, the dress being almost see-through. I sauntered outside, handbag in toe, and walked around the corner to where he'd parked his car. As soon as Mr. W. saw me coming, he jumped out of his vehicle, smiling of course, heading towards me and completely ignoring my hand gesticulation to stay just where he was, as he pushed the button on his key-fob to set the alarm system on his car. He was presuming, and rightly so, that we were headed up to my lovely bed for a three-hour fuck session. Wrong, Mr. Wong!

"Stay there!" I shouted, as yet again I held my hand up like a cop directing traffic.

He stopped dead in his tracks,

"I wasn't joking about the car date" I yelled, although I kept my voice quite low in case any of my neighbors were eavesdropping. "You can't come in tonight, Mr. W." I told him, "The place has some issues with ants and they sprayed chemicals all over the upper floor and they told me not to breathe any of it in and wait until tomorrow to return. I might have to find a hotel room."

His face changed color. I think he thought I expected him to pay for that room, something I know he would never do because he always goes home to his wife and kids. I preempted his next question.

"No, I am not suggesting we go to a hotel. I expect we will just have fun in your car"

His face lit up again, relief being the order of the day for him!

"Oh, we go in car?" he said, excitedly.

I gave him that 'DUH', look, rolling my eyes backwards into my head. He understood immediately. His key-fob came out of his pocket, he turned round and hit the unlock button and the doors opened. I got in the passenger side and he got in behind the wheel.

"Where we go?" he asked

Well, it was always a three-hour session with him so I suggested we go behind my complex, just as I'd figured out earlier that evening when our texting back and forth had begun. He was keener than keen to impress, and with his erection almost bulging from his old worn jeans, he hit the accelerator as I guided him to the back side of my complex. Now, bear in mind, my complex isn't that large, and it isn't that private, but there is one spot at the rear end of the lot that backs onto the 73 freeway, which, thank goodness I do not hear from my particular apartment. I suggested we pull in there and then begin. He was more than compliant to do what he was told. He parked the car, we both got out and then re-entered into the back seat of his car, a 2019 Ford SUV. As soon as my backside hit that seat, it began.

Now, on all of my dates, especially with new people who I've never met before, I always get paid up-front before anything begins. No money, no honey!

Mr. W. has been around 15 years or so, and I never ask for money beforehand, he just pays at the end of our session. He's never let me down and the fee is well-known to both of us, $400 for one hour, $1000 for three hours.

My legs had already been spread, and Mr. W. was feasting on my panty-less vagina. He loved to go down on me. On a typical date, he'd lick me into submission several times in the first hour, then he'd fuck me and then he'd repeat the licking well into the third hour. I didn't mind, more tongue and less thrusting, makes an E$cort all wet and bursting!

I was enjoying him immensely, well, maybe not, but he thought I was, and was about to climax for the first time, (I can cum and cum and cum if someone licks my clit properly), when, with my head bent backwards in pleasure, my wetness now streaming and my eyes focused solely on the freeway bridge behind the car, I see this kid on a skateboard, staring, no, ogling, tongue hanging out his mouth, looking right at me through the rear window of the car, about 10 feet above us, motionless, frozen to the spot, smiling and unable to comprehend exactly what he was witnessing. I didn't know what to do. I couldn't stop Mr. W., he was too far into his own demise, licky licky fucky fucky cummy cummy payee payee, and frankly speaking, I was too into what he was doing to really care about the kid. My reaction was to blame my weirdo roommate with the house guest, swearing under my hot panting breath, never to forgive him for this, ever! The kid wouldn't move for what seemed like an eternity, but eventually he got bored and as Mr. W. took out Mr. W. Jnr from beneath his old jeans to cover him in a condom and then fuck me, the kid lost interest and vanished. Mr. W. continued in his usual manner, with his very small penis, fucking me like crazy and then came in less that 5 minutes. He removed his used condom, threw it out of the car's rear window, and then began licking me again. By now, the first hour was long gone, and we were entering hour 2 and then 3. $1000 here we come!

The session over with, Mr. W. handed me the envelope I'd been expecting, THAT envelope, the one with my cash.

I opened it. $400 was all that was in there. WTF??? He got out of the back seat, I was still lying there, trying to re adjust my dress and wipe up all my bodily fluid off his seat, drove the car round to my unit, asked me if I needed anything ese, then opened my door to let me out. No word on why he'd short-changed me, or when I would see him again. I thought back to my diary, remembering how many guys would do this to me when I was 15 and 16. They'd fuck me, leave me and never care less what happened to me after that. I gave Mr. W. the dirtiest of looks. He knew there was an issue, but shrugged it off, got back into the car and drove away. I was $800 down. What should I do?

When I got into my home, I wanted to kill weirdo roommate, I wanted to grab him by the balls and drag him through the apartment until they fell off. Rightly or wrongly, I put the blame for my loss, solely on him, and his stupid house guest. My diary suggested this wasn't the first time that I'd been duped, my head told me that this wouldn't be the last time either. In fact, there have been may times, too many to count, but this one, the one with Mr. W. my trusted client, really hurt, and even afterwards, some three days later, I was still hurting. I received a text from Mr. W. about a week after that session asking why I had a sour face when I'd opened his envelope. I never replied. When he comes around looking for hot pussy next month, perhaps I will tell him then, but perhaps not. I am such a wuss.

Anyway, my diary, yes, THAT diary. I have no idea why I even started to write it. It's so long ago, and my mind suggests I did it because I wanted to keep a sexual record, perhaps unconsciously at the time, and that it might be important one day, at least to me. That day seems to be now. I do recall sitting in one of my old apartments trying to calculate the number of guys I'd fucked. I think I was 34 at the time and in need of some entertainment as I sat eating pizza one evening. The TV was shit, so I turned it off and began making notes, counting men, ex-lovers, sexual partners but I ran out of paper and my pen dried up before I'd even completed that list. I didn't realize then that my diaries were still available to me and just sitting up in an attic waiting to be re-read. When I moved home 6 months later, I found them, but I never read them. It wasn't until I decided, or should I say, until I was persuaded, to write this memoir, that reading my old diaries made any sense to me at all. Well, not that it matters, but when I did finally pick up the very first volume and began recounting, through my very poor use of English language skills, the things I'd written all those years ago, I realized it made sense to articulate some of the things that happened to me way back then because I feel that they shaped my life as it stands today. Maybe, upon reflection, I have always been 'into' sex, either with men or women or both, or maybe I'm fooling myself and I just like the thrill of the chase and the monetary compensation, either way, sex is my life and it seems it always has been. I was crap at school, and even to this day, I read very slowly and my math skills are shit. I wanted to be elsewhere, not sitting in a classroom all day. I do remember that my friends sort of relied on me for any kind of sex education, which I gladly gave them for a small fee, but again, my skills and knowledge were limited at that point in time, although I certainly was an expert at giving blow jobs, which to this day, are my specialty! No one, and I mean NO ONE, gives head like me.

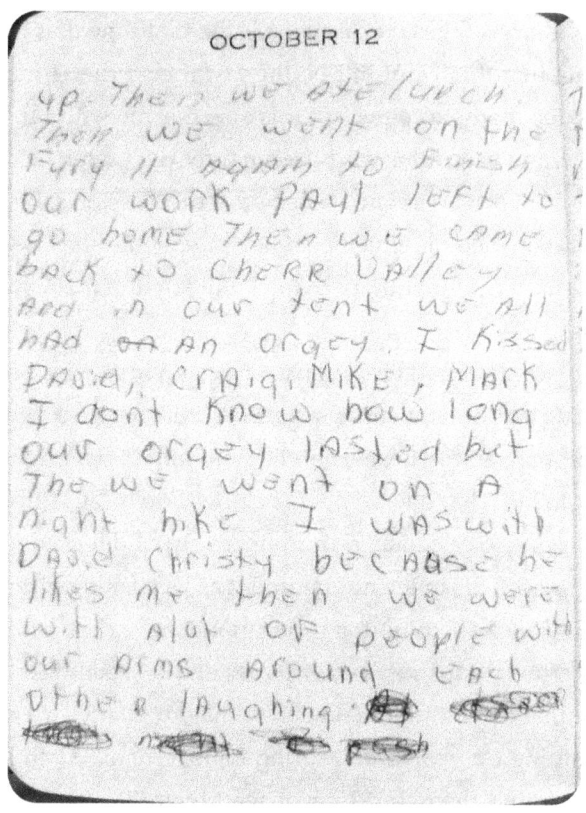

As you can see, to me, kissing was an orgy. Not only could I not spell, not only could I not do math, I didn't really know the meaning of orgy! Kissing several boys in one day was as good as it got. I have sat and read my diary several times recently, and honestly, I feel it's better than a Seinfeld episode. Some of my perspectives in life at that time were naïve to say the least. I remember one day we were all round at my friend Michelle's home and I just wanted to touch Eddie's penis. Eddie was one of my school friends. I sat around all afternoon fantasizing about that day. In the end, he and I fucked, again, we were about 14 years old, so you can only imagine what that felt like.

> DECEMBER 20
> moved in with us. She has
> the first room. Bye
> DEAR DIARY - Dec 19
> I went to Natatlie's with
> Kelly. It was ok we just
> screwed around. Nat. likes
> Bob Erikson I want to
> make out with someone
> Lori made a ramp Randy
> and Eddie were over.
> Carol told me Eddie tried
> to go down her pants but
> she wouldn't let him. But
> he went up her top. Dam
> I wish he liked me. I'd
> go down his pants I
> would. Bye.
> DEAR DIARY Dec. 20
> I got in the shower to go to
> Michella's house. I went
> cross the bridge and Sherri

The thing was, my hormones were running wild. I was into music of all genres and occasionally smoked a joint or two, but only if one of the other kids could find the weed we all craved, but in general, sex was for me, big time and the thrill I craved continuously. My first experience which I told you about earlier in the book when I lost my virginity, was crap, but as the years passed, of course, experience made way for enjoyment and understanding and sex became the thing I wanted to do most. I made a list, about ten years after that diary extract, and I counted back, as best I could, just how many guys I'd fucked from 13 through to 23, remembering that Dave and I were with each other for 6 years, 16 to 22. I got to 176 men, and I know I missed some out. I was wild, totally wild. I even stopped writing my diary because it became too revealing. 176 men! That's a lot of dicks, and many gallons of sperm. All unprotected sex by the way. I was 17 when I fell pregnant for the first and only time in my life. 17 is young, but at the time, when I realized I'd missed two periods, I never thought much about the pregnancy or the state of being pregnant other than I couldn't fit into my tight Levi jeans, which pissed me off more than the thought that I was carrying Dave's baby. I worked at Wendy's at the time, serving burgers and cleaning tables. I lived with my older sister, and it was she who advised me to terminate the pregnancy. But the Levi jeans thing just got to me, as did the situation with my mother and also the man who made me pregnant, Dave. Both were culpable in making me lose my mind. I went into work, the day I realized I was 'up the stick' and after telling Dave, who really didn't give a shit, my mood was fouler than foul. I was cleaning tables, when suddenly I went off the rails. By 'off the rails' I mean I really just lost the plot. I was taking some empty cups off a table and about to throw them into the trash can when the whole idea of being pregnant at 17 and the concept of becoming fat and unwanted at such a young age, drew this horribly psychotic image inside my head. I picked up the trash and just threw it across that Wendy's restaurant, right in front of all our customers who were sitting quietly eating their lunch. The manager, Jerry, came out of his office behind the kitchen. I remember it as if it was yesterday.

"What the heck are you doing BLONDIE?"

He was livid, I was shocked and I was fired on the spot. I had to call my mother to come and collect me. She arrived, I was crying, she was distraught that her pretty little daughter could be so irresponsible and that's when I told her. I just blurted it out. "Dave made me pregnant." With tears running down my face and anger written all over my body, I realized that my mother just didn't give a shit.

Abortion

Before I begin this chapter, I would suggest that all you 'pro-lifers' reading this book, stop reading or just turn to chapter 4. You're not going to like this story. In fact, the one thing I cannot stand here in the USA, is the sheer hypocrisy that lies in our society. During the short time I was pregnant, 'Planned Parenthood" were my saviors and I don't know what I would have done or where I would be now, without the help and counseling they provided. I cannot say enough about how well and how nicely they treated me, and also, how much they were there for me, when others around me just didn't want to know, or ran in opposite directions, as far away from this pregnant bitch, whore, slut, they all used to adore. My surgery was a fuck up, but I will come to that, the people there at the clinic though, well, they were the best. I will never forget them and it saddens me now, today, that all their funding is being taken away by rabid right-wing pro-lifers, most of who have no idea what it's like to be 17, pregnant and abandoned by all who you believed cared about you.

My pants grew tighter, and unprotected sex seemed only natural. Dave and I were bonking day in and night out. It was non-stop sex. His place was our sanctuary, and my mother and step-dad couldn't do anything to stop us. I would often use spermicide cream, but in general, we were too careless and just wanted to fuck each other's brains out, which we did regularly, sometimes two to three times a day. I never thought much about contraception, it just didn't feel right with me, and anyway I was so young and fancy free I just didn't care what happened. The 'withdrawal' method had worked for so long, I thought I was invincible and seriously incapable of ever having any kind of accident, or as I used to say back then, 'oopsie!'.

But then, bang! It happened. At first, denial, then belief, and then, well, then it was just 'oh shit' and a complete meltdown at my place of work. That meltdown had taken weeks to manifest itself to the point of the violence that consumed my insides and my raging hormones just exploded, obviously in the wrong setting and in front of people I should have never disrespected. My full-on tirade, now that I think about it, was so childish and brattish, but probably scary too for those who witnessed it, and I can only imagine what the circumstances would have been if I'd done that in this day and age, the age of social media, instant uploads, phone videos and the wanton desire for 'followers'. I would have probably been jailed or elevated to 'cult' status. Back then, people, I believe were more tolerant, and on that infamous day in Wendy's they all just stared at me as if I was Regan from the Exorcist. I think they found me funny, until all the condiments and empty paper cups began flying at the speed of hate, across that restaurant. When my mother arrived, I was in tears. By the time she left, (I had been fired by then), the whole place knew I was pregnant and I could feel their sympathy oozing from underneath each cheeseburger lying dormant and uneaten on the occupied tables where my audience had sat in fear of their lives, but perhaps grateful for the entertainment they'd received and the story they would relate to all their friends and family that particular evening.

The clinic, and I call it a clinic, but it was more like an office building, in Irvine, was cold and 'lifeless', pardon the pun. We sat, my mother and I, in front of another 12 girls, some younger than me, some older, but all were very alone, even though some had parental or marital support. I was in a daze. I knew I had made a mistake, but surely it wasn't mine alone? Where the fuck was Dave? The answer, nowhere to be found. He'd fucked off, also in denial, telling me to 'get rid of it' and taking no responsibility at all, something he'd eventually regret and apologize for, but only after it was all over and he wanted to fuck me again one evening in that not-too-distant future, when he was feeling horny.

As I sat there, all alone, at least in mind and body, my only thought was "I would be able to fit back into my tight jeans again!". I was so childish and so very innocent in so many different ways, and I was also so vain and selfish, something I grew to understand as I matured. My jeans were the only thing that mattered to me as they wheeled me into the operating room, where within minutes, my pregnancy would end. It didn't take long, and it wasn't that painful, and before I knew it, I was back with mom and ready to go home to begin another chapter in my very sad and careless existence. Or was I?

My conscience was clear, but after 5 days and a call from the clinic, it appeared my fetus wasn't free and clear of the life it never had or expected.

"We can't find any remains proving we actually terminated your pregnancy" they told me. I hadn't a clue what they were trying to tell me. After I handed to phone to my mother, she explained to me that every termination is analyzed in a lab to ensure they'd extrapolated all human remains from the womb. In my case, they couldn't find any proof the fetus had left my womb. I was told in no uncertain terms that I needed to come back in immediately to have a 're-do'!

"You have to be fucking joking!!" I shouted at my mother, as I threw my empty ceramic coffee cup towards our kitchen window, just missing her head by about an inch.

Sure enough, within the hour I was back at the clinic, dragged in screaming by so-called adults who wanted to make sure they hadn't fucked up too much.

"We believe the 'baby' (yes, they called it a baby) is still in your fallopian tubes"

"WTF does that mean?" I asked, as they put me onto the gurney and took me back into that little room where all their equipment lay in wait. I felt like a piece of meat, an experiment, an aberration, and I felt completely let down by life in general.

"Lie back and think of someplace nice, somewhere you love to go" said the voice behind the mask.

And as this vacuum-like noise began to vibrate around the room, I thought of a ride, my favorite ride, at Disneyland, and my mind went blank. It only lasted 2 minutes, but when the lady took her mask off, and I came back round from my most 'happy' of places, I was told they'd terminated my 'baby' and that I could go home to rest.

As I walked out of that clinic for the second time, in front of a new crop of 'unfortunate' mother's to be, I smiled and then I began to cry. My tears were not being shed for my loss, but for the knowledge that I was free to start a new life under new circumstances, and with fresh perspectives. Only that didn't last long, and within days, I was back to my old ways, and more importantly, I was back with Dave. He had no remorse, my mother had nothing but remorse and me? Well, I just wanted to fit into my jeans, never knowing that the opportunity to be a mother myself, had just passed me by. This would be the only time in my life that I carried a child, even though it was only for a few weeks and under the most awful of circumstances, but it would be an event that would leave an indelible mark on my character and more importantly, my soul. I have never returned to that Wendy's, not even to eat, but I'm sure I left a huge part of me there on that day, the day I just lost it.

The Red Onion and Other Joints

When I was in my teens, and then into my early 20's, my friends and I used to frequent a club, close to where I lived, called the Red Onion. The Red Onion was a great place to go and enjoy a few, 'illegal' beers, some shitty food and great rock bands, who would play into the early hours of the night and allow us all to dance our hearts and our teen years, into oblivion. We had so much fun in that place, and fun was the order of the day after my 'baby' mishap. Dave and I were together for about 5 years, and in that period of time, I rarely cheated on him, and I believe that same philosophy applied to him, although I will never really know. Once or twice, I would stray, and once or twice, I enjoyed the 'change of scenery' when I decided to fuck someone else, notably someone I picked up at the Red Onion.

The Red Onion was part of a chain of restaurants, all with the same name, started in the 1940's in Los Angeles and expanding south into Orange County, as the owners franchised out their brand to ten other locations, including Huntington Beach, which is the place I would end up frequenting on a regular basis. It was probably the rowdiest place in the OC, and one of the most infamous, for many reasons I won't get into in this book. My task was always simple, simple until I was 21 at least. I would park up outside, or be driven there by one of my friends. We would go regularly, but only Friday and Saturday nights. I would always be bra-less and either in the shortest of dresses, or in jeans. I do have the most perfect tits by the way, not sure if I mentioned that and as you know, I never wear a bra, so with that in mind, a bra-less, 19- or 20-year-old, with perfect tits and nipples protruding, walking into a club/restaurant, with 2 or 3 females, also dressed to thrill, was, for most of the guys who were in that club purely to pick up a chick and fuck her, the highlight of their weekend. We all looked great, and we looked great ALL of the time. I am a blue eyed blonde, with not only perfect tits, but also great legs and a killer body, so what man wouldn't want to buy me liquor and fuck me? The answer was simple, no man could refuse me, and on most weekends, I drew a lineup of men along the bar, most of whom were handsome 20 somethings and all buff, asking, no, begging to get me what I wanted from a well-stocked bar and then hopefully to get what they wanted after that, which was inside my panties. Some were successful and some were not. Those who failed, would try and try again, because frankly the crowd at the Red Onion was almost the same every weekend for many years. You knew most of the regulars by first name. You knew who had herpes, who was an alcoholic, who was married and who had a big dick. It was just part of the scene, a scene that became very familiar to me and at times, very appealing, both financially and sexually. I was at Junior college, close by the Red Onion, when I began to spend my weekends at the bar, because that's what college kids do. They want to drink, illegally of course, they want to get high and they want to fuck. I was a perfect match for that 'want to' mind set. My ambitions were limited, (by my own choosing), my libido was on fire and my looks carried me anywhere I wanted to go. I could charm the head off any man's penis, with or without having to fuck him. One look at my tits, always exposed in some manner, whether inside or outside my clothing, turned on even the prudish of men. There was one guy in particular who used to sit and ogle me every weekend and he would never offer to buy me a drink or even come over to chat to me. He just sat there staring. This went on for months and I remember one Saturday, after drinking far too much, which seemed to be my MO on most Saturday evenings, I sauntered over to him and asked him flat outright, "would you like to go half with me in a baby?"

The guy, I think his name was Roger, nearly pissed his pants, and he certainly spilled his beer all over the floor but after that he never looked at me again, not once, and his perverted gaze would sit squarely across the other side of the bar for ever more. I had my ways and methods of dealing with morons, and no one, not one person in my group of friends, had more one-line comebacks that were better than mine. I was the queen of the picky-upies and one-liners. I could pick up any guy I wanted by just looking at them quickly and seductively. I could get any man to buy me anything I wanted in that place, with a quick glance at his crotch and a gentle smile, and it took me to a different sexual level at such a young age. I was the queen of that domain, I knew it, and so did all of my friends. I sat down recently and made a list of all the guys I fucked from that restaurant. (Yes, writing this book has encouraged me to produce lots of lists of guys I've fucked. Just out of curiosity of course!) Remembering I was with Dave for a couple of the years I went there, I still managed to bag over 160 others. Quite a feat, and although I remember most of their names, which is even more of a feat, there are still some blanks that I am trying to fill in, and my five-page list, may end up as 6.

Car dates began at the Red Onion, and they never ended. I could go outside into the parking lot with a guy I'd just met, fuck him in the backseat and sometimes on the hood of his car or truck, then go inside, my pussy still dripping from the fucking it just received, and do it all over again with another guy. I was so uncontrollable. I would have competitions with myself to see how many guys would fuck me in the same night and then the following weekend I'd go back and try and beat that record. It meant nothing to me, the sex, that is, nothing at all. It was sex, plain and simple and I loved it. The only difference back then was, I wasn't getting paid by those guys, they just bought me food and drink. The payments would begin later in life, but often I wonder what my financial state would be now, if I'd charged them all back then? I'd be super rich, or perhaps not. I am not good at hanging on to money. It seems to desert me as quickly as it finds me. They, the guys at the Red Onion, used to joke with me. They'd say things like, 'How does a blonde turn the lights off after she has sex?" And in unison, the answer would go flying across the bar room. "She shuts the car door!!"

There were so many other quips just like that one, and I didn't mind at all that the guys thought I was an easy lay. In fact, it empowered me even more to be as outrageous as I could be. My car dates became legendary in that parking lot, and although, when I look back now it seems like a terrible way to live, I think at the time I had more fun then, than I have ever had since. I was carefree, and I was happy, and even happier that my slim fit jeans never grew tight around my waist, ever again.

Some crazy stuff happened in that club and nothing crazier than the time I took on two guys in the back seat of a Ford Mustang, which probably had the smallest back seat of any vehicle on the road at that time. There was one guy on my left and one on my right, both trying to penetrate me at the same time. In the end, and after the car was seemingly on its last legs from all the friction we'd created, both guys just decided to cum all over the rear side windows, leaving me, fool that I was, exiting the car, half naked, and very unsatisfied, sperm dripping all over the tee shirt those guys had stripped me of, a tee shirt they'd removed from my body to expose my tits, but then had used that very same shirt to clean the mess on both windows. Sticky mess? More like a whitewash!!

There was another infamous club nearby, called Confetti's, run along similar lines to the Red Onion. Booze, broads, shitty food and music.

Yes, again, I was famous for my car dates at Confetti's, but on one particular night, and you might want to Google this, I was walking into the club when I bumped into two beautiful women who asked if they could join me and my friends at our usual spot inside. Turned out they were at college nearby and had made a promise to both themselves and their parents that they would be inseparable all night, guaranteeing each other that they would stick together no matter what happened and then return home together, no matter what, hand in hand, just as they'd arrived. Only because of their looks, they were two stunners, they were asking for trouble at Confetti's, where men were outnumbered by women, two to one, and any woman with a nice pair of tits, hell, anything with a pair of any kind of tits, left herself wide open for the pick-up and fuck routine that most of the guys who came to Confetti's were honored to perform. They didn't care what they did. With the odds stacked in their favor, if one woman didn't fuck, another would. We all wanted sex, and we all wanted good looking guys. The guys all wanted to suck and fuck and so battle lines were drawn and the two ladies who walked in with me, it was their first visit, had no idea what they were in for. They'd been warned by someone though, someone who'd been there before them, hence their cautious approach to me at the front door asking for company. I could smell the fear on their breath, but also their excitement too.

My evening started with a bang, not literally, but just as I paid for and collected our first round of drinks, I was approached by this great looking, buff, blond, hunk of a man.

"Wanna dance sweetie? He asked. I didn't, but I told him in no uncertain terms that if he stripped naked outside for me and showed me his dick, I'd consider it! On most occasions, guys don't know what to do when I blurted this out, but on this occasion the guy concerned grabbed me by my arm, pulled me to one side, came right up to my left ear and whispered,

"You have no idea what I will do for a dance with someone I think will be a great fuck"

I was so turned on by his charm and his ability to breathe passion into my left earlobe. This guy was a charmer. I got chills down the back of my neck. After he released my arm, a motion that gave me much needed relief, I began walking back to my table, drink in hand, and wet between my legs.

He followed me over to where my friends and the two girls who'd accompanied us inside the club were sitting, all the time, offering words that were just a complete turn on to me.

When I got to my table, I put the drinks down, and the guy, I think his name was Sean, looked right into the eyes of one of the two ladies who'd come in with me, and pointed.

"You!" she looked up, "You remind me of springtime, please dance with me" It was a demand, not an offer, and as funny as it sounds now, not only was she smitten, I was too!

She accepted, and off they went. I could see out of the corner of my eye that she was happy, but I could also see that her friend, the one left sitting beside us, had a look of trepidation written squarely across her face.

My evening turned into the usual farce, picky uppie and then fuck.

I got home around 3 AM that night, fell asleep and then rose around 10-AM the next morning. I was alone, I think, but had to get showered and dressed because at that point in my life, I owned a candy truck, yes, a candy truck. As if my pussy wasn't sweet enough!! I used to roam the streets of Orange and surrounding areas in that truck, parking up outside office buildings and selling lollypops, bags of hard candies and chocolate bars. I'd been doing that for about a year, making a decent living, picking up the odd handsome guy and generally having some fun, when on this particular morning, the morning after the night before, my route took me past Confetti's night club. Only stop on my weekly roster I really loved, because opposite the club was a huge office complex, filled with people who could really afford to spend big with me. This particular morning, once I'd parked up and locked the van, I entered the office building, expecting my usual crowd of sweet-toothed admirers to line up inside the building and purchase my wares. Once the receptionist made the announcement that I was in the lobby and ready to sell, strangely, nothing happened, and instead of having 40 or 50 people line up to buy candies, only one elderly lady showed up. I didn't know what to do, because, as I mentioned, this had always been one of the better stops on my route, a stop where people would spend upwards of $100 at a time, but on that particular day, nothing!

I never thought too much about it until later that evening when I returned home, having had a more than successful afternoon selling at other points on my route, but deep inside, I knew something hadn't been right at that first stop when no one had showed up to purchase my sweets. I turned on my TV, poured myself a glass of wine, sat down, and then nearly fell off my couch. There, right in front of me was an image, an image I immediately recognized and an image I just couldn't believe. The 6 o'clock news was half way through an article on a murder, not just any murder, but the murder of one of the girls who'd accompanied me into the club the night before. Her picture was right in front of me, emblazoned on my TV set for the whole world to see. I sat down on my sofa in a state of shock and just listened. As I said, you can Google the case, it's horrific, and I don't want to get into the gruesome details in this book, but that girl was mutilated, close by the same office building where no one had showed up that day to buy my candies. The whole scene had been caught on the CCTV cameras that surrounded the building. It turned out the reason no one showed up for me, and I found this out at a later date, was because they were all encamped at the back of the building watching the Police clean up the murder scene. They got him, they knew who he was from all the footage that had been captured on camera, and I knew who he was because he'd try to pick me up before ending up with her, but there I sat thinking, 'shit, that could've been me', shaking like a leaf and unsure of what to do or who to call.

It took me many months to get over that experience, deciding there and then to make the Red Onion my place of call for the foreseeable future, and the only venue for picking up guys. My thoughts and prayers still go out to that young lady. There isn't a day that goes by that I don't think about her, and I hope that her family are doing well and that the guy who killed her is still rotting in jail.

The Galaxy! Oh boy, what a place that turned out to be. Again, a total dive bar, where, back in the day, we could go there, meet people, get high, get drunk and never be judged by anyone. One night I was driving home from one of my 'dates'. The guy had tipped me well and I'd decided to pop into the Galaxy to have a drink and maybe meet some new people. As soon as I sat down at the bar, this guy came up to me and is his southern drawl, offered to buy me a drink. Once I'd made it clear I only fucked for money, he was happy to drive me back to his place to have sex. We arrived around midnight, and when we got to his front door, I could smell an odor, which I thought at first was coming from him, but when he opened his front door, I realized it was coming from inside his home. It was disgusting.

"You got a dead body in there?" I asked him

"Why? Can you smell something?" he replied.

"Are you being serious?" I continued," Dude, your place stinks!"

He couldn't smell anything and was looking at me as though I was stupid.

"There's no way I'm going inside to fuck you. Let's just do it in the car"

So, we did. Right in his driveway. It was over in 4 minutes and he drove me back to the Galaxy, where by now, this Doors tribute band was in full swing and everyone was getting high to the beat of their music. Smelly guy parked up outside, paid me, and then after I got out of his car, drove off in the huff. I decided to go back inside. This club had 7 private rooms on the upper floor and one of those rooms seemed to be empty, or so I thought. I was looking up from the ground floor, the music was blaring and people were bouncing around everywhere, other than in this one room. I decided to go upstairs, walking straight into that 'empty' room, only to find this guy and female partner, going at it on the floor. He was fucking her doggie style, with both of them facing in the direction of the stage on the lower floor. They never saw me come into the room, but when they realized or sensed I was standing right behind them, the guy withdrew, looked at me, smiled and asked if I'd like to make it a threesome.

Why not? Right?

We all went at it, Jim Morrison's lyrics floating in and out of my ears as I was being fucked by this man called Cliff. At that point in time I didn't know his name, but by the time he'd cum inside me, twice to be exact, we were the best of buddies and his girl, Pru, had left for pastures greener.

"Want to go to Vegas with me this weekend?" he blurted.

"Honey, I only fuck for money. You got a freebie, but Vegas will cost you $2000 for the weekend"

"OK" he replied. "I'm in"

Cliff became one of my regulars, telling me, even today, he thinks I have the best pussy he's ever fucked, and he should know because he's been fucking it for many years, and even though he's gone through 3 wives in that time, he's never left me for any other E$scort!

Good times, bad times, but yes, much simpler times. You could say and do what you wanted, within reason, and there was no Woke or Cancel culture, no MeToo and no QAnon. What indeed has happened to our society? Being able to move without the threat of a law suit or someone filming you for the social media account to increase their following? It just didn't happen then, making it easy to be who you really were and not who anyone expected you to be.

It's all going South if you ask me, and I don't think it's ever going back to the way it was. On the other hand, the internet has made my job a lot easier and I'm now more accessible than I ever was.

My Career Path

I went to a local junior college after I left school. It was all I could afford and all I wanted to do at that time, not knowing where I really wanted to go in my life or what career path lay ahead. At no point did I ever believe I'd become an E$cort. In fact, I hadn't any idea what an E$cort even was or what an E$cort did back then. I think I wanted to work in commerce, but honestly, I cannot remember that clearly how or why my career path took the turns that it did.

Wendy's, Burger King and Baskin Robbins, filled my youth with temp jobs during summer vacation breaks from high school, giving me the means to pay for the 'finer' things in life that I really loved. Weed, shoes, more weed and of course, spermicide! Gosh, my sex life was so good back then. I would fuck anyone who looked at me and showed the slightest intentions of liking me. One glance in the right way, and I melted, my pussy opened wide and we went at it. Most of these men ended up being one off fucks, but some, the chosen few, lasted a little while longer.

My first job, real job, and not one where I was cleaning toilets or dirty tables filled with leftovers from fat people who ordered and ate too much but never finished anything, was doing word processing and secretarial assistance for a team at Toshiba America, in Irvine. I'd ended up attending two different junior colleges, both in the Irvine area. The first one, Irvine Valley, taught me the basic skills in word processing and typing and also how to speed read. I left that college after fucking one of the teachers in his car to get a better grade. We were caught in the act and even though I was 18, he got fired and I didn't get a better grade. When I was 19, I transferred to Coastline Community, in Fountain Valley, and decided to pursue my real estate license, which, after some toil and hard graft, I achieved. But, real estate at 19 years of age, or maybe I had just turned 20, wasn't for me. Dave and I were in turmoil. He wanted rid of me and I wanted rid of him. He was fed up with my infatuation in other men and I was sick and tired of his jealousy. It was a certainty that relationship was going to die its very own timid death, the question was simply, when? I dumped him, but I dumped him gently.

"It's fucking done Dave!" I shouted at the top of my voice as we drove through the local Micky D's for a cheeseburger and fries. I think he spilled his coke all over my bra less tits, then begged me to allow him to lick it all up. I was done, and he knew it, and by the time we'd paid and left the confines of that drive through, I'd made him pull over, stop with his begging, I then got out the car and walked off never to set eyes on him again, or so I thought! I needed a job, and I needed one badly. I had skills, more than just cock sucking skills, which I swear to you, are my forte. No one, and I mean nobody on this planet, sucks a cock better than me. I applied for several jobs, all involving secretarial work, and swore inwardly that the first company to offer me employment would be where I would end up. I knew I wasn't gifted in anything other than word processing and sex, so why hang around looking and waiting for that perfect job? I saw no point, and neither did Toshiba, and before I knew it, after just one interview where this man interviewing me kept staring at my nipples, which were on full beam poking through my thin summer dress, stood up and shook my hand with a 'welcome to Toshiba' kind of grin. After such little effort, (I don't think I said more than 2 words at that interview), I got the job! My nipples did all the hard work, something for which I will always be grateful for.

And on that particular day, the day I passed the interview, my working life began in earnest, each day, more mundane than the next and certainly not as good as the last, but a job was a job, and I decided to give it my all, both in and out of the office, something I always believed in. If you're going to do something, do it well and be the best.

Toshiba was a superb company to work for. I was there 6 years in total and honestly, it was a huge error in judgement to leave. If I'd stayed, and yes, I realize everything is clearer with hindsight, I would have been rich by now, not rich beyond my wildest dreams, but certainly very comfortable and in a lot more of a secure position financially than I am in right now. My daily tasks were quite mundane and honestly the job was easy to do, but when, after 5 years my friend

Susan decided to start sending out her resume to other corporations, I too like the sheep I was, began to do the same thing. The grass is always greener, right? Around that time, Sean, a guy I'd met at Toshiba about a year earlier, started to take a real interest in my tits. He would follow me all over the office, gazing endlessly at my nipples, both of which were left to roam freely under my thin and skimpy dresses. After I left, I was told they were the talk of the office on a daily basis. Sean, innocent Mormon that he was, just couldn't take his eyes off them, until one day, as boldly as I could, I walked up to him in the middle of Toshiba's kitchen/eating room where we all went to make coffee, chat, consume lunches or just hang around to have a break, and said to him, "Want to fuck me and my titties Sean?"

Poor guy almost fainted, went redder than a beetroot, then calmed down enough for us to both laugh it off. We decided there and then to go on a date, which hopefully would fulfill all of Sean's fantasies.

Sean, being a Mormon, had never been on a date, and the guy was in his mid 20's! This was something I'd found hard to believe, but sometimes the real truth is often hard to fathom, and after deciding he'd take me for dinner one evening, we had the most interesting chat over a steak and fries at one of our local hostelries.

"You've never kissed anyone?" I berated him. We were both on our third alcoholic beverage by this time. At least I was, I'm not sure Sean actually drank anything. I was suffering from a yeast infection that evening, and was trying to flush it out by drinking one beer after another. Sean was mesmerized by my tits; I could see his eyes venturing south towards them every time there was a pregnant pause in our conversation. Eventually I just went for it.

"Come on Sean, admit it, you've never had sex, you've never kissed any woman, and you've never looked at a porno movie, so with your eyes firmly on my tits for the past 6 months, what would you like to do to me?" "I can't have sex until I am married. It's my faiths requirement that I remain a virgin until I find the right woman to settle down with" he replied, "but," he paused, "I WOULD love to go down on you" he said, as he smiled while looking incredibly embarrassed.

"What would you know about going down on anyone Sean?" I asked him, knowing all the time he was dying from sexual frustration.

"Just would like to try it" he said, quite lamely.

Knowing I had a yeast infection kind of put the kybosh on that idea, but the look on his oh so innocent face, and the want that was written in his eyes, made me reconsider.

"OK Sean, let's get out of here and go somewhere where you and I can get closer." Sean limped out of the restaurant with a huge erection bulging from between his legs, visible from 300 yards to anyone who cared to gaze at his crotch. He was so excited and ever so nervous, I thought he was going to cum in his pants before we'd ever reached the exit door. We got to his car, and I unzipped his pants and grabbed his balls, and before I knew it, the rear car door was flung open and we were entwined as one on his back seat. I was undressing him, and he was undressing me, until, when both of us were naked, he paused and sat straight up, his erection, showing no signs of retreating.

"You going to fuck me?" I asked

"No, I can't" he was stammering as he said this.

"Well, big boy, what are you going to do?"

He pushed me back down and went at it with his tongue, he was inside my vagina and his tongue was performing tricks on my pussy the way I thought his penis should. I knew there was an odor of sorts coming from my yeast infection, but Sean didn't seem to care and after 25 long and wonderful minutes, he brought me to climax like the pro he was aiming to be, using his fingers to finish the job.

"Where did you learn to do that? I asked him, as he lay back on the rear seat smiling like a Cheshire cat.

"My mother!" he quipped, and we both laughed.

He was happy, I was happy and Sean never stopped smiling for the next three months That was all the time we had left together before my resume was picked up by another company and I left Toshiba for pastures new. I never did understand how Sean wasn't turned off by the smell of my yeast infection, but I did understand that he fulfilled a lifetime ambition by sucking on my tits and then making me cum with his tongue and fingers. I often wonder what became of that man. I'm sure he's still a virgin, but if not, I hope he found someone who smelled better than I did that day.

My life then took a strange turn. I went to work for a company involved in real estate, and just as I mentioned earlier, pastures new were not often the pastures green. I ended up stuck in a cubby hole of an office in San Jose, (which was 350 miles north of the OC), commuting each week from Orange County. I hated it, and all I did was type reports. It was so boring and I began very quickly to regret that I'd left Toshiba. Again, I started to send out my resume and low and behold, within a week, I got another job offer, this time from a company based about 5 minutes from where I lived, in Costa Mesa. Same idea, property management, but their offering was much more attractive and lucrative than the company I was about to leave. I found solace in the learning experience I was given, leading to prospects, both financial and promotion, that my last company would never have offered.

I had no office romances at either of the two companies I just mentioned, mainly because my sex life outside of work was in full swing. I was sleeping with at least 1 different guy every 4 to 5 days, and often more. My steady relationships were lasting about 3 months, but even then, I found myself straying and shagging other men while trying hard to keep up appearances with those who wanted more steadiness from the romantic side of life. That wasn't for me. I was far too wild to remain faithful to anyone, something I was about to find out would be to my benefit in later years, when E$corting came to the forefront of my career path.

I was 2 years into this job, and I was quite enjoying it, but yet again, was becoming restless on more than the odd occasion. In life, some things just happen, and in my life in particular, that 'other' thing seems to just happen all the time. We used to have this lady show up every two weeks to the office lobby. She sold candies. She was the representative of a Colorado corporation called Mountain Man Nut and Fruit Company. I loved her, her name was Wilma, and she liked me. We'd chat for a while when she'd show up with her delicious selection of sweet treats for us all to taste, and hopefully purchase. She'd have a line of people all waiting to be served and as her visits grew more frequent, our friendship became quite solid. Wilma and I shared a passion for men, and we'd gossip endlessly about who we'd fucked or who we wanted to go out with. I used to set her up with guys from my office, and she'd end up thanking me by giving me free candies if she slept with them, which was more often than not. And then, one afternoon, with my sugar craving at its peak, she never showed up as planned. I had her arrival dates all marked out in my calendar, months in advance, in order to ensure the continuity of those delicious treats on my desk, treats which I just adored. On this particular afternoon however, she just didn't show, nor did she show up 2 weeks later when her next visit was due, and I began to worry.

I called Mountain Man and asked what had happened to her. I knew she was making great money, (she'd been very candid with me about her takings and profits when we were sitting chatting one afternoon, showing me just how much she made weekly) and I also knew she loved the job. Mountain Man gave out specific routes to all its agents, mainly women, split up in Zip code fashion to avoid cross pollination of all these office complex's spread across the OC. Wilma of course had the route that came into my office building, but the guy on the other end of the phone told me she'd vanished without word, leaving them high and dry, and that they were actively trying to fill that route with another employee.

"I'll do it!" I shouted at him down the phone.

"You will?" he replied.

And so it began. I became one of 8 females representing Mountain Man in Orange County California. I had training, I had a van, I had a storage unit, I had a sales route and I had a new life. Freedom! Freedom from the daily grind of 9 to 5. Freedom from a boring office job, and best of all, freedom the dress and behave any way I wanted, with clients I would come to adore and who adored me in return.

My route took me to my old company. I'd successfully replaced Wilma, and for the next couple of years, my pussy wasn't the only sweet thing in the OC! People just loved me. I had lines forming outside all the office buildings I serviced, in anticipation of my arrival. I had men by the dozen, just ogling me and my great tits, and more importantly, I had them spending thousands of dollars on sweet treats they didn't really want or need. I had one guy in particular, I think he was in insurance, and he'd come to my 'party' every two weeks, in the reception area of the office building where he rented a room, and spend $1000 just to fill up the jar on his desk. He was a one-man band, so I have no idea what he did with all that candy, but I do know that he tried to date me for over a year, until he got the message that I just didn't fancy him. Once he realized that, his purchases fell by 90%! It's a shame really, because I wanted to fuck him, but my conscience wouldn't let me, which is hilarious considering all the other crap I was into at the time. Many men would flirt with me, and even some women, and many would fail in their attempts to bed me. I was so into fucking, but not with any of the people I met on my route. After all, they were clients, and mixing business with pleasure? Well, at that point in time, and for what reason, I do not know or recall, but my boundaries were rather strict.

The candy business soon took its toll on my psyche and my personal life and after 4 years running around Orange County in my van, I decided it was time to bail and to try something else. I had no idea what that something else might be, and I also didn't want to just give up my candy route for nothing. I put an Ad in a local paper trying to sell my route, and within days I had a buyer. After four years of toil my route was worth a whopping $1000, which not only made me feel sad and worthless, it wasn't enough money to even put a dent in what I owed. My debts were large and completely unaffordable and my ambitions were burning a hole in my head. I took the $1000, pocketed that cash and went home and opened the yellow pages to find another job. Around that time, stripograms were the rage. Remember them? People would have parties, order a stripper, who came dressed as a cop, the birthday boy thought he was being arrested, carried off for some bogus crime he never committed, and then suddenly the cop would undress and bare all, giving the birthday boy the surprise of his life.

I knew I could do this and I'd also heard that there was huge money to be made doing that particular job, stripping, which I knew I'd be good at. Just ask the 150 odd guys I'd fucked. I had seen one or two performers at birthdays I'd attended, and thought, why not?

Yellow pages opened at Entertainment, and eyes fixed on one Ad in particular, I picked up the phone. That Ad, which would change my life forever, was emblazoned in Red and simply read, Entertainers Required

I'm Not A Hooker

I was cautious when I picked up the phone to dial that number, but also extremely excited and a little naïve

"I saw your Ad in Yellow Pages" I said, as the lady with an extremely nasally voice answered the phone with a simple "yes, how can I help?"

I honestly expected them to be friendlier, after all, weren't they supposed to be a 'party' company? Sending nice people out to do funny things for celebrations?

"Name, and age please" was all she said.

I replied, and she continued.

"What do you look like? Describe yourself"

And I did.

"Meet me at Denny's (a restaurant that was close to my home) at 2 PM please and dress nicely. After that I will decide on how we proceed, if we proceed"

"What's the job?" I enquired

"Parties" was all she said.

Her voice sounded so weird, as if she was holding her nose while she spoke. When I put the phone down, I couldn't stop laughing because she sounded just like a cartoon character, and one that could be on any Loony Tunes show.

I arrived at Denny's a little early. I didn't know what this woman looked like, but she'd insisted she'd find me. It wasn't going to be difficult, the restaurant seated around 100 people and I was the only 20 something blue-eyed blonde sitting at a table. Everyone else, and there were only around 15 others', was in there mid 60's!

Her name was Sandy, and she arrived just after 2. I knew who she was as soon as she walked in the door. Mid 40's, but kind of dated the way she dressed. Bleached blonde hair, glasses, a frown on a face that looked like it could use a good iron to take all the creases out and bright red lipstick that could have made her visible from the moon, it was brighter than bright.

She spotted me, of course, from the moment her eyes looked up from the floor she seemed to be continually gazing at, though for what reason she was doing this, I would never know. It was as if she wanted to remain anonymous as she walked through the restaurant towards me.

"BLONDIE?" she asked

I wanted to say, "well duh!" because who the heck else in that place even came close to resembling the description I'd given her, but I politely stood and shook her hand.

There would be no small talk.

"Well, aren't you the pretty one?" she noted, without even the semblance of a 'hello, how are you?' coming from beneath those bright red lips.

"Follow me!" It was a command, not a request.

And without too much more to think about, she stood up and walked towards the bathroom. I followed like a puppy dog, all the time wondering what the fuck was going on. We entered the ladies, and she locked the door.

"Strip!" Yet another command.

I stripped down to my panties, obviously I didn't have a bra on, as I already told you, I never wear one.

"Perfect tits, great body" she looked me up and down. "Dress!" she commanded.

My audition seemed to be over, but what the fuck had that audition been for? I was about to find out.

We left the bathroom and headed back to a table. We sat. Then the questions began to flow.

"Married?" she asked

"No"

"Boyfriends?"

"Several"

"Kids?"

"No"

"You like sex?"

"Yes" but as I responded to her questions, I was curious why she'd asked them in the first place.

"Ever had an STD?"

"No"

"Been checked by a doctor?"

"Yes"

"Ever been paid for having sex?"

"No"

"Would you like to be paid for having sex?"

And that's when the penny dropped. This was an interview to become a prostitute, and she was the 'pimp'.

I was on the verge of walking out, but she could tell by the look that had come up on my face that was the case and as she read my mind she uttered the following words, words that made me stay in my seat and words that changed the rest of my life.

"You're not going to be a hooker darling; you are going to become an E$cort. Do you know what an E$cort is?"

I had no idea, and so I told her that I didn't. She began to explain.

Sandy had this very annoying habit of repeating herself. She would ask the same questions over and over again, but for the purpose of telling this story, I have vied away from repeating them like she did because I think you would find it very frustrating to read everything twice over. But believe me, by the time we'd arrived at this explanation of 'E$cort' I was frustrated beyond belief with her repetition.

"An E$cort my dear, is a lover, a friend, a companion, a muse, all wrapped up in one beautiful package, which you are, and then offered to very rich men for their private entertainment, either for an hour or for longer periods of time, depending on how long they would like to spend with you. You are not a hooker, a whore, a prostitute, you are a very approachable young lady who deserves to be paid for the use of your assets, which consist of great tits, a tight pussy and super conversation. You will go on nice dates to nice places with nice men and have a nice time. You will be treated like the queen you always thought you were and you will be paid handsomely for doing so. I get to set the rates, make the bookings, vet the clients and you do the easy part, drinking, eating and sleeping with whoever I decide is best suited to you. You will go on dates with thin men, fat men, black men, white men, Catholics, Jews and anything in between. You will collect the cash, after the date, and then you will pay me. Am I making myself clear? Any questions?" I sat and thought about this for a few seconds.

"So, this isn't a stripping job?" I must have sounded so meek and naïve to her, which would have also been evident on the dumb expression I had on my face. She laughed, and then began again.

"What part of 'E$cort' didn't you understand? If you'd like to walk away right now, feel free to do so, but honestly darling, with your looks, you'll make a small fortune"

"How much?" I asked

"We, as in my company, do all the bookings, and you get paid for fucking the clients. Although honestly, some guys don't want to fuck, but that's another conversation. We ask $300 per hour from each client, I get 40% and you get 60%"

I did the math.

"How many clients per day do I see?"

"Depends on how successful you become. In the beginning it's going to be one or two but if you're good at this, and your clients repeat and then tell their friends, I think you can probably see 4 to 5 a day." This to me was a 'no-brainer'

Getting paid to fuck was really a dream. Inside my head I had already thought about the 150 plus guys I'd fucked in my life and the math at $300 per fuck per head was mind-blowing.

"I'm in!" I told her, with a certain amount of enthusiasm oozing from my dollar infused veins. And with that, the meeting ended and Sandy, after repeating herself another 5 times, told me she'd be in touch with the finer details in the next couple of days. As she left and we hugged, she said to me

"With your looks sweetie, you'll be rich within 3 years."

As I drove home, still in a daze and still doing math in my head, all I could think of was 'what am I going to tell my parents and sister?'

Pictures and a Date

Sandy called me 48 hours later. I had my first date. I was both excited and very nervous, but hey, it was just sex. My only issues, mental issues, focused on the great unknown. What if the guy was smelly, ugly, dirty, or just plain boring? Did it really matter? I thought about this some more and in the end, I decided to cast all aspersions to one side of my brain, and focus on the financial compensation and windfall that was about to enter my rather baron bank account and hopefully improve my frugal lifestyle. The math, again I went over and over this in my own head, was mind-blowing. I figured that if Sandy got me a minimum of two dates a day, and I worked only 5 days a week, I was going to make more in 3 months than I made in a whole year being a PA! I would be so happy if this actually happened, but back then, concentrating on the penis ahead, the unknown penis of a man I had never met before, I was gearing up for a worst-case scenario, a date I was beginning to dread, and a date that I may just run away from. As the time to meet up with him drew closer and closer, my silent trepidations became louder and louder.

Sandy had promised that she'd take pictures of me so that potential clients would be able to ogle me before they fucked me.

"Part of the fun is they masturbate with your picture and build up this incredible desire to see you in person. Most of them fantasize about the woman they are going to fuck, before they actually fuck them, and that makes for some very interesting phone calls" Sandy had said.

She'd wanted a head shot, with my face blurred out to protect my privacy. A full body shot, in a bikini, and one that was naked but with my pussy blurred out to avoid breaking any pornographic laws and also to tease any prospective clients. She also wanted some sexy poses in lingerie and high heels, all of which I duly obliged her with. The 'fun' part was now over, and I felt like a million dollars, (photography can do that to a woman), and so, without too much more fear, I drove to my first date, scheduled to take place in a hotel room near John Wayne Airport in Orange County.

Remembering, in those days I drove an old banged up Toyota Camry, when I arrived at the hotel, I had to find the self-parking garage, I didn't want any Valet to see me or to drive my beaten-up wreck of a car. Discretion, I had been warned, was of the utmost importance. I was instructed not to bring any unwanted attention to either myself or the client. There were very few people with cell phones in those days and when I arrived at the hotel, I already been advised of the room number to go to. The client had given Sandy all the relevant info required during her very thorough vetting process, and all I had to do was follow instructions. I was told to look nice, but not to dress too provocatively, and to never bring attention to myself when sauntering through hotel lobbies. With my naturally bleach blonde hair, something that makes me stand out anyway, it would always be hard to keep a low profile because most men and women are really attracted to that facet of my body, a fact of life, fortunately! My blonde locks have taken me through more closed doors than any other part of my anatomy, well, other than my great tits! And so, all dressed up, with a little handbag under my arm, mid-range heels on my feet, a rather short skirt and a see-through blouse and shawl, which covered my bra-less tits, I entered the hotel lobby and made my way, as stealthily as possible to the elevator. My new life was about to begin with a bang!

I knocked on his door, he answered, we spoke for a few seconds, he paid me, we fucked, I left. That was it! All my concerns were for nothing. It was simple, beyond easy and it lasted less than 35 minutes. I wish I could sit here today and tell you a wonderful story about how he fucked me or how he smelled or how he was a gentleman, but it was completely uneventful, and, thank goodness, it was over. I was no longer an E$cort virgin, I had been christened and it had been one of the most uneventful experiences of my life, other than I had made $300, $120 of which would go to Sandy. I felt rewarded and yet I felt deflated, only because it had been so easy, so incredibly mundane and I hadn't suffered one little bit, even mentally. I'd left the hotel having been fucked by a complete stranger who I'd probably never see again, and never did. I told myself I should have done this job years ago, the math from the money I could have made in my 20's was really burning a hole in my pocket and in my head, but oh well, this was going to be my new life and I was determined that I would get rich from living it. I had no ties, no ambition to be married or to have kids and I was ready to fuck my brains out until I had enough cash to be comfortable for the rest of my days. Oh, the best plans of mice and men, as they say! It just hasn't worked out that way, but you'll discover that as you read on.

Things changed on my very next date. Sandy hooked me up with 2 guys at another hotel, this time it was one of the best hotels in OC, I won't name names, but there's a spectacular bird that skims the oceans in CA, and probably in many other places, and the hotel was named after this bird. Anyway, the call with Sandy had been clear,

"There are 2 guys, in 2 rooms, both adjoining, and they both want to 'play' with you. Bring all your toys and plenty lube because I think you're going to be fucked from here to LA and back, at least twice!"

She was full of enthusiasm when she called and after she'd told me how much these guys were going to pay me, so was I. I could earn in 2 hours what it had taken me a month to earn at Toshiba.

I prepared in the way only I could prepare. I bathed, and washed my hair. I dressed to thrill and I smelled great. My little overnight bag was packed with all my great toys, toys for men and toys for women, because I didn't know what kind of fetish these guys would have or exactly what they would want to do with me, and it was better to be prepared than to arrive without the appropriate 'tools of the trade'. Oh, and I also had my bottle of Moist Lube. That bottle, oh boy, shaped like the best vibrator, only better. I never went anywhere without it, and by the way, it is THE best lube on the market, and one that I swear by. I swear by Moist for two reasons.

1, when applied, no matter how dry or turned off I might be, it allows any sized penis to enter me effortlessly.

2, the bottle acts as a sex toy and is a perfect fit inside my vagina when a vibrator just won't cut it.

I often thought I should be a poster child for Moist, my slogan being,

"Moist gets me through every dry spell"

Well, the older I got, the more Moist I used, and I honestly never use any other brand, so Moist, if you're reading this, call me, my agent is ready and willing to make a deal!

It was time to leave my home and time to have fun. I drove down 55, the local freeway, towards the beach, all the time thinking, 'I hope this is better than the first date I had', but also realizing that this business might be fickle and one had to take what one was given. If it was a baker, a butcher or a candlestick maker, or even a rich preppy type billionaire, they all had the same dick and its only variance was in size and shape and whether they could use it or not.

Arriving at the hotel, I parked up, there was lots of self-parking, and I took my bag out of the trunk, put on my best smile and headed towards the reception area. Again, I was given a time and a room number to go to, and as per usual, I was bang on the money as the clock stuck 9 PM.

5 floors up, turn left and knock on the door.

He answered.

I entered.

The second guy was there, inside the room.

Small talk, check around for any sign of law enforcement, and then down to business.

Both guys were straight, I could tell, and the second guy was in an adjoining room. The door was open to that room and I could see clearly inside it, but no matter the view, an up-close inspection was called for, just in case!

I marched inside, followed by number 2. Number 1 stayed put.

The room was clear, in my opinion, but you just never know, so a further look behind a closed bathroom door and then a little peek outside the window onto the balcony, and I was done.

"Satisfied?" they asked in unison

I was.

Down to business.

"Right guys, what's it to be?" I asked

"Threesome!" they shouted back in unison.

"Money upfront please"

And with that command, a wad of $100 bills was laid on the table. I'd not seen that much cash since I was selling candies, and in fact, after I counted it, when our session was over, I think it was my largest daily take of all time, and to this day, it still is.

These guys were game, and were up for a great time. We began.

"Drink?" number 1 offered

"Yes, make it a large tequila, I need to fit both of you inside me at some point so relaxation is vital" I joked.

Number 2 lost his smile. "WTF?" I thought to myself, and presumed that somewhere in the not-too-distant future, we might have an issue.

We drank, they began kissing me and undressing me, and I had 4 hands all over me. It was fantastic. I was sucking number 1's dick while number 2 went down on me, and I was thinking at that point that lube would not be required. I was so into it. We started to fuck. Number 1 led the way, but number 2 was soft, and couldn't get hard.

"Oh, Oh, do we have a problem?" I asked him.

He got all pissy and sort of went into a huff. At the same time he was going all huffy on me, he was trying hard with his right hand to rectify his softness by playing a 'five finger boogie', a tune I'd always known to be an effective remedy for most men with issues. "Come on honey, don't be shy, be hard" I told him. But it wasn't working. Meanwhile, number 1 was banging my pussy hard and with so much vigor, I thought he or I would pass out before I climaxed, which had crossed my mind several times in the first few minutes of the pounding he was providing. He fucked like an animal. Number 2, in the meantime, made a request.

"Can you masturbate for me?"

"Sure honey, whatever works for you. I am here to please"

I watched closely as number 1 pulled out of my vagina, trying hard not to be annoyed that his fun was being interrupted, and as soon as he was clear, the Moist bottle was out of my bag and I began doing tricks with it, tricks that neither of them had ever seen before, well, certainly not in person. That bottle is just the right shape and size and before I knew it, number 2 was turned on like a light bulb and ready to fuck. Number 1 however, had sort of lost his urge, and seeing him look at number 2 with a certain amount of angst and disdain, made me even more determined to get him back up and running to ensure one of them could be in my ass and the other in my vagina, simultaneously! Commonly known in the trade as a DP, double penetration. I sauntered over to number 1, took his cock in my mouth and hey bingo! We all went at it again. We had sex in the first room, then in the second room, then on the couch in the first room, and the bath in the second room and it went on and on and on. We fucked until 4 AM, when, at that point in time, I had blisters coming from my knees from kneeling down on the carpet to be fucked doggie style, and my vagina was so red raw, I didn't think I'd have sex again for a month, if ever!

These guys were wild, and so was I. It had been to the best sex I'd ever had, up to that point in my life.

At 4 AM, after we stopped, I asked them if they wanted to go again, but if they did, they'd have to pay me more money. They agreed, but wanted me to stay with them, a kind of MFM sandwich in bed, for a few hours to let them recover. We slept for 5 hours and at 9 AM, the party started again, but this time, the two guys were spent, and we didn't go that long. Long enough for one of them to cum in my mouth, but again, number 2 had been rendered useless. He kept pleading for me to get out that Moist bottle, but by that time, my pussy couldn't take another orgasm, even if they'd both put down $5000 in cash. I was shot, my pussy was shot and my mind had been blown, just like my clit!

We all showered and dressed and the guys invited me for breakfast. We ate together, all still half drunk, and then we parted ways. As I was leaving, number 2 followed me out to my car and asked,

"Hey BLONDIE, any chance I can have that Moist bottle?"

I couldn't believe it, but in the interest of letting his right-hand rest and a bottle do all the work, I surrendered it with much love and then gave him a kiss on the cheek. I got in my car, drove home and slept for 22 hours straight. It had been one of the wildest experiences of my entire life and I'd loved every minute of it, thinking that if this was how E$corting was going to be, my life was going to turn out perfect, and I'd be a happy bunny for many years to come.

I called Sandy before I fell asleep and reported back. I never told her about the 'extra' payment, I didn't think that was any of her business, but in the long run, that was a mistake, and one that would come back and haunt me in the future.

I saw these 2 guys just that one time, and to this day, I have never heard from them again. I didn't know if they were friends, work mates or brothers, but it didn't matter. I satisfied their every desire, I think!

I need to tell you that while I am recalling all of these stories, it's like talking to my psychoanalyst, going through my life story in front of a mirror, remembering the good, and the bad, although there have definitely been far more good times than bad, I think! But what this is doing is bringing me to a point and place of guilt over Moses.

Moses, the love of my life since this time last year, my latest steady boyfriend. The more I recall, the more I feel guilty over this relationship between him and I, a relationship that's relatively new. I keep thinking about Moses and how I've known him for so many years, although only intimately for a year and a half, but how much I like him and how he knows nothing about what I do. When I write these stories, each one seemingly better or worse than the next, Moses is always on my mind, and it's driving me insane. What would he do if he realized this was the real me? An E$cort, fucking day and night behind his back, and then fucking him. I just don't know. I have told him, because he asked, that I made a ton of money on the stock market and don't need to work, but I'm not sure how long that story will hold. The crux of the matter is, when I realize how many guys I've serviced, Moses, for what it's worth, seems special to me. He's never asked me for anything, and he gives me everything I need in life, and when writing this book, I simply wonder, 'where had Moses been all of my life and why am I still doing this now I've found him?' More about Moses will follow, but it's very strange how my thoughts go back and forth between the past and present, leaving me with pangs of guilt and a lot of pleasure too.

Back to my real job though and another current client.

Mr. Wong came over last night, something he does once a month as I mentioned earlier, and as per usual, Mr. Wong loves his cunalingus. My roommates were home, it was 10 PM. I have had issues with roommates over the past couple of months and again, if you recall, my last date with Mr. Wong, ended up in the car, and not in my home. "Fuck it" I thought, when he called me last night, "if I can't entertain in my own home, what's the point?" He arrived around 8.45, and he brought with him two of my all-time favorites, Wendy's spicey chicken sandwiches and beer, Miller Lite. He snuck in through the back door, my roommates were in their own rooms. I opened the door to my bedroom, and kind of 'threw' him into the room and onto my bed. Remember, I've known him many years and can do this to him without much of a reaction. I shut the door, and yes, I thought of Moses. I'd just spent the most amazing weekend with Moses, great sex, great conversation and more great sex, and now, well, now I was about to fuck Mr. Wong, and fuck him for a measly $400. I hadn't worked that month so when I took the booking I only did so for the money, and of course because Wong was a regular who I know would be pissed if I refused to see him. Not that I haven't turned him down in the past, it's just I can tell from his voice when he's really in need of a release and when he just wants to fuck because he's bored. On this particular night, he needed a release, I could tell when I spoke with him, and so I obliged. I have other clients like this. One guy, Jim, from the local car repair shop, likes to fuck me on Fridays, and when he fucks me, on top and in front of all his tools, he loves to cum on one of his car mechanics towels. Disgusting I know, but that's his thing. And not only that, he cums more than any other man I have ever met, just gallons and gallons. Anyway, when he calls me, I can tell by his voice what he needs and if he really needs it, and depending on my financial situation on that particular day, I will decide whether to show up and fuck him or not. Mr. Wong, on this day, needed a good seeing to, but yet again, I would have to be patient while he 'went down' on me, and this time, I was determined, it would not be for hours. We ate, we drank and then the fucking began. It was 9.17, I looked at my clock, and by 10.05, with Mr. Wong stuck in first gear amongst the remnants of my shaved pussy and over sensitive clit, was given his first warning.

"Get your tongue out of there and come up and fuck me." I warned him, "I've told you before, I can only take so much of that, just stick your cock in and fuck me." He replied, again, his broken accent cracked me up, before he went up my crack! "So solly, so solly, now I fuck you, and I do it velly hard. You will ruv it"

It was over by 10.15 and by this time, not only was my clit sore from all his tongue rubbing, my pussy was dry because I hated every minute of him fucking me as I lay there and thought of Moses.

Things were about to change though. I ushered him out of my room, quietly, so as not to wake the natives. He fell down the stairs! What a racket he made, half-drunk slurred speech, at half volume, wasn't enough to wake anyone up, but oh, what a scary moment, remembering not one of my roommates knows what I do, but they ALL know Moses.

Mr. Wong got to the back door and handed
me my envelope. I took it and ushered him out.
"Happy new year, I whispered"
And he was gone.

I opened the envelope and was shocked to see a wad of cash. He'd left me $1500, and all thoughts of Moses temporarily vanished from my guilty conscience!

"Wow, what a night" I thought to myself. "Moses would be proud" but that was the last thought on my mind, the guilt returning post haste to leave me with yet another sleepless night worrying about how and if I would ever tell Moses the whole and truthful story of my existence.

My thoughts drifted back to those first days with Sandy, and that first 'extra' payment I'd received and the funny thing was, nothing had changed, other than the 'John's' I was now fucking.

Men are strange creatures and think that by extending some extra cash, I will love them more than the next guys who pays to fuck me. It's all BS, and in fact, I can never understand what brings any man to pay me the amount they do, never mind extras, but honestly, I am and always will be eternally grateful for the horny and often dumb creature, man, who God placed before me to make my living!

I Don't Like Surprises

As the title of this chapter says, I do not like surprises, I hate them, other than when Moses brings me gifts, but that's rare and his gifts are normally buckets of KFC accompanied by endless supplies of Miller Lite. He knows how to treat a lady!

I've had a few surprises in my E$corting career, some good, most have been bad, but some of the bad one's have been horrific. Broken condoms, guys pulling condoms off while fucking me and not telling me until their cum is filling up the inside of my pussy. I've seen smelly cocks, dirty cocks that haven't been washed in weeks, which I then I have to suck, and the worst of the worst, guys who cum in my mouth and whose sperm tastes of rotten eggs. Did you know that some guys have cum that actually tastes good? Some don't, and during my rise to infamy while E$corting, I have changed my policy to state quite clearly, NO CIM, no cum in mouth. Most of the men I see now abide by my decision, and some even alert me in advance if they think there's even a remote chance they are going to 'overshoot' and break my allocated rule, but in general, I am now safe from swallowing horrible, crappy tasting cum.

One of the biggest surprises I ever received was so bizarre that it's definitely worth writing about.

I'd been working for a few months with, "I will repeat myself twice", Sandy. Things were going well, and she was providing a suitable number of mainly up-market older gentlemen who paid handsomely and often paid more, just to be with me, but there were times where I would go off on my own and fuck the occasional man without telling Sandy what I was doing. I was kind of testing the waters to see if it would ever be possible to go out on my own and perform all of

Sandy's duties, as well as my own, and cut her out completely, leaving me with 100% of my take. Her cut really ate into my earnings and being quite savvy, from a business standpoint, it was beginning to make little sense to me that I should pay her as large a percentage as I was. Don't get me wrong, she earned her cut, she really did, but my thought process always took me back to my number 1 question, which was why pay her if I don't have to?" She did all the vetting, the advertising, the arranging, but I felt I was gaining enough experience to do all of that myself, and with that thought always in the back of my mind, I played away a little, offering a slightly reduced rate to men who I found on my own, either in bars or clubs or Craigslist. I would place a small ad, just occasionally, under a different name and with pictures that bore no resemblance to me at all, I'd wait for the replies to come in. It was from one of those Ad's that I received a phone call from a number in Indiana, a number I didn't know. I recall it was a very pretty afternoon in OC, and I'd just come back from my work out at the beach. The phone was ringing and the caller ID was showing a 260-area code, which left me staring at that number thinking, 'who could that possible be?'. Honestly, I didn't even know where Indiana was, and I didn't care.

I picked up. Remember, there were no smart phones or text messaging back then, only phone calls.

"Hi this is Blondie"

"Blondie this is Bruce, I have been admiring your

Ad's for quite a while now and I'd like to meet you"

"OK" I replied, "where are you located?"

"Well right now I'm in Ft Wayne Indiana, but I am originally from the OC and will be in Florida all next week, and I was wondering if, em, if I bought you a ticket to come to Daytona Beach, if you'd meet me there?"

"Daytona? Are you fucking joking?"

"No I'm being serious. I'll buy the ticket, but you need to rent a

car, which I will also pay for, and then I'd like you to drive to where

I'll be and I'll also pay you double your going rate as a minimum"

"Double? How do I know you're being serious?" I asked

"I'll send you a deposit through Western Union, and also

arrange your ticket to Daytona, then you'll realize I'm serious"

"OK, show me" I told him.

"Stay by your phone and I'll get back to you within the hour"

This was crazy, why would anyone want to send me a ticket to Daytona and the bigger question was, why would I even consider going?

An hour passed by.

Next call went something like this.

"OK I need your name and your address and the closest WU

office to your home and I need to know if you can get up to

LAX for the flight I'll book, and then I can arrange your travel. You

can't get to Daytona flying out of John Wayne Airport unfortunately"

"How long will I be away?"

"4 days. I will pay you $1000 per day and remember, it's all cash and the only proviso is, you need to rent a car. I will tell you where and how to rent it, but that's non-negotiable, you have to do this for me"

"OK Bruce, let's do it"

When I uttered those words, 'let's do it', something inside me said, 'what the fuck are you doing you stupid bitch', but I gave Bruce all the info he required and I waited for another hour until he called again.

"You're booked, and $500 has been sent to you for collection at the WU office in Irvine. I will see you at the weekend in Daytona. I'll be staying at the Mirabelle Hotel on Daytona Beach, so just come straight there and straight up to my room. I will give you the room number the day before you leave. The car should be hired from Dollar, and you should hire it for a week. I need you to hire a full-size car please. Whatever it costs you, I will pay it back when you arrive. Are we good?" he asked.

"How do I get you if I need you?"

"You don't. Listen, I have been fantasizing for weeks about you and being inside that tight pussy of yours, so don't let me down."

"What do you do for a living?" I asked him.

"Government work" was all he said.

After all was said and done, I moved my lazy butt as quickly as possible down to the WU office in Irvine, and low and behold, the $500 was sitting there waiting for me, along with a reference number for a Delta flight leaving from LAX to Atlanta and then to Daytona, two days from then. $4000 in earnings for 3 days' work in those day was a fortune to me, and with that in mind, my excitement boiled over as I took the $500 and headed straight to the closest bikini shop to get myself kitted out for my trip to Florida.

Thinking back now, I was a complete idiot, but at the time, it all made perfect sense for me. The guy saw my Ad, loved what he saw and then summoned me to come visit him, paying everything in advance. What was wrong with that? The answer was about to be revealed.

I packed my bag and left for the airport. Bruce had called again to re confirm the time and the hotel and room number, he was obviously already there, and yet again, he was insistent that I rent a car, a full-sized car, from Dollar, at Daytona airport. I told him I understood all the requirements and that once I'd landed, I would grab the car and come over. All his intentions seemed to be sexual, and he kept reminding me exactly what he was going to do to me once I arrived. I was pretty excited and he seemed to be extremely horny.

My flight was great, and I drank a lot. It was free, sort of, the guy next to me kept looking at my tits, and again, as per usual, they were bra-less and hanging in the right direction. He was ploughing alcohol down my throat, all at his expense, in the hope I would blow him in the bathroom of the Boeing 737 that took us into Atlanta. I took the drinks he offered, but never provided him with any 'extra' service! I changed planes, and flew into Daytona.

Arriving around 6 PM local time, I immediately got on the shuttle bus to the car rental facility. On the bus, I started rummaging around in my hand bag looking for my driver's license. It was just after 9/11 and you needed a license to board any flight, a new rule initiated by the Bush government after the attacks on New York. I had the license when I got on the plane, but now, as I sat on that bus heading to the car rental facility, I just couldn't find it. Panic set in.

We arrived at the building where all the rental companies were housed, I got off the bus, found a bench to sit on and started to take all my luggage apart, piece by piece. No License! No matter where I looked, it just wasn't there. I went inside, found the Dollar rental stand and asked the lady behind the desk if she could help. Together, we went through everything in my case and hand bag once again, and we found nothing. Sweat was rolling down my neck on to my back. I didn't know what to do. The Dollar rep called Delta, and told them what had happened, just in case someone had handed it in or I'd left it on the plane and a flight attendant had reported it as missing. She gave them my home number, but at that point in time, no one had found it and I was completely stuck. I had no way of renting a car, no way of getting back on a plane and no way of getting to the hotel where Bruce was. I was in complete melt-down mode.

The kind lady at Dollar asked me where I was going, it was now past 7.30 PM, and I was late. I gave her the address and she told me that she'd drop me off. I was delighted that anyone actually cared that I was stranded and as she seemed to be going right past the hotel where Bruce was staying, I accepted her offer with open arms. I would need to figure out how to get back to CA without my license, but that would be in 3 days, so I got in her car and we drove off. The hotel wasn't that far away, I'd say 15 minutes max, and when we arrived, I thanked her with all my heart and got out the car, headed to the hotel reception and found a bathroom, spruced myself up and headed directly to the room number Bruce had given to me.

I knocked.

"Who's is it?"

"Blondie"

Silence

I could hear him coming towards the door.

The door opened.

"Why are you late?" he was high as a kite. I could tell.

"Hmmm, long story."

"Where did you park the car?"

"Can I come in, and HELLO to you too!" I said sarcastically.

He backed away from the door moving himself inside towards a king-sized bed that looked as if it hadn't been made in weeks. There were items of clothing strewn all over his room, drug paraphernalia too and to top it all off, the room stunk of weed and meth. This was a disaster, and my stomach sank.

"Where's the fucking car?" he shouted

"I didn't get one"

"WHAT?" He shouted directly at me with such volume, that I thought the roof was going to cave in and it also looked like he was about to physically assault me. I stepped back. I was scared, but only for a short moment until I realized that this guy was a real softie. Don't know how I knew, I just did.

He continued to rant, and was extremely abrupt.

"Where's the fucking car bitch? He was high as a kite, and it looked like his ass was floating above his elbows!

"If you calm down and offer me some of your weed, I will tell you what happened"

He looked at me and relaxed a little, then we both went over and sat on the edge of his bed. He pulled out his 'stash' offering me a joint, and we both began to smoke. I realized then that I was in no danger at all and his bluster had been for effect only. I explained to him the issue with my driver's license and how I couldn't rent the car because I'd lost it on the plane. I told him about the lady who'd dropped me off and then, and only then, did I ask him for my 'donation' for coming all the way from LA to Daytona. He was about to respond when his room phone rang.

"Yes, she's here."

Silence

"No, the bitch lost her driver's license on the plane and couldn't get one"

Silence

"Yes, well…."

Silence

"No, I am not going to pay her"

Silence

"OK, understood, yes, I will do that"

He put the phone down and told me,

"No money for you since you didn't get the car"

"WTF has the car got to do with me coming here?" I asked.

"Can't tell you, but the boss says fuck you and not to pay you"

"The boss???" Who the fuck is the boss?"

Doesn't matter, I do whatever he says, and he says not to pay you"

"I'm lost here" and I really was. "Why would you not pay me because I never rented a car?"

We were both getting high very quickly, his weed was GOOD.

"because…" and he was beginning to slur his words, 'because we take the car you rent and we dismantle it and ship it to another country. It's what we do"

"It's what you do? What the fuck do you do? Who are you? Who's the boss?" I was losing it fast. I was getting high, I was tired, hungry, had lost my license on the plane, had no return ticket and was being fed all of the BS about selling my supposed rental car to another country after it was dismantled? I was so confused and not in the mood for any more of the crap I was being fed.

"OK Bruce, if that's really you name, you need to get me a plane ticket back to LA in the morning and find me a room for the night."

"Can't do that, the boss won't allow it"

"Then get the FUCKING BOSS on the phone"

I shouted so loud that Bruce cowered in retreat, showing signs of fear from my tirade. He upped himself from the dirty bed, went over to the room safe, pulled out some cash, threw it on the bed and said,

"Just fuck me bitch, there's enough there to last all night" I looked at the cash, thought about swiping it all up into my bag and making a run for it, but by then I was too far gone on weed, so we both lay back on the bed, fucked, fell asleep and then repeated that same process about three times more as the night wore on. First thing next morning, Bruce was still out of it, and I was wide awake, I picked up enough cash from the wad of notes that were still lying on the bed, got my things together, went outside to reception, found a cab and headed to the airport. My chance of returning to LA without issue, were of course multiplied by the fact I had no license, the fact that these guys were probably dangerous crooks, and the fact that I had taken his money and vanished, and the car situation, whatever that was, was still playing on my very confused mind.

To be honest, I cannot remember clearly how I got home, but I did. It involved my boyfriend at the time breaking into my apartment and sending me a fax, I think to a 7/11 shop in Daytona, showing my birth certificate, my passport and then I took this to the nice people at Delta, but frankly, it's hard to recall exactly what it was that they did that allowed me through security and onto a plane bound for Atlanta and then LA, but I did get on and I did get home. I was still high from the night before, and the effects of Bruce's weed were blurring my mind at that point in time. All I remember is, that with a few good deeds from a few good people, everything worked out in the end. When I arrived home, I had 16 messages from an irate Bruce, threatening me with all sorts of unmentionable and unrepeatable, unpleasantries. But he was the least of my worries. I couldn't go to the cops, because my E$corting activities were illegal and so I sat down, took out my computer and googled several scenarios before, BINGO, I found what I was looking for.

This was a gang, operating out of Florida, calling E$corts from all over the USA, to come there, to Daytona, Miami and Orlando, to rent cars that would be stripped bare and sent to foreign countries for cash. The gang used E$corts because they knew that we couldn't go to the cops. Dozens of unsuspecting women, including me, had been conned. Eventually this gang were caught and jailed, but from that day onwards I was looking over my shoulder for any signs of gang activity that might come back to haunt me. Surprises? No, I don't like them at all, but that one was one of the worst things that ever happened to me and to this day, I still shiver when I think about that room and that man, a man who gave me nightmares for years after and who's face is ingrained into my mind and will be there until my dying day. I was lucky to get out of that situation with all my limbs intact, others weren't so lucky, something you can find if you do the research yourself, but thankfully that whole issue really set me up to take more care in what was about to be a meteoric rise in my good fortune.

But before that rise, or perhaps assisted by my rise to better days, was my friend Terry and his fascination with taking all of us, by us, I mean several E$corts and our buddies, in his giant limo to the Long Beach Grand Prix every year. You'll learn more about Terry later on in this book, and even today, we are still great friends. Back then, we were great buddies. Terry though could be a complete asshole. We would often go out to have fun and before I realized what was going on, he'd either dumped me for some other chick, leaving me stranded without a ride home, or he'd take me home and then fuck one of my friends, just to piss me off! His adventures to the Long Beach Grand Prix though, were legendary. Don't get me wrong, the experience in Florida with the rental car scam was bad, but this one year at the Grand Prix, was ten times worse. It began in earnest, with Terry picking me up in his Limo as promised, a limo that was larger than my condo at the time. Already packed inside, drunker than I could ever explain, were a few blondes, brunettes and redheads. It was 9 AM on a Sunday morning, and the fun had already begun. Terry, sober as could be, was directing the entertainment, with boobs and shaved pussy's, flying around freely in the back seat of this monstrosity Terry called a Limo. It was more like a house on wheels. I got in, was offered some champagne, and woof! Off we went at full speed up to Long Beach. The ride took about 35 minutes, and when we arrived, the crazy bitches in his back seat, exited Terry's limo and headed straight for the bar. It was now around 11 AM and the race wasn't due to begin until 2 PM, you can therefore imagine the carnage these women were about to create. 6 or 7 incredibly gorgeous ladies, setting out to meet rich men, tits flying, no underwear in sight and a need to get fucked for money or love or just for fun. Take your pick, these ladies were on fire! After several hours of drinking, eating and even fucking in the back of the limo, we all settled in to watch the race, something I found incredibly boring, and then, about 10 laps from the finish, Terry decided to fuck off back to Huntington Beach, with some of the girls. Ironically, Terry decided to leave ME at the track! I was so pissed. I was sitting alone in one of the bars trying to call Terry to come back and get me, but his cell phone was off and there was no chance of him answering until he'd fucked all 4 of the women he'd taken with him. Yet again, that moron had dumped me for no good reason, without any means of transportation back to Huntington Beach, without money, without any sense of regret. What an asshole. I was so upset.

Leaving the racetrack, I found a sushi spot across the street and decided to go inside to see if I could at least bum a ride off some kind gentleman, in exchange for a blow job or quickie fuck. As I walked into the restaurant, I bumped into this guy, who looked me up and down, stopped back to check out my nipples for a second time, and then offered to buy me a drink.

"Fuck that", I said, "is there any chance

you can take me back to Huntington Beach?"

He looked at me, all the time keeping his eyes focused on my tits, but wanting so badly to look me in the face, knowing that was seemingly an impossible task. I spoke again.

"Dude, would you take your eyes off my tits and take me home please? My date left me here and I don't have any way of getting back unless you take me" He nodded in agreement and then motioned for me to follow him, which I did, all the way back to his truck in the parking lot behind the sushi place. He then spoke for the first time.

"You gonna make this worth my while?" he asked.

"What do you want?" I replied

'$50 and a chance to take you to dinner" he said.

"Deal"

We got into the truck and made our way to the 405 South, all the time, in silence. This guy just didn't want to talk. About ten minutes passed and suddenly, without warning, he reached into the side of his door, into a kind of hidden glove box, pulling out a 9mm pistol.

"Whoa, big man, what the fuck?" I shouted.

He said nothing, while pointing the barrel of his gun right at my face, between my shocked eyes.

"When we get to your place" he asked, "are you going to fuck me?"

"Of course," I replied. With his fucking gun in my face, what else was I going to say to him? I had nothing more to add, other than a quick prayer to the Almighty and a few Hail Mary's thrown in for luck. "I'd fuck you without that gun being pointed at my face Dude, but it's a bit late for that request now!" I told him.

I gave him specific instruction as he drove, hoping for relief in the shape of a passing police car, which never materialized. I was ready to jump out the door if one came withing 100 yards of this dickhead's truck.

"Turn right, go left, straight on" I said, while looking all over for law enforcement.

We got to my home. His gun was still pointing right at me.

"Right" he said, "get your ass in the back seat, and don't try anything silly"

It was a command, which I willingly obeyed. At that point in time, I grew a pair, as they say in the trade, finding the courage to confront him.

"I'm a fucking E$cort you asshole! Do you think I don't fuck other guys for free? I normally charge $300, but with your gun pointed at my face, I think I will charge you double." This totally confused him, telling me immediately, the guy was stupid, uneducated and also unable to comprehend any type of sarcasm. He blinked and hesitated. I saw my opportunity, and I opened the passenger side door and bolted, heading straight for my complex's swimming pool, where I knew there would be other people mingling.

"He's got a gun!!!" I shouted, as loud as I could, repeating that phrase several times.

People began to take notice, and the moron who'd kindly driven me home, even though I'd had his gun pointed at me the whole time I was there, took fright and drove off at the speed of light.

Before I knew it, I'd calmed down, with the assistance of some of my wonderful neighbors, and then I'd realized that I hadn't taken the guy's license plate number. Now I couldn't report him for kidnapping, or threatening behavior or assault with a deadly weapon. Would I have done that anyway? I doubt it. I tried to stay away from the law as much as possible. My profession dictated that.

My cell phone rang. It was Terry.

"You fucking asshole" I shouted, "you abandoned me, I got kidnapped and threatened by a guy with a gun!" I was crying now. All Terry could say was, "we're coming back to your place for a nightcap, get the tequila ready"

He didn't give a shit. Never did and never would. Another great escape for yours truly and yet another day in the life of being friends with Terry. Yes, as I mentioned, I hate surprises, I really do, especially one's where guns are involved.

Sandy Shafts Me and I Move On

It wasn't that I never liked her, as I've mentioned before, Sandy was just a complete pain in the ass, her voice, her endless repetition and her inability to know exactly when to talk and when not to. The when not to, in her case, seemed never to happen, and after about three months of listening to all her crap, which included the repetition of many different instructions,

"Take 92 to the 405, look right at the exit marked Sand Canyon and up in the hills, you'll see a pink house. That used to be mine"

20 times she told me that!

OR

"Honey, don't forget to look your best and brush your teeth!"

That one was told to me over 100 times, and sometimes she'd say it three times a day depending on the number of dates I had.

OR

"Sweetheart, I used to be very rich and then I decided it was time for a change because I lost all my money when I got divorced" Maybe 4 times a week?

OR

"Don't forget to come to my room at the hotel with your cash before you go home!"

That one was every day, 5 times a day, even if I had no dates!

The thing was, she seemed to live in hotels. She did! I never saw her any other place except the hotel room she'd booked for that night. I'd no idea how she lived like that or indeed how anyone could live that way, and in the end, I said 'fuck it', I'm out of here. My decision was enhanced by a fortuitous meeting with a male E$cort called Randy, yes, I know, forgive the pun, but he was, and probably still is, one of the best fucks I ever had.

Sandy called me one afternoon and gave me the address of this condo in Newport beach, and that's the day I met Randy. We hit it off from the moment I walked into his home and although my rates are normally $300 for one 'pop' and not for MSOG, multiple shots on goal, Randy and I went at it all afternoon and into the evening, ending up going out for drinks, dinner and then more fucking, which after all the drinking, became 'on the house' fucking. I didn't know it then, but Randy was a male E$cort, and after I found that out, which was several weeks later, I just couldn't understand why he needed to pay for sex? After all, wasn't he getting enough of it already? By the time I found out about Randy's past, my days with Sandy were numbered, and one evening, as we both lay naked in bed, sweat pouring off us after another raucous session of wild uninhibited fun, I told Randy that I was thinking about quitting Sandy's stable and finding someone else.

"Do you know anyone……" I asked him, just on the off chance he might have some contacts from his former life. (Randy had quit the E$corting game about three months prior to our meeting, but I had no idea of his 'status' the first time we fucked), "…..anyone who I could go to for management? I need to get out of what I'm in and find a better deal"

"I do, as it happens, and I think you'll love them"

"Them?"

"Yes, a husband-and-wife team, Sophia and John. Look them up in Yellow Pages, Amoramia is their company name."

"Will they talk to me?"

"Just tell them I sent you" he said. With those words of encouragement ringing in my ears, Randy took his erect penis and entered me once again and we fucked for another 2 hours.

When I got home that night, I opened the Yellow Pages, remember those days? For those of you who don't, before the internet, every household in the country received a Yellow Pages book free of charge, which was at that time, your only outlet to every phone number, for every business in your area. E$corts, took up a whole section, maybe 6 pages of phone numbers, but Amoramia had a whole page on its own, yes, one whole page! I couldn't begin to imagine what that might have cost? The page was unique. It had the Amoramia name emblazoned in the center of the page, and their phone number discretely positioned at the bottom left, small and insignificant, but visible all the same, and that was it! No other information.

Sandy was history, I'd already told her I was done, and despite her protestations, we'd split on amicable terms and she'd understood I was moving on. This happened all the time in the industry. Girls came and went and that vicious cycle seemed never ending. My issue was, how to call John and Sophia, the owners of Amoramia, and ensure that they saw me without thinking I was Law Enforcement. For you, at home, this might seem trivial, but at that time, it was so hard to make people in our industry feel comfortable because of the Heidi Fleiss case that been making all the headlines in LA. No one trusted anyone, other than themselves or their inner circle, and it was just difficult to make people believe that you were genuine and seeking work in an industry riddled with liars and snitches.

My opening thought was just to pick the phone up and tell them Randy had recommended me, but then I thought to myself, what if there were two of us? Two is always better than one, right? Not just me, but me and a friend, also someone who wanted to be under new management, someone who was as good looking as me, and someone who would come with me to the meeting? Hopefully, and in my mind, Sophia and John would be less intimidated and two is always less suspicious than one. That was my theory and I was sticking to it.

I picked up the phone, shaking like a leaf, and Sophia answered. I explained to her in great detail my time with Sandy, a conversation that didn't last overly long because Sophia was hooked and wanted to meet. I told her I would bring Rosita, and Sophia agreed that would be in everyone's best interest because they were already looking for more girls to expand their business. We picked a meeting place, Starbucks in Anaheim, and set the date for our get together.

Rosita, a friend of mine who was also an E$cort and looking for someone to manage her, had agreed to join me after I'd explained my dilemma to her. Beautiful Rosita, who is so tall, about 5'11", slim and exceptionally pretty, had second thoughts about joining me, but in the end, after a few kind words in her ear, agreed, and we both set off two days later to meet our new partners. Although Rosita was really never comfortable about coming with me, she did so as a favor in the end, and happily it all worked out.

Sophia and John both showed up, ten minutes late, but dressed to thrill.

She, Sophia, was a stunning Asian lady, with long dark hair, slim muscular legs, great tits, probably fake, and a St John Knits business suit, clinging tightly to her wonderfully shaped figure. John, well, he was in jeans and a tee shirt, but boy, he was a great looking guy, and from the off, I was deeply attracted to him.

With all of the compulsory greetings and small talk out the way, both their eyes and our eyes scanning Starbucks for any sign of Law Enforcement, we got down to business. Rosita and I sat while Sophia, who was doing most of the talking, explained how Amoramia operated. They had a stable of around 20 regular girls, all working LA and OC area. Rates were similar to Sandy's although Amoramia would take a little more from our cut, and Sophia explained that they were far more professional and spent more on Advertising than Sandy ever would. Rosita and I agreed that would work, we all shook hands, hugged, although John's hug was a squeeze too much in my opinion, and we left. My new career, the one I'd begun just three months prior, was about to take another turn under new management. I just hoped it would be a good turn. On the way out of Starbucks, Sophia suddenly remembered that she hadn't given us any names for her Ad's. I suggested she use my real name, and she refused, and after a few back and forth attempts to come up with something, and knowing that I'd been selling Candy for 2 years, Sophia decided to call me Candice, a name I still adore, even today. Candice though was how my life at Amoramia began, but I didn't really ever get used to that name, it was too much like a 'stripper' name for me and too similar to the game Candyland, that all the kids played when we were growing up, but I kept it for a while, and Rosita, who was now Rosita-Ann, thought that it was cute and slipped easily off the tongue. Again, we all hugged and left, and I went home and waited for the phone to ring. I had high hopes with Amoramia, they seemed professional, competent and well-organized, and I believed, from what they'd told me and the spiel Sophia had spouted that their clientele would be a step up on anything that Sandy had procured for me over the past months, and honestly, that wouldn't have been hard. Some of the men I'd met had been of 'inferior' quality for sure, and I now had high hopes for the future.

Things started slowly, but within week, I was seeing at least 4 guys a day, and sometimes more. The quality of men on my dates was definitely a huge improvement over the dates Sandy had provided and I found myself flitting between hotel rooms at 5-star resorts, mansions, stuck way up in the hills of

Orange County, and extremely spacious houses that were close to the all the local beach areas. I could be in Long Beach in the morning, yes, men want to fuck early in the day as well as late at night, and then was asked to drive to the San Fernando valley, and then back to Irvine. I was traveling about 1000 miles a week in my car, something I hadn't planned, but my goodness, the cash was pouring in. I met rich dudes, richer dudes and often, although not as often as I would have liked, I met billionaires. Tips outweighed fees, ranging from $1000 to $3000 if I performed well, but the underlying trend I learned with all my new clients was that they all preferred to contact me directly, and not book me through Amoramia. Most appreciated my skill levels were extraordinary, in and out of bed, and when I left them gasping for more, they all begged me to give them my phone number so they could contact me at will and without the hassle of calling Sophia. In the beginning I refused, mainly because I felt a certain loyalty towards Amoramia, but as time went by, I began to think it might be to my benefit to do so, pocketing all of the fees rather than a third. But after putting these thoughts to the back of my mind, (although they were always festering and really never went away), most of the time I would just plough on regardless and realize that if it wasn't for Sophia and John, my life might be completely different.

    I was invited to an office party in Irvine one evening. A regular building, where, from the outside, nothing out of the ordinary seemed to be happening. A few people from one of the office units inside that building had decided to invite a few of us 'party' girls over to share in some celebration they were having. Sophia and John had arranged for a posse of girls to attend, of which I was one. When I arrived, and by the way, Rosita, or Rosita-Ann as she was now called, came with me, we were ushered into an elevator and taken to the 15th floor, and that's when all Hell erupted. The elevator doors opened and we got out and turned left and then entered this huge office where we were confronted by lots of guys, some standing alone and ogling us as we walked in, and some with 2 or 3 girls on each arm, all very pretty by the way. After being offered a drink, champagne, Rosita and I began to explore and what we found totally surprised us. Guys were fucking E$corts, or we believed they were E$corts, in the bathroom, on the desks and in front of the other 100 or so people in attendance. I knew at that point that this was a 'free for all' event where anything was acceptable. After about 30 minutes, a man, whose name was Guy, came over to chat with me. He was some kind of investment banker and our conversation was quite enlightening. He informed me, (and while he was informing me there were three women fucking this one dude on the desk next to where Guy and I were standing, pussy juice running freely down their legs and onto the top of that desk which now needed polishing), suggesting I should put all my savings, and I had about 30 grand in the bank at that time, into a company called DFJ Italia, and that I could double my investment within a year.

"Could this possibly be true?" I asked myself.

Our conversation led to sex, not on that cum covered desk, but in the back seat of his car, and then more sex, in his bedroom and then even more sex in his lounge, as my evening turned into a $2000 tip and a sex-fueled adventure across Orange County, ending up at Guys large home. Guy fucked me so ferociously, so wonderfully, and with such passion that evening, my pussy was red raw from feeling his huge cock, (9 inches), pound me relentlessly and his insatiable sexual appetite, seemingly never ending and honestly, quite thrilling. In the morning, or should I say early afternoon when we woke up side by side in his back room, on his rug in parked right in front of an ornamental fireplace, I made him coffee and then sat down, naked, next to him. I asked if he would give me more details on the DFJ company, which he did, before fucking me one last time, increasing my pay packet to $3500 and telling me to send him all the cash I had and he'd take care of opening a trading account on my behalf. Guy was a good man, and did what he'd promised to do, and my savings began to increase, although not as rapidly as he'd promised, until one day, about 6 weeks after meeting him, my savings just vanished and I found out I'd lost everything. DFJ Italia turned out to be a Ponzi scheme and I turned out to be one of its thousands of innocent victims, losing everything I ever had, and more. In the blink of an eye, it was gone, all of it. I was devastated, and depressed for weeks and weeks and to this day, I don't think I ever got over the shock of waking up to find out I had nothing left. My loss was minimal in comparison to other people's losses, but all the same, my life's savings were gone, and I was penniless, more or less, even though Sophia and John were still sending me out on plenty of dates. I just hoped I would one day make back all the cash I'd lost, but at that point in my life, I had little hope and even less faith.

My new and improved lifestyle had grown accustomed to certain 'luxuries' and those riches, now gone, although small in part, seemed to have a way of disappearing on me with regularity. Something that's held true even to this day. Whenever I get flush with cash, that cash finds, more often than not and through no fault of my own, a way of vanishing before I've had any opportunity to accumulate vast amounts as a buffer to live my life, although I suppose if you really look at each occurrence, it really was my own fault or just my stupidity. I really can be a ditz!

During the time I worked with Sophia and John, I had a boyfriend named Kevin, who knew nothing about my life outside of our relationship. He believed I was selling candies around OC, and that often I had to work nights just to make ends meet. How silly was I, believing that Kevin would never find out about my secret life? I had two cell phones, one for Kevin and my other friends and one for Sophia and John, and my work life. I kept that second phone hidden at all times, checking it as often as I could, but discreetly and never in full view of any of my friends, family, or Kevin. I'd been with Sophia about 4 months, when my popularity at Amoramia skyrocketed for some unknown reason and their calls to my second phone became more and more frequent, in fact, they became rather annoying. Annoying perhaps isn't the correct word, but I'd be out having fun with Kevin, doing boyfriend girlfriend things, when I'd sneak away to check my work phone to find the calls were coming fast and furious from Amoramia. It was a complete distraction and it spoiled any loving moment that I was having with Kevin, so I just stopped answering the damn thing. That pissed off Sophia and John to the point where they'd literally threatened to fire me if I didn't respond to their messages and start to tow the company line. Their clients, emphasis on THEIR, were too important for me to ignore their constant calling, and THEIR clients required servicing, because time is money, etc etc. I hated the fact that and I was beginning to dislike the two of them, even though they were truly professional and only had my financial interest at heart, along with their own bottom line of course. I was making a lot of money at that time, and in my own mind I felt that if I missed one or two appointments or calls, who would care? Certainly not me. After all, how much could I spend? Well, I could spend tons and I could lose even more, but that wasn't the point. I was meeting men by the dozen, and every day I'd receive offers to travel, to go to dinner, to be at a certain hotel or home to fuck, but none of it mattered while Sophia and John were piling on pressure on me to work more and more and to extend my pussy where no pussy had ever gone before! I was magic, and all the men I fucked told me that. My pussy was the tightest they'd ever fucked and they all loved it. I was on a roll, I was on a high, I was onto something, and I was about to take advantage of it.

On My Own

I reckon it was around 8 months into my relationship with Amoramia when the wheels came off and the walls came tumbling down. My relationship with Kevin was one I just didn't want to give up and Sophia was becoming extremely irritated with me because I refused to pick up her phone calls when I was with him. This left her scrambling to find other girls to fulfil the appointments I was missing when I was out with Kevin. I got lectured by both her and by John on several occasions, and they made me feel like I was back in high school. I always believed it was none of their business that I had a personal life outside of E$corting, but they believed otherwise, and now, some 15 years on, I can see their point of view a lot clearer than I could back then. Back then I just thought, 'fuck it, and fuck them, this is my life' and I continued to do my own thing and lead my own life, without their permission. They hated that and, unfortunately, it all came to a head one sunny afternoon, an afternoon that I won't ever forget.

Kevin and I were out on a boat in Newport Beach harbor, having fun, getting drunk, making out, and my phone was ringing nonstop, the Sophia and John phone, not my personal one. I kept hearing it vibrate, and so did Kevin. I always had it on vibrate, silent, but vibrate, and even though that was the case, depending on where I'd left the phone, either in my handbag, in the glove box of my car, or, as was the case on this particular afternoon, my beach bag, if the phone was situated at the wrong angle, in the wrong position, and ended up leaning against something hard, you could either hear the vibration or not. That afternoon, unfortunately, we could both hear it. It was a never-ending symphony of monotonal annoyance.

"What is that?" Kevin kept asking.

I deflected him for as long as I could until his curiosity got the better of him and when I went to the other end of our very small boat to re-bait my fishing rod, Kevin swooped in, opening my bag and finding my other phone. His face was filled with dread as he looked at me and asked me, very nicely, "what's this?"

"It's a phone" I said, while shrugging my shoulders

"Yes, but why do you have a second phone?"

Right at that precise moment, the phone vibrated once again.

"Who is Amoramia?" the caller ID didn't lie.

I shrugged again and grabbed it from him. I put it away and said very little, and then the bombardment arrived.

Who, where, why, when, etc etc. And the phone kept vibrating. It was as if I was in the middle of a very bad dream.

I answered it, Kevin was right next to me.

"I am busy!" I shouted, and I cut the call off. The phone rang again. "Fuck, can't they take the hint!" I was now shouting at Kevin, not the phone. He'd gone from having a very red face, a product of all our alcoholic consumption, to having a very white and scared look on that bright red face. He was worried, I was worried, Sophia wasn't giving up.

"I cannot talk right now!"

"Do not hang up" Sophia said," I just want to let you know you're fired. We don't want you anymore. When you're not so busy, call me and I will explain why, we can arrange to meet up so you can return my cell phone, and end this relationship formally" the line went dead.

Kevin asked me what happened. I gave him some BS about having another phone because my mother bought me a gift and I couldn't take it back so she always called me on that number. He knew I was lying. We didn't spend too much more time on the water, we kind of packed up in silence and made for the harbor. I could tell he was pissed off, and he knew I was hiding something. We got back to shore, he took me home and I never saw him again. He refused to return any of my calls, my attempts to see him in person were blanked, and eventually, I gave up. Such a shame, he was nice, and I believed we had a chance to be much more than just boyfriend/girlfriend.

I called Sophia to arrange a meeting, thinking I would try to iron out our differences in person, but she was adamant, and told me I was no longer employed by the agency. They knew about Kevin and told me I couldn't have both a boyfriend and an E$corting life. There was no further discussion between us, and my termination was complete. I didn't owe them and they didn't owe me, but my phone belonged to them, so Sophia said that John was going to come and get it. I immediately took the phone, copied all the names and numbers onto a notepad, deleted them permanently from the phone, then put the phone in a bag for John to collect. He arrived at my home 45 minutes later, I didn't want to talk to him and he didn't want to see me, he took the phone and left. Copying those numbers was the smartest thing I'd done in years. I was in demand and all I had to do was to make a call to each of the 200 odd clients I had in the hope they would support me in my new venture, my self-employed E$corting venture. I would now be classed as an independent E$cort from then on in, something that I never regretted and something that again, changed my life for the better.

 I decided to place Ad's in all the different media formats available at that time, and the one that brought me the most success in the early days, OC Weekly, was my first port of call. My Ad was simple, and concise, and I changed my name to the name with which I'm known by today. Candice was gone and Blondie had arrived. With all guns blazing, nipples and pussy at the ready, my life became hectic. I called all of my old clients and told them I was now operating on my own, and that they should call me directly and not to call Sophia at Amoramia if they wanted a session. I offered them a one-time $50/hour discount to do so. Most of them did this without questioning why or if or who and the rest just vanished. That's the thing about this business. Often, you'll have clients who come back again and again, and sometimes, it's just a one-off for them. They want to experiment, try something new, or just get relief from the boredom that's set in with their marriage or other relationship. Once they get that out of their system, they never return. My regulars, however, those who need to see me more often and can't get enough of what I do to them, the ones who came with me at that time, well, they have stayed with me, most of them, to this very day, and I am honored they chose to do so. The Ad ran and ran and ran and my client list just expanded to the point where I had over 1500 contacts in my address book. I was being fucked from North to South, to East and then back West and I had nothing but cash in my bank account again. Life had taken a turn for the better, and not before time. My personal life was non-existent because of all my time was spent being fucked by clientele. Morning, noon and night, 7 days a week, I was having sex. My pussy though, well, she was a trooper, coming through on several occasions when I thought that she would just dry up and frizzle into extinction. Thank God for Moist, my go-to get out of jail card! I was meeting rich guys; very rich guys, and some not so rich guys, but we were all having a blast. Free this and free that, so many gifts, so unexpected, but so appreciated, my wardrobe was expanding, my bank account was expanding and so too was my ego. I just couldn't do anything wrong for a while. The loss of the 30 grand that Guy had pissed away for me, seemed insignificant as I raced through life buying what I could with the money I made from sex, pure sex, raw and wonderful. I was loving every moment.

As time sped by, the internet became my source for advertising. Things were changing and changing rapidly. Sex was becoming real mainstream, only because of the internet and the ease at which it was available for everyone, even minors. I often had offers and calls from underaged horny boys, but that's another story.

The OC weekly, ah yes, what a gem of a publication. My lifesaver, and sadly, no longer with us. When I began my solo career, I placed an Ad, a very small Ad, in the back section of the OC Weekly. The back section, probably the last 2 to 4 pages, was dedicated to men seeking women, women seeking men and so on, in other words, dating and sex. I was the smallest Ad on any page, a little box, about 1 inch tall and 2 inches wide, and all it said was,

"Blonde By the Beach"

"949-555-1212"

Nothing more.

All the big agency Ads were large, and some were just garish, but I kept mine small for two reasons. The first reason was, I had very little money to burn, and the second reason was subtlety and independence. If life had taught me anything thus far, it was not to go shouting from the rooftops. I was an E$cort for goodness' sake, not a plumber or electrician.

Again, the internet was a thing of the future, this was around 1998 and although sex was beginning to raise its head (pardon the pun) on line in the early days, OC Weekly and other such publications were still the go-to place to advertise my services because very few people had internet access and fewer still had laptop computers. The iPhone was still some 6 years away and people still read magazines! OC Weekly came out once a week and it was free. It was given away at gas stations, convenience stores and many other places around

Orange County and most of its articles referenced what was happening in the OC on that particular week. I, like a lot of other people, just adored reading it, and I kind of directed my personal social life around some of the events I'd read about in the magazine. Life back then was a lot simpler than it is now, but also a lot scarier. The internet brought a little more security to my profession, enabling me to check IDs at the touch of a button. Back then, I would receive calls, about 50 a day, from my little Ad, and really, I would have no idea who these guys were. They could have been anyone from any profession, including Law Enforcement, and I wouldn't know until I met them. I was leaving myself wide open for solicitation, but honestly, thinking back to that particular time in my life, I really didn't give a fuck. I was interested in partying, fucking and making big bucks. The possibility of jail time for soliciting sex, well, that was just part of the risk we all took, and when I went solo, after Amoramia, I just wanted to ensure my bank account was replenished daily, which it was. I was traveling all over the county again, meeting guys in hotel rooms and also at their homes. Most of my clients were married, yes, married, and yet they still invited me into their homes. They would fuck me in the same bed they slept with their wives, something I never cared about, but I'm sure their wives would, if they ever found out. Around that time, I was also planning to move to a new home, well, not a home, but a room inside a home. Omar, who is now my good friend, owned a huge house in Fountain Valley, and yes, the OC Weekly was his choice to advertise this massive room he had vacant above his garage. Yours truly was the first and only application he received and we agreed to meet at the house so I could see what it was I was going to rent. $600 per month was the deal, and that was crazy cheap at the time, and right within my limited budget. My plan was to eventually purchase a home, which I was saving up for, but at that point in time, I never had enough in the bank to secure a deposit on my dream condo near the beach. I always wanted to live close to the beach, hence my Ad, which always read, "Blonde By the Beach", but as Fountain Valley and Omar's place was only a few miles from the sand, that is where I was headed and where I hoped I could live until a home purchase became affordable.

Omar's home was huge, and I don't mean huge, I mean HUGE! One of the largest I had ever seen. Omar himself, was a great guy and so friendly, making me feel very welcome, from the moment I got out my car, both nipples at full beam, with Omar staring right into my cleavage, to the moment I left, shaking hands and agreeing that I could move in a few days later. Suddenly my whole life had changed. New place to live, new phone number, new Ad, new clients and new hope that one day I would make enough to retire and live, in comfort, forever and a day. All my friends were either married or living with someone and I had no choice but to room it on my own. Omar's place was a real find. I discovered that he traveled a lot, in fact twice a year he went to Australia for 3 weeks at a time, on business. From the information he'd given me when we first met, I knew that his house would be empty most of the time giving me the freedom to really do want I wanted and come and go as I pleased, without anyone questioning why or where I was going.

After moving into my new room, which by the way, was above Omar's garage and at least 800 sq feet, very large for a room in the OC and extremely large for $600 per month, I was driving to the gym one morning when my phone rang. I had a very small cell phone, not a flip phone, remember the Motorola flip phone? I didn't like them. I preferred a regular small rectangular device, and one that fit in my purse without making it look bulky. Anyway, I pulled over thinking it was my sister calling, at first glance, the number looked like hers, but when I answered, it was a man's voice.

"Candice?" the voice asked. I still went by that name to my old clientele. I decided further down the road to change it for good, but for the sake of continuity with all my old clients, Candice was still who I was. New clients called me BLONDIE. Confused? Imagine how I felt? I would get calls for Candice, calls for BLONDIE, and when I returned them, if the clients left messages when they couldn't get hold of me, I didn't know by what name I should introduce myself by. It was often funny and kept things very interesting.

"Yes, this is she" I replied

"I'm Barry, and I saw your Ad, and I'd like to meet up. Do you have an in-call?"

Well, I sat there looking at my phone, lost for words. What the fuck was an in-call? I had never heard that term before. This was certainly a first for me and I really didn't know what to say to Barry, so after a few seconds of silence and Barry shouting down the phone "hello, hello, are you still there?"

I just blurted it out, "yes Barry, when would you like to come?" not knowing what the fuck I was talking about, but knowing I would soon be educated and that Barry would be the man to enlighten me.

"Are you free in about 2 hours?" he asked, "I'd like to come over"

'Come over?' I thought to myself, come over where? And then it clicked. In-call, my place, my home, my hotel room. Ah ha! Light bulb moment.

"Sure" I replied, "it's going to be $400/hour Barry and my address is…." And I gave Barry the address to Omar's house.

Before I knew it, I was turning the car round and heading back home. I needed time to get ready for Barry and time to ensure that Omar was where he was supposed to be, AT WORK! My mind began racing.

"In-call, Omar, shit, I invited a client to fuck at Omar's

home. What if I get caught? What if someone sees me?"

I had no idea what I was going to do if Omar was still home, but I did know that Barry now had my home address and was on his way over. What if I misjudged him and he was a cop? I was so quick to accept this In-call invitation. Maybe I shouldn't have been so forthright?

Arriving back at the house, thankfully Omar was gone. As time was of the essence, I prepared for my date with Barry as quickly as I could, keeping watch out of my windows, just in case he was a cop and not a real date. I didn't know what to expect, and when his car finally drove up and parked in the driveway, I could tell by the way he expressed complete surprise at the size of the house, that Barry was just a regular guy looking for sex. Phew! My relief was incredible and now, my job was to make Barry cum and get him out of there asap.

Better thought than done!

Barry entered, and we hugged.

"Nice place" he said, as he trundled into the hallway, looking up and down at all the fancy décor.

I ushered Barry upstairs and into my room as quickly as I could, all the time thinking that Omar could walk in at any moment, unannounced. We made ourselves comfortable on my bed. Barry began.

"$400 you said, so here it is" and as he said that he took 4 crisp $100 bills from his jacket pocket.

"Thanks Barry, now why don't you get naked and we can begin?" I ordered him.

"Is this your home?" he continued. All I wanted to do was fuck him and make him happy and then get him out of there. Barry had other ideas, and the poor guy must have been nervous. I carried on the conversation.

"Actually, it's owned by a friend of mine. I just rent this room"
"Oh, so you do all your in-call here?" as he said it, his eyes rolled to the back of his head as if he was somehow disgusted that I might have fucked more than just him on my mattress.

"Yes, I do, is that OK with you Barry?"

Barry nodded and then proceeded to undress. He was right down to his underwear, when he spoke again.

"Foot fetish." he blurted out.

"What??" I shouted.

"I have a foot fetish; I hope you don't mind?"

I had no idea what the fuck a foot fetish was. In those days, no one talked about a foot fetish, now of course there's a fetish for everything and everyone. I was bemused and shell-shocked.

"Barry, what would you like me to do to you? You don't want to be fucked?" I was really confused and Barry knew it.

"Candice, just let me suck your toes, one by one, and then rub my dick in between your feet and I will be as happy as a sand boy in shit"
I burst out laughing.

"Glad you find this amusing. I am happy to take my cash and go
somewhere else"

"No Barry, no, stay. I'll do it, I've just never been asked by anyone to do this before. If I laugh when you're sucking, it's only because I am ticklish. I just washed my feet so they are nice and fresh for you"
And with that, Barry, the crazy fucker, (well way back in 1998/99, I thought he was nuts, not so much 2019/20), began sucking my toes. One by one, he placed them in his mouth like he was about to eat a popsicle. Into the mouth went the small toe, and he'd lick it and kiss it and then move to the next one, repeating this process 10 times and then starting again. I'm not really one for clock watching, but after the second round, I was so bored. I thought it best to speed the proceedings up, so I reached down to feel his cock. It was soft.

"Barry, why are you doing this when it's not making you hard?" I asked

"Wait" was all he said, as my big toe came out of his mouth for the 3rd time. It was all wet and sticky and getting cold just sitting in fresh air as Barry grabbed hold of his cock and began to masturbate.

"OK Barry, this is getting weird. Why don't you let me do that to you?"

"Shut up, I know what I'm doing and I know what I want" he was so demanding.

I sat there like a spare pussy at a wedding, while Barry stroked his cock up and down, eyes closed, humming a tune while he worked his magic. Then, about ten minutes later, his penis sort of got hard and he placed it between my feet again. Well, no lie, as soon as that cock got near my toes, it went from 2 inches to 6 inches in 1.2 seconds! It was as if it had been fertilized in the best plant grower ever made. Zoom! Erection! I rubbed my feet up and down his cock for less than 30 seconds and BOOM! Barry came buckets, all down my freshly washed and sucked toes. There was so much cum, I thought I'd been given a new pair of yellowy white slippers!

Barry finished off with this massive sigh and then lay flat on the bed, exhausted.

"Barry, I hate to rush you, and I hope you enjoyed that, but I have another client coming" I lied.

"Oh, oh, so sorry" now he was embarrassed and he obviously didn't realize that although he'd paid for an hour, he'd only been with me 40 minutes, but I wanted him out of there, just in case Omar returned.

Barry kind of ran away, dressing super quickly, putting on his shoes and hugging me goodbye. I saw him out the front door and then spent the next 45 minutes with my feet draped in a foot bath cleanse! To date that had been the strangest day ever in my short E$corting career, but I was certain more would follow, I just hoped they weren't all going to be as weird as Barry, but I was wrong on that count too. Over the years, fetish and roll play, which is also classed as just fetish, has become more popular than ever. I have had guys want the following, and try not to laugh too loud, these guys are genuinely serious when it comes to this stuff, and I have grown to respect their preferences and not to judge.

I had one guy come to see me who wanted me to me to stand on his face, call him names, bad names, a list of which he gave me before we began, and take polaroid pictures of him as I did this. At first, I refused, then I complied and the tip he gave me was enormous. I didn't even fuck him.

Another guy came to see me and wanted me to kick him as hard and as often as possible in his stomach before we had sex. I just couldn't do it, so he grabbed an ornament from one of my shelves and inflicted as much pain as he could on himself by beating his stomach repeatedly until it was bruised and then he begged me to have sex with him, which I dually did. He writhed in agony as

I bounced off his tummy, but again, at the end, left fulfilled and happy and also left a huge tip!

I don't do roll play and I am not a dominatrix, but I've been asked many times to perform those fantasies for clients who are willing to pay large sums of money to be beaten, bossed and ridiculed. All in all, I am now more open to fetish requests than I was back then, when I'd just started E$corting on my own, but some of the other girls who do this for a living have even wilder stories than mine. One of my best friends, I will call her Miss R, used to go to a mobile home just outside Anaheim Hills here in CA, and stick a can of beer in this guy's asshole until he bled. She never fucked the guy, who was a drug addict, but he'd pay her $300 to $400 every time she went there. She told me the smell at his home was so bad that she'd wear a gas mask before entering, but she did it often enough to buy herself a new car, just from that job alone.

Yes, men are strange, and this was just the beginning of my journey as a solo E$cort, and more great things were about to happen to me. I often sit and think about the days before the internet and somehow, they are kind of missed, especially by me. There was so much naivety back then, so much trust and so much we didn't know. Now, with everything available at the touch of a button, nothing is sacred, you can even watch a penis going in and out of a vagina with a camera that's been placed inside that vagina, thus leaving nothing up to the imagination. Everything is so well documented. Life has changed, and I am not sure it's for the better. What I do know is that the oldest profession in the world is still the strongest and probably most everlasting profession available on this planet.

Violence and Abuse

There have been times over the past years where I've felt completely at ease with some people, and other times where I've actually feared for my life. The gun episode being one of those times. In general, people, well, men, clients, are respectful. For the most part, I can tell on the phone whether I think there might be an issue and I always have the opportunity to cancel the booking or indeed to not even accept that booking. I have remained true to my gut when making these decisions and more often than not, I have been proven correct. There was a time when I was prepared to accept all bookings, my financial situation dictating that necessity, but as the years progressed and experience kicked in, I became more choosey and more skeptical when receiving calls from men I thought might be problematic. Intuition certainly helps and there's been more than one instance where I got it completely wrong. I began to understand how some young girls can get trapped as 'sex slaves' in an industry dominated by violence and abuse at certain levels. There are men running brothels, Pimps who run whores, and men who just want to fuck underaged girls they've captured or flown in from poorer countries. All of these types of guys are to be avoided. I've had close shaves, some too close for comfort, but men do really dominate in this industry and these men are by the part, not nice.

 I had one experience, early on in my solo career, when I received a call from a guy asking if I would come to his office and perform for three of them. Three office workers in Irvine California, sounded an OK gig, and they'd offered me a ton of cash to do so. After talking with the guy, who had a remarkably soft and sensual voice, I decided to make the appointment happen, and we arranged a time and place. When I showed up, I was completely surprised by how nice of an office he actually had. It was modern, clean and set amongst other similar structures in a serene business district of Irvine. I was quite relieved when I arrived because I knew there were good and bad parts of Irvine and I really didn't want to drive to the seedier side of town.

I remember it was around 8 PM and the building was empty, but when I got there, one of the guys was outside waiting for me and he kindly opened my car door and assisted me inside. Their office was right next to the main lobby and offering an easy exit back to my car if need be. This in itself gave me a sense of relief because if anything went awry, I could escape in an instant, or so I thought.

The party started. We will call them the 3 Stooges. One was fat, one thin and the other just tall, so tall in fact, he towered over me by at least 2 feet, and I'm 5'7"

The conversation began, and I could tell they'd already been drinking for quite a while and there was that pungent odor of 'weed', hanging restlessly in the room. They'd cracked a few windows to get rid of the odor, but I could still smell it.

"Drink?" Mr. Tall offered

I accepted, and Mr. Thin poured me a bourbon, and Mr. Fat began to taking his pants down.

"What are you guys looking for tonight?" I asked. I was used to being asked to perform all sorts of perverted acts, and honestly, these three guys looked like reasonable human beings so I didn't anticipate being asked to do anything I hadn't done before.

Mr. Tall said "we want you to suck us all off at the same time, then we will all fuck you"

"A triple blow job?" I asked, still smiling and still contemplating no issues.

"Yeah, 3 cocks in your mouth at the same time" came the reply from Mr. Fat.

"And how am I supposed to fit all three of you in my mouth at the same time?"

And that's when I realized I might have an issue. I could just tell from their faces that violence of some kind was in the air. It's something I'd learned from watching all the bar brawls I'd witnessed over my life, when a man or men get that look, trouble is in the air. I had to make a split-second decision, to stay, or not to stay?

I needed the cash badly, I really did, and greed got the better of me, I think?

"Right gentlemen, here's the deal" I said and as I lifted my dress off my body, revealing my nakedness and of course my perfect tits. I continued speaking. "One in my mouth and one in my pussy or nothing at all. Number 3 can masturbate and wait his turn"

They all looked at one another, and they looked again.

Mr. Thin sauntered over.

"Suck this" he said, as he placed his smallish cock in front of my mouth. The other two were laughing, and then, as I began to grip Mr. Thin's cock, I noticed Mr. Fat leave the room.

Did I mention the cash? Probably not. They had this large bag filled with cash, all of which was supposed to come to me, or so I thought, and all of which was just sitting there on one of their desks waiting to be picked up and pocketed when I was done. I'd been told there was 3 grand in that case, and with the money in mind, I took Mr. Thin's cock and began to rub it and suck it. When I'd began, and with Mr. Fat already out of the room, Mr. Tall came over to where I was sucking off Mr. Thin and he began holding my hair and pushing my face in towards Mr. Thin's cock. It wasn't a friendly push either, it was kind of violent, sending Mr. Thin's cock all the way down my throat and making me gag. I had men do this to me before, but never with this much force. All the time they're doing this, they are egging me on with slanderous and unwelcomed comments.

"Come on bitch, swallow that cock"

"Let' me see you puke"

"You're nothing but a slut and a whore"

And this went on and on and on and while Mr. Thin was fucking my throat. He was getting harder and harder and more violent with every stroke. I knew at that point I was in real trouble and with Mr. Tall holding me in a kind of Police grip, with both hands behind my back as if he was about to cuff me, I had no means of escape. Mr. Fat had now returned to the room, and they switched positions, with Mr. Fat putting his cock in my mouth and Mr. Thin leaving the room. I didn't know what the fuck was going on and this vicious cycle repeated itself again and again, and always with one of them out of the room. After about 30 minutes of taking this nonsense, they stopped. Mr. Fat had cum, Mr. Thin was lying half naked and high on top of a desk and Mr. Tall was jerking off so he could cum on my face. It didn't happen. He stopped. "Go get cleaned up," he said, as he threw a bunch of cash at me.

I let the cash fall to the ground, because I knew I could collect it later before I left. I cleaned up in the ladies' room, came back and all the fun began again. All I could think about while they banged their cocks into my throat, was the cash and what debts I would pay off with it once this was over. It seemed like hours had passed, but it was only about 45 minutes, and I noticed, when I arrived back from the ladies' room, all three were laughing and joking about something. Which seemed related to me and or my well-being, but whatever it was, it went right over my head. I was shattered, and ready to leave. They'd booked me for 2 hours and I wanted to be nice and to fulfill their requests, but the violence which they'd extended upon my poor throat had taken its toll.

"Anyone want to fuck me properly?" I asked, hoping that maybe one or all of them would just fuck me in my pussy. None of them did. They were all spent.

"Can I go now?" I asked.

They laughed, and Mr. Tall came over towards me, handed me $100 and said "fuck off whore"

I was too nervous and frightened to fight with them about the cash, I was shaking like a leaf, and so with the $100 in the palm of my hand, I grabbed my dress and panties and shoes and ran. I got to the car, breathed a sigh of relief, still shaking, and started the engine. I could still smell each and every one of them, as I drove home in a panic, tears running down my face. As I approached the freeway, I reached into my glove box to pull out a CD to relieve the tension in my body, not just any CD, but my favorite CD, a Judas Priest Best Of collection. I reached into where the CDs were supposed to be, and I reached again, remember, I was driving while doing this. Everything was gone. My CD's my gum, my photo's that I kept in the car. Nothing was there! The bastards had stolen everything while I was being throat fucked. I remembered now that only 2 of them were in the room at the one time while the 3rd was someplace else. They stole everything I had. Fuckers! I got home and couldn't sleep. I hadn't been paid the promised $3000, and they'd also gone through my car and taken everything. I didn't know what to do.

I went round and round contemplating my revenge and I couldn't fathom what I would do that would compensate for both the loss of cash and also the loss of all my personal belongings.

First thing next morning, with my head a little clearer, I had a plan. I went back to the building I'd been at the night before, knowing the 3 of them had to work there, and I walked straight in and asked for security. The head guy came out, the head security guy.

I sat for 10 minutes and told him the whole story. He was very understanding and very sympathetic.

He told me that he'd get to the bottom of the matter and he believed he knew who the 3 Stooges were.

About 48 hour later, I received a call, a call I hadn't expected.

The security guy had come through for me. He'd located the culprits, all of my belongings and some cash they'd thrown in after he'd insisted he'd report all of them to senior management if they didn't pay up. He was a lifesaver. I drove back to the office block, where he met me outside, handing all of my things back to me in person and also passed me $1000 that he'd taken from the Stooges.

I was so grateful and I told the guy that I would fuck him for free whenever he wanted. He never took me up on that offer, but I had learned a valuable lesson from that whole experience, and a lesson that would stay with me even today. I never again would take a job like that unless all the money was paid up front, my car was locked with the keys hidden and my ground rules set out in advance in order that the violence was averted.

And then there was Joey. Joey was a hoot, at least he started off that way. I met him the first time at his hotel, a lovely 5-star hotel in Dana Point California and Joey was nothing but niceness, all wrapped up in a package that smelt of money. We went out a few times, in fact we had great sex on 4 or 5 different occasions, for which Joey paid me $1000 per pop. Things with Joey were great, but what I didn't know about him, and what I was about to find out, was that Joey was a coke-head, and not only that, his temper was just vile. One summers evening, about 3 months after we'd met, Joey sent a Limo to pick me up from my home. We were going to a concert, it was a concert at the Irvine Center, but I cannot remember who the band was. We took off, it was around 6 PM, and Joey began the evening by going down on me while the Limo driver shut the center partition and looked the other way. Joey had paid the guy to drive us around all evening, taking us to dinner and then the show and then taking me home. Joey was single, no attachments at all, and was incredibly handsome. After he licked my pussy into oblivion, he decided he wanted to fuck me, there and then, with the limo driver still going around in circles waiting for Joey's signal letting him know to pull over so we could exit the limo and have dinner at a pre-booked restaurant near Laguna Beach. Joey, before he got out his dick, took out some cocaine, asking if I would like to join him in snorting a line. I refused and as soon as I refused, he started to get mad. Without warning, he rolled down the central partition, and told the driver to take me home. I was in a state of shock and couldn't understand what was going on.

"You don't snort, we don't go out" was all he said.

I never did cocaine, ever, and I wasn't about to begin that evening. We reached my house, and he asked me to get out the limo. He paid the limo driver to go and park somewhere and he followed me inside. By this time, we were really at the stage where he wanted to fuck me and I wanted him to go, but he'd not paid me yet, so I let him come in, and that's when the violence started.

Joey spread his cocaine stash in even lines on my dressing room table and snorted 4 out of the 6 lines he'd laid there. He was high as a kite, in fact, his ass was higher than his elbows and he was flying. Next thing I knew, and believe me, I wasn't expecting any of this because, as I mentioned, I'd been out with him several times, and he'd been in my home previously, but this behavior was new to me, and honestly, quite uncharacteristic, his cock was out and then the abuse began. He started throwing me around the room, not violently at first, but forcefully, shouting profanities, all aimed at my profession, as his eyes seemed to just pop from his head. It was something to behold and something to be scared of, but at the onset of this tirade, I thought it was just amusing. The amusement that I may have had in the beginning soon turned to sheer terror, as Joey, with the weight of his body pinning me down on my bed and the sheer strength of his grip making it impossible for me to get up or to move a muscle, or to reach for my cell phone to call for help. Before I knew it, and before he could get his dangling cock inside me, he pulled me up, ushered me over to the bathroom, threw me in there and then used a pair of handcuffs I kept for roll play which he'd taken out of one of my dresser drawers, to cuff me to the sink taps. Then he closed the door and went back into my bedroom, smashing ornaments, mirrors and other furniture, until he'd exhausted himself and decided to was time to smash me instead. I was shitting myself, locked up, cuffed, with no exit, no one at home and no chance of escape. I decided to try talking to him, but that just made things worse. He came into the bathroom and pulled up my dress, then he fucked me, a fucking that I can only describe as brutal and bordering on rape. Us E$corts know the difference, and this time, there wasn't much difference.

The fucking went on for hours, in fact, by the time he finished, it was well past midnight and well past any chance I'd had of getting out of this situation intact. Joey went back into my bedroom and passed out on the bed, with me, still locked up and unable to escape, weeping my poor heart out in the bathroom.

Some 7 hours later, this would be about 13 hours after he'd initially collected me, Joey woke up and had no idea where he was. After a few minutes spent getting himself oriented to his surroundings, he called out my name, and at first, I was too frightened to reply. He obviously knew where he was, my place of course, but he didn't know where I was. He stepped into the bathroom, where he found me on the floor handcuffed to the sink. With total disbelief on his face, he came marching over to the sink and spoke

"What the fuck are you doing in here tied up like that?"

He had no idea. I explained to him what had happened, but he didn't believe me at first. Then, as he watched the expressions on my face turn into more tears, I think he got it. He uncuffed me, took me into the bedroom and apologized profusely. He then wrote me a check for $5,000, called the limo driver and sped off, never to be seen again.

Joey's check bounced, which blew my mind, and Joey cut off his cell phone and vanished. Some 3 years later, one of my E$cort friends told me she'd met a great guy and they were going to be married. It was Joey! I tried to warn her off him, but love is what love is and she went ahead with the ceremony. I found out that after about 5 months of married hell, Joey overdosed and died, leaving my friend penniless and permanently bruised, inside and out, and regretting every moment of her decision to marry him.

My last story in this section involves a 4-some on a Super Bowl Sunday, way back in the day, and certainly after the two bad experiences I just listed above. It wasn't so much the violence that I remember this for, but the lack of violence, because the guy who I was with, a 6'8" white basketball player, and his two friends, one a woman and one another tall black guy, had been shooting the shit for hours, telling me just what they intended to do to me after they picked me up that Sunday afternoon. Their language was so abusive, I almost canceled the date, but they'd offered me $1500 to come out with them, fuck all three of them, yes, the woman too, and to watch the game, which by the way, I remember none of. From the experiences I'd had with the 3 guys and with Joey and with the kind of verbiage they were spouting during numerous phone conversations we'd had to set up this date, I was kind of nervous that yet again

I was getting into something that might be dangerous. The white guy, we can call him Matchstick, and I'll explain the reason for that name as we progress, would come on the phone and explain in great detail what he'd always wanted to do to a 'dirty fucking blonde bitch' like me. He was extremely descriptive and at first, I thought he might be joking, but after the second call, the one where we'd end up confirming all the details for our date, he'd put the black guy on the phone, we can call him Assassin, because that's the impression I received after he told me he was going to 'shoot his load' in some kind of manner that would harm me. I thought he was amusing, but again, as that call progressed, my uncertainties rose to DEFCON 4 as humor turned to fear. I had no idea there would be a woman involved, well, not until they all arrived to collect me just after 1 PM that Super Bowl Sunday.

A Buick large enough to be a spaceship arrived, with all 3 of them on board. It was a huge limo, sawn off in the center just to enable the manufacturer to extend it. The vehicle was uglier than heck, and jet black and also in need of a good cleaning, the guy who was driving the limo got out, and went to open the rear door to let me in. I was standing curbside, close to where I lived, waiting patiently for them to show up, and when they did, Matchstick, wearing his best suit and a chauffeur's cap, was driving! It was hilarious, and it certainly put my mind at ease, believing now that these two morons were just pranksters. Matchstick greeted me with a bow and then handed me the $1500 fee. I asked them to wait for a few minutes as I took the money back to my room and deposited it in a locked safe, I'd purchased. They were still waiting and goofing around when I came back and that's when I realized there was also a woman inside the limo, we will call her Linda, because she looked and acted like Linda Lovelace, the big porn star at that time. She was very pretty and Assassin was quite into her in many ways that I cannot describe. He was fingering her in public on top of the trunk in broad daylight as I approached the limo for the 2[nd] time after dropping off the cash. I found out later, she wasn't even an E$cort, they were just dating!

We drove off, with Matchstick in full command of our Super Bowl experience.

In the back of the limo, Assassin and Linda were already 'at it', leaving nothing to the imagination and often looking up from between her legs where his tongue was now rampant, Assassin would speak and offer me a commentary.

"Just getting to the good part now Blondie" he would say and then 2 minutes later, while coming up for air, "She's nearly there, Blondie" and then again, as Linda screamed as she came, "Told ya, Blondie!" he would boast.

This went on for fully 25 minutes until Matchstick pulled up outside a home in Orange, and we all got out.

"Where are we?" I asked.

"Beer stop" Assassin said, as he shut the limo door and led the way into this nice townhome. Matchstick was already at the front door and opening it with one of 25 keys he had on his key chain. He looked like a Jailer with that set of keys, and perhaps I should have named him that?

We all trundled into the house and Matchstick went to the fridge, took out a 6 pack and offered us one each, and then, well, then it just kicked off. The abuse again,

"You fucking whore, you slut, just come upstairs and fuck all of us" Matchstick was loud and obnoxious and I was nervous and not a happy bunny. Linda seemed surprised and sort of calmed things down again, but as she did, Matchstick grabbed my free hand and pulled me upstairs, where, followed by Assassin and Linda, we all ended up naked and fucking on his bed. Matchstick took off his clothes and yes, guess what? His penis was the size of a……, yes, matchstick. I couldn't stop laughing and realized there and then that the abuse he was spouting was a cover for having a small thin dick. It was embarrassing, for him especially, and no wonder he had to pay for sex. He was a huge tall man, with a dick the size of my pinky finger. It was hard not to laugh and hard not to say anything as he tried to insert his penis into my vagina. He couldn't do it, and as Assassin and Linda began to fuck again, Matchstick became more and more annoyed with himself and in the end, he gave up, went to sit on a chair next to his bed and drowned his sorrows with more beer, continuing his insults as Linda, now bored with Assassin, came to me and licked me out, probably the best fucking by a woman I'd ever had. Assassin and Matchstick in the meantime, were locked in a kind of physical brawl at the other side of the room, all over what, I will never know? So, while Linda and I were having a jolly good old time, the two of them were punching six bags of shit out of each other and blood was flowing freely, which was more than I could say about anyone's seamen!

I came, Linda came, and the two guys calmed down and went out of the room to attend to their wounds. Linda said little, but I could tell this wasn't the first time she'd been through this scenario, and it wouldn't be the last, and thank goodness I was paid up front and had left the money in my safe at home. When the two guys had patched themselves up, bandages were the order of that particular day, we all settled down in the lounge and watched the game as if nothing had ever happened, with Assassin and Matchstick looking like they'd been involved in a WWE event and me and Linda, holding hands and locking eyes and wishing for more.

Yes, violence is uncalled for in this industry, but unfortunately, it's a fact of life and sometimes, part of the business.

Cute 'N Sexy

Since I was a child, I've been told I am cute, in fact, it was drummed into me by my family from the age of 5, and I can remember clearly, everywhere we went, my mother telling strangers, 'Look at my cute daughter'

It became embarrassing, and also repetitive, until I was around 13 or 14 when my breasts began to blossom and my face filled out and my sex appeal just appeared out of nowhere. I was then maturing into what I would become, cute'n sexy, and that's the way it would remain, right up until today. Everyone tells me the same thing, and without wanting to sound big-headed or vein, I think they are all correct in their assumption. Ask any one of the thousands of guys I've fucked, most will tell you, yeah, she's cute and she's sexy, and I often just hear it when I'm in a bar or restaurant with Moses, those words seem to echo all round. I have never let this go to my head, honestly, and most of the time it bypasses any self-esteem I might seriously have, but it's always nice to hear those words, and it's always nice to believe they are true.

Cute led to sexy, sexy led to horny and horny led me to where I am now, a fuck bunny, for anyone who can afford me. My ageing process has been slow, and I am so grateful for that, and I rarely do anything to stop the natural progression that life has thrown at me. I veer away from any procedures, Botox, Dermabrasion, Collagen and breast implants. I decided long ago, you get what you get, and you're stuck with it, so make the most of it and flaunt it while you still have it. Now, it's not to say I haven't thought about doing any of that stuff I just mentioned, and on occasion, I've been presented with opportunity, trades if you like, where someone will call me, offering me something from their business in return for sex. They see my picture on line, look at my golden locks and great tits and think that if they offer me some kind of body enhancement, I will fuck them in return. It doesn't always work that way, but I remember one Valentine's Day eve, many years ago, I was walking home from a bar, on Feb 13, and my cell phone rang. The lady on the other end of the line was to the point and explicit.

"Hey honey, saw your Ad, I'm Spa Jeanie, you may have seen my Ad's and I want to ask if you're interested in doing a trade?"

She had a foreign accent; I think it may have been Russian and she took me completely by surprise.

"What kind of trade?" I asked

"Honey, you're just a gorgeous woman, my boyfriend and I have been perusing the local E$cort Ad's and we keep coming back to yours. He's so horny luvy, he's always horny and even though I'm only a couple of years older than him, and in my early 30's, I just cannot satisfy his sexual appetite. I want you to do that for me. I want to offer you something in return, and it's not cash. You open to a trade?"

"What's the trade?" I asked, intrigued and ready to be disappointed.

"Have you even seen my Ad's sweetie? The one's offering the cosmetic peels? They rejuvenate the skin like nothing else on earth and they cost a fortune. It takes an hour to do and lasts up to two years, costs $700 and I'll give you one if you fuck Spa Jimmie, my boyfriend."

"Sounds tempting, but what will that procedure

do to my skin and how long does it take?"

"Takes an hour, so you have a choice, you can Fuck Spa Jimmy first and then do the procedure or the other way round, you decide? Are you up for it?" she asked

Well, I didn't have too much else going on that particular Valentine's Day, so I agreed to do it and we made a time to meet at her place the following evening. In the meantime, I Googled her and her Spa, of which she actually owned 2 places, close to each other in Irvine CA. The procedure itself got great reviews and seemed to be exactly as advertised. When I read up on what Spa Jeanie was going to do to my skin, I was quite excited and looking forward to my 'date' with her boyfriend Jimmie. She seemed a decent lady when I spoke to her on the phone and I had high hopes that she'd not only make my skin prettier and more youthful, but my whole being cuter and sexier too!

I dressed up for the occasion. I put on my best white blouse with red hearts emblazoned all over, positioned in such a way that some of the hearts covered my bra-less nipples, a red mini dress and red high heels, and I got into my car and drove to Irvine. When I arrived, I was feeling sexier than ever and when I saw where Jeanie and Jimmy actually lived, I was blown away by how nice the apartment block was. Brand new, upmarket, close to all the shops, nicely situated and best of all, plenty of parking. Excitement rose up inside me as I pushed the 4-digit code to enter their building and made my way up to the top floor. I got out of the elevator and walked briskly towards their front door. My heart was pounding, and I didn't know why. I never got nervous before a call, but for some reason that all changed on this particular adventure.

I knocked.

The fun began as soon as Jeanie opened that door. She was stunningly beautiful. 5 foot 6, slim, blonde hair down to her shoulders, about 30 years of age, wonderful skin, great boobs and legs that ran for miles. When she opened the door, hugged me and kissed me on the cheek, there seemed to be an instant attraction between us. I knew straight away that Jeanie and I would become intimate, not sure when that was going to happen, but I knew it would.

"You're so cute!!" she exclaimed, "and sooooooo sexy!"

I replied, "Honey, you're just drop dead gorgeous, and I cannot wait to meet Jimmy"

As I said that, this hunk of a man, Jimmy, appeared from behind the living room door. By this time, Jeanie had closed the front door and all three of us were left standing in their hallway. Jimmy was over 6 foot, and looked like a walking Ad for Men's health magazine. He was completely ripped. His Abs were a 12 pack and his biceps were enormous. I couldn't help but stop and think why on earth they'd wanted me there in the first place? I mean, surely these guys fucked like bunnies every night? If I was living with Jimmy, we'd never get out of bed. It was the strangest situation, and one that I kept reminding myself, I wasn't actually getting paid for!

"Follow me" came the order from Jeanie.

We entered her bedroom, where a huge king-sized bed awaited our arrival. The room was so clean and tidy, the bed, freshly made, sheets that were crisp and deliciously soft, probably Egyptian cotton, and a vanity unit next to that bed, covered with as many sex toys as any lover of sex could ever want. I was wet, and getting wetter, and nothing had happened yet!

"Would you prefer we do the procedure first and then have sex later?" Jeanie asked.

I didn't know what I thought. I was so enamored by the two of them, I was looking left and then right at her and then him and all the way back again. Who was the more beautiful? I just didn't know. I wanted both of them, I wanted them there and then, and I think Jeanie could sense that my sexual appetite was growing, in a good way of course. "Um," I was stuttering now, "I think the sex?" but my answer was far from positive and certain. Without procrastinating any further, Jimmy came slowly towards me, his muscles bulging as he walked. I was so turned on, and it showed. Jimmy began fondling my tits, which were free and loose beneath my see-through white blouse. I was dripping wet, and raring to go. This was perhaps the biggest turn on I'd ever had in any of dates I'd been on so far. I was just mesmerized by the 2 of them, willing Jeanie to get involved too. Unfortunately for me, she left the room, without saying anything, and I was left alone with Jimmy.

The fun began. He took off my blouse and began sucking my nipples, then he gently picked me up and laid me down on their bed. He began to undress himself and I willingly assisted. As quickly as I could say 'fuck me Jimmy' , he had a condom on and was inside my dripping wet pussy. It was amazing, he was amazing, thrusting in and out, playing with my clit, teasing me again and again with his cock. As I lay there, orgasmic sensations flowing right through me, all I could think about was Jeanie. And then right on que, she came back into the room, naked. It became a threesome for the ages. Jimmie was fucking me; I was fucking Jeanie and Jeanie was just enjoying it all by exaggerating her vocal prowess every time I licked her clit. Fabulous wouldn't be the right description. Amazing, well, it was beyond that. I couldn't believe my luck, and all thought of payment or procedures to follow, evaporated with every thrust Jimmy made inside me. He was huge, and he knew how to use it. Boy did he know. I found out later that Jimmy was younger than Jeanie, and Jimmy could go and go and go. I envied Jeanie, living with such a stud, and I envied her even more with her ability to trust her boyfriend and watch him fuck another woman, albeit for money. This was fun, so much fun, I didn't want it to end, which, sadly it did, after Jimmy came inside me for the 3rd time. After Jimmy was done, and spent, Jeanie became friskier. She took me to her side of the bed and while Jimmy cleaned up, she licked me all over, and after that we started using her toys. I orgasmed several times more and Jeanie, well, she came more than 10 times in a row. The juices were flowing, the bed sheets soaking wet and soiled and me? Well, I was in sexual heaven.

When it was over, I had my procedure, and I left. I wanted to stay, and I think they wanted me to stay too. The funny thing is, I have never heard from either of them since, and I now know it was nothing other than a complete romp and distraction for both of them, something I can appreciate, but nonetheless, it saddens me that I never got an opportunity for round two. The procedure Jeanie did on me lasted about 8 months, and during that period of time, I did look cuter and sexier than ever before, even if it was all in my own mind, but the whole experience that Spa Jeanie brought to the table and obviously into my life, left an indelible impression, not only on my sexual libido and my face, but also on my soul, and it's something I'll be eternally grateful for until I leave this earth. A once in a lifetime sexual experience that placed a new 'face' and perspective on life!

Parker Arizona

Since I turned 13, the longest period of time I've ever gone in my life without having sex with a man, is about 10 days. Yes, 10 days, and that was only because I was sick. I have had an amazing sex life, and one that I can only brag about, and want to brag about. That is, if anyone else would like to listen? If I was a man, and thank God I'm not, I would be declared a national treasure and a stud. Because I'm a woman, things are kind of frowned upon and some people might describe me as a hussy or a slut or a whore, which I am not. I am a woman who knows what she wants, sees opportunity and grabs it with open arms. I am a lady and at all times, I am honest. I love my body and my body loves sex. I was born to fuck; I was born to make love and I was born to please. When the good Lord opens the doors of heaven for me, and I know he will, he's going to offer up a long list of men whose souls I have saved or salvaged, because I let them into my vagina and I made them feel good and wanted. I have given a love-life to thousands who thought that their love-life was over. I have pleasured and been pleasured by those very same men, and at the end of the day, I feel great about my contribution to mankind. This merry-go-round of sexual exploration began at 13, and it has carried on to this very day, as good as, if not better that it was back then, experience playing a huge part in the way I perform and view my sexual experiences and exploits. As my age has progressed and as the lines on my face have deepened, although, honestly, I still look great at 57, and probably will, well into my 60's, I am more comfortable now in and out of bed than I ever was before.

Parker Arizona, a small town nestled on the border between Arizona and California, it's two sides, split by a river, one side in CA and the other, obviously in AZ, but either way and either side, my den of iniquity and my grounding for what would become my career.

My sister, who is 4 years older than me, had a car, and I had ambition. My sister drove, I slept. My sister had a boyfriend, I had many, and with all of this in mind, let me tell you how Parker became my own personal fucking paradise.

The town of Parker was introduced to me at the tender age of 16, by Marie, my sister, one sunny afternoon in May of 1980. She had a boyfriend called Robert, and his father Syd and his father's girlfriend Darvy lived in a trailer park, 4 miles outside of Parker, on the California side of town. As I lived full-time with Marie, rather than her try to find ways to go to Parker without me, leaving me alone with my several boyfriends in her home in OC, she decided to take me to visit Robert's dad and asked me if I'd like to bring a friend with me. One trip to Parker turned into two trips which turned into many trips, as each time I went down there, sitting comfortably in the back of her car, being fingered by David, my boyfriend at the time, I grew to love the place more than any other place on earth, including the place where I live now. To this day, I still go there bi-weekly, and to this day, I still have as much fun as I did back then when I was just a young girl. The trailer park was decent, and Syd, Robert's dad, owned a home, which was actually a trailer, a fairly nice trailer, but oh my goodness, the things that went on in that town and especially in that trailer park, are stories of legend. Darvy, Syd's girlfriend, was one of the most insane people I have ever met, and she was fucking Bill, their neighbor from across the way, without Syd knowing of course. I knew, my sister knew, but Syd, well, he was oblivious for years, and it was happening right on his own doorstep. The situation just was like a TV soap opera, bodies popping in and out of trailers each night and people fucking different people at different times according to work schedules and desire. Hilarity overcame my need to puke, every time Darvy would sneak across the park to fuck Bill. She was out of her mind, but not on drugs, just in a crazy kind of way, but she didn't care and she made it very easy for herself to get caught, which, she eventually did.

One evening, when David and I were going at it in the back of my sister's car, it was about 10 PM on a Saturday night, Syd, who by now had found out what Darvy was up to, produced a homemade bomb out of nowhere, snuck across the lot to Bill's trailer, placed the bomb in the back of his truck and then detonated it, not only blowing the truck into a million little pieces, but also destroying part of

Bill's trailer while he was inside it fucking Darvy! The two of them, Darvy and Bill, fled like criminals on foot to the other side of town, not knowing what the hell just happened, but realizing someone had spilled the beans on their little secret and taking no chances that Syd was going finish the job by shooting both of them in the head with one of the several guns he kept locked up in his trailer. Guns! Yes, this is when I leaned to shoot, ride ATV's and motorcycles and fuck like a bunny, more so than when I was in OC, and boy, even though I was good at it in OC, I became even better at it in Parker. Parker was different. It brought a different outlook into my life. It opened doors to the kind of men who really turn me on, men like my current beau, Moses. Long hair, muscles, tattoos and a love for heavy metal music. Parker had all of this in abundance, and more. After I split with David from OC, I continued to go to Parker at weekends, fucking guy after guy, and honestly, there were so many men in that town, I could never run out of new cocks to suck and fuck. But apart from my sexual exploits, which I will come to in a moment, there was also some really weird shit going on there that I had the misfortune to witness, first hand.

About the same time I started to frequent Parker, a cult, or maybe it was a type of religion, who knows, also began to have its gatherings there. These people, the one's from this cult that I used to see down at the river, were very weird, performing all kinds of rituals in front of all of us, the party goer set. They were all dressed the same, white shirts, or blouses, black pants or dresses, and what looked like orange sneakers. We'd see them all the time, in the town, at the river, on the campsites. Totally surreal. It made the news, a lot, only because this was something very unusual for the local media to talk about. One afternoon while I was at home in Orange County, I watched in disbelief on TV as they reported that this whole group of people from that cult had committed suicide in Parker. About 60 of them had died, and I remember watching this and thinking, "oh my God, I saw all of them 48 hours ago! I was standing next to some of these people', and now they were all gone!

There was a sandbar on the river, somewhere between Parker and Havasu City, yes, a sandbar, where all the boats congregated and where all of us 'party people' went crazy. So much incredible stuff happened on that sandbar that I could write a chapter on that alone. One of the strangest things to go down was one afternoon when I was sitting on top of a boat called The Desirous, owned by my friend who's first name shall remain anonymous, but who had the last name Shell. We were partying like crazy and I'd just been fucked by a guy who I called Long Haired Terry. He had a huge schlong, maybe 9 or 10 inches long, and every time he fucked me, and he fucked me many times, I had to go back up on deck, undress and jump in the water naked, just so pussy could cool off. He was wild, and he could go for hours at a time without coming. When he did cum, he could spray his cum more than 6 feet across the room. It was amazing to watch but the shower was something to avoid. Often enough he would get his cum in my hair when he ejaculated, and I'd have to shower or get into the river and shampoo it off. He was a great lover, but also had no idea when to stop thrusting and lost so many of his girlfriends because they just couldn't take the pounding any longer. I, on the other hand, just loved it, and the harder and longer he fucked me, the more addicted to his cock I got. We'd just finished one of those legendary fucking sessions, and there I was, all red and raw and desperate to jump into the Colorado river. I marched upstairs, serenaded by two of Terry's friends, who'd stood outside his bedroom door on the boat getting their rocks off as he fucked me as I moaned my way through and hour and a half of penile torture, shouting through the door as loud as possible, 'my turn next' and 'fuck me please', and not interested in how ridiculous they might be looking at that point in time, but determined, so determined, to get me into the sack. I got to the top of the stairs, jumped out onto the deck, and stripped. Jumping into the river was by that time, a pleasure, and I swear, you could hear the sizzle off my pussy as it hit the water and began the soothing process of cooling down in that wonderfully cool water. It was just like a cartoon. No sooner had by body submerged into that cool elixir of fresh water and that feeling of orgasmic bliss, when suddenly and from out of nowhere, another boat arrived on the scene, coming dangerously close to where I was paddling, and two guys on the edge of that boat threw me a life-vest and rope. Instinctively I grabbed the rope, to this day, I have no idea why, and off I went, soaring into the air, fully naked, tits and ass bouncing all over the place and landed square in the middle of their deck as they both hauled me in like a fish and opened the boats throttle as we sped off. I had no time to assess the situation, and in my 'birthday suit' had absolutely no desire to. The two guys, we can call them Captain Kirk and Captain Pugwash, threw me a large beach towel, but not before ogling me all over, then they brought me a beer, super cold of course and the fun began.

"I'm Captain K" the first one said, and we are going to entertain you for the next couple of hours. I wasn't frightened, I was intrigued. This was Parker, and nothing but good things happened in Parker, well, except that cult suicide perhaps, the one I'd watched on TV?

They parked their boat on the AZ side of the river at a deserted beach. They fed me liquor, lots of it and they were very friendly. By now they'd managed to rustle up a bikini from inside the boat and also procure the services of two other ladies, both drop-dead gorgeous and willing to play. The fun began. We all decided that since we were so drunk, a five-some would be the way to go and decided that Captain P would lead the way. Both he and Captain K had generous sized members and when they stripped, the two other ladies, began munching on them in a manner that suggested they'd not eaten for days. They devoured those cocks from top to bottom and with two hard dicks looking straight down the barrel of three wet pussy's, the fucking began in earnest. There was me and Captain P and then me and Captain K and the other two joining in just for fun. I was double penetrated, they were double penetrated, I was then on top of one of the ladies and being chewed out by the other and all this was going on while boats, one after another, were just drifting past, taking stock of the unbelievable scene that was our boat. We fucked on deck and in full view of all of them, blind to anything other than the great sex we were all having. The fucking went on for hours, really it did, and by the end of it, both Captains had come and gone twice, both ladies, maybe 12 orgasms each and me? Well, I was so out of it, so high and so drunk, I really hadn't counted when I'd cum and then where I'd gone. We stopped as quickly as we'd begun and they started the boat and took me back to Long haired Terry's boat, about half a mile up stream. Terry was standing on the edge of the port side of the boat when I arrived.

"Where the fuck did you go?" he shouted, as he looked at both captains with some disdain.

"Upstream with friends" I answered. I knew from the look on his face that Terry just wanted to blast the two captains into the middle of all eternity with his shotgun, the one he kept below deck and the same one we used when we went shooting in the desert, and I knew I had to diffuse the situation immediately to avoid bloodshed. Terry was definitely the jealous type.

"Terry, I was cooling off my pussy from the incredible fucking you gave me and these two lovely gentlemen picked me up and treated me to a nice couple of hours in a spot that I'd never been to. "I didn't think you'd care" and as I said this, the two ladies, my compatriots from our mega fucking session, came up from below deck and Terry relaxed. Once he saw them, his temper subsided as his brain realized the two captains had partners. Little did he know what kind of partners they really were!

Parker was synonymous for adventures like that one. As an old mining town, there were hundreds of wild Donkeys roaming freely, a byproduct of days gone by when they pulled carts to and from the gold mines, now left to live and breed freely, and just a friendly reminder to all who came to Parker that there was life before sex and debauchery. One evening when I was in the Sundance Bar, a guy I knew left drunk, got on his motorcycle, collided with a donkey on a dark road and died. Not the first or the last to do so. Donkeys were, and still are, everywhere. They're a tourist attraction as well as a hazard. I've even seen drunk guys sitting chatting to donkeys and asking them for sexual favors, although I have yet to see anyone fucking one! The three main bars in Parker are the Sundance and the Roadrunner and Foxes, all are dive bars and are a lot of fun to frequent. I've had several hook-ups in all those bars that have led to semi long-term relationships and many, perhaps too many to count, sexual affairs or as they say in the trade, one-night stands.

One of my long-term relationships was with a guy called David, not the Dave I was dating, this was David, and David owned a boat called Screwdriver, although the only screwing I ever witnessed David doing was with me on his boat. He was an animal in bed, but a gentle animal. He couldn't hold his load for more than a minute or two, most men can't but we can do a chapter on that later on in the book, but David was gentle, kind and loving, even though his inner self wanted to be brutal when it came to sex. We'd hooked up in the Sundance bar and fucked on the first date on the deck of his boat, yes, we were drunk, and then we fucked in his bed and then we fucked in the desert and then on the boat again. This went on for months and as David lived close to me in CA, about 40 miles, we used to hook up at my place or in hotels or back in Parker on his boat. One day I was sitting outside my home in OC when a lady drove up and parked right outside my gate, taking her time to get her shit together before stepping outside the car.

"Are you who I think you are?" she asked

"And who do you think I am?" I replied

"Blondie?"

"I am"

"May I come in and talk to you, I am David's wife Cindy"

Dave had a wife! WTF??

We'd been going about our business, admittedly it was monkey business, for two months when this lady appeared. Cindy was nice, well-spoken and very calm. It appeared that David had been having extra-marital affairs for several years, and had been caught every time by his wife, through his own carelessness and her ability to smell a rat. Why she was still married to him, I had no idea, but after chatting with her for twenty minutes, my affair with David ended on the spot. I never saw him again. Yes, Parker had its moments and in general it still does, but it gave me the grounding I needed to wake up and realize that sex was my passion, my love and my future and sex was something I should be charging for. It happened so quickly and it happened for the best, but the early years in Parker, all the fucking I had done and the money I could have been making, suddenly made me realize that E$corting was the way forwards, and even though it took me until my early 30's to make it happen, I know that Parker was a catalyst in helping my career in the sex industry materialize and then blossom.

So-Called Friends

In all the years I've been E$corting, I have picked up and also lost, many friends. When I say 'lost' I don't mean they died, I mean that they disappeared from my life for one reason or another. Most of the ones I have kept are with me to this very day, but the ones who have passed me by, well, they will never return, and I hope that one day, most of them will come to terms with what they did to take advantage of me at the time and how they should have remedied that before our friendship faltered. You see, I am a nice caring giving human being, probably too nice. I was brought up that way, I know while you're reading this you may have formed a different opinion of me, but trust me, even though I have had a wild and adventurous life, I am still a nice person, and through and through, I really do care about people. I have been taken advantage of by so many, for so little, from the age of 13 onwards, and it's never stopped. Most of my friends, my good friends, realized at an early age that I am reliable, honest and trustworthy, some however, took advantage of my softer side and even though I have persevered with relationships that were incredibly broken, as I have grown older, my tendency to trust people has worn thin. Age has ushered in a kind of hardness that wasn't ingrained in my personality when I was younger, and I have to say, I quite like it, although I never use it. I let things bubble up inside me and then I laugh them off or vent to someone I trust, in the hope that venting will make my sadness vanish. When I became an E$cort, my friends were all in the E$corting business. It just happens that way, and frankly, the E$corts I have known and know now, are all really decent ladies, well, most of them anyway. I've met people that left me inspired, I've met some who left me broken, but for the most part, my E$cort friends are my family. Those of us in the E$corting industry had an unwritten code, share and share a like. If we had a client who we were fucking and that client wanted to have a change of partner, then we would all recommend each other and take a cut from whoever he decided to go to. The cut would be a small cut, maybe $50 per pop, but it would be on going and never ending. Normally most of the girls would honor this rule, but some didn't and the ones who didn't, well, they just never received any more referrals, and word soon spread around our community of their unwillingness to share.

And then there was Jamya.

This is a lady, Jamya, who broke all the rules, all the molds and all kinds of fucking records. It's a story that needs to be told, and one that will blow your mind, just like she blew the thousands of cocks she ended up fucking. Her only saving grace, in my humble opinion, is that she has better tits than me. I would love to post a picture of her tits on this page, but she'd end up suing me, so I will try to describe them.

If you can imagine a teardrop shaped 36 C, perfectly formed, set of boobs, with beautiful pinkish rose-colored nipples, nipples that were constantly erect, with every inch of those boobs, soft and smooth and rounded and ever so delectable, that was Jamya's tits. THE best set of tits I have ever seen, and probably WILL ever see, and I am talking from first-hand experience here, I sucked those nipples and played with those tits until my heart was content. Whenever the two of us went out together, no one spoke to me, they all ogled Jamya and her tits. When she went braless, every room she entered became silent, with every man's jaw dropping in unison at the site of those tits. Everyone wanted to fuck her, and everyone did. But, let me begin at the beginning.

I had a friend, a good friend, who knew a guy who was rich and well-known and in the casino business. This was the deal. He owned a boat, a yacht, and he had a friend called Joelinton. Joelinton knew my friend Kat, and Kat knew another lady who was unknown to me at the time, called Jamya and her pal Kristin. You see where this is going now? Neither did I, until one afternoon Kat called and told me that rich guy was taking Joel and a group of women to Manzanilla on his boat. Manzanilla is in Mexico.

"Can you get me on that boat?" I pleaded and while I was pleading, Kat was telling me that the women 'quota' had already been filled.

"Kick someone off Kat, come on, you know me and you know how much fun I can be?"

And she did. Kristen went sayonara, and I got the last spot on the luxury van to the airport, and that is when I met Jamya. She sat next to me on that van and we instantly hit it off. From the moment I saw this blonde goddess, I mean it, she was stunningly beautiful, I fell in love with her, and she with me, and I knew at some point on that trip that we were going to make out.

The journey began innocently enough, a van ride to the John Wayne airport where a Gulfstream jet awaited. The plane was magnificent and held ten people. We all boarded, no security of course, settled in and took off for Mexico. I was in my element. I just couldn't believe that this was happening. The two-hour forty-minute flight ended all too soon, with all of us drinking champagne and eating incredible food and just having the best of times. We disembarked, and headed for a bus that would take us to his yacht. Again, there was very little security and no one in Mexico really cared about our passports or driver's license as the immigration officer walked up and down double checking our tits! The yacht was the largest boat I had ever seen. It was ten times larger than anything I'd been on before and when we boarded, I was mesmerized by how clean it was, how friendly the crew were and nearly died when I found out there were 7 bedrooms! My immediate thoughts turned to what I would have to do to get fucked in each room and honestly, that thought really turned me on. I wasn't getting paid, but I was getting a two-week vacation for free and so if anyone on that boat asked me to do anything, no matter how perverted, I decided I was going to be up for it.

I won't describe the yacht in great detail because I know you would prefer to read all the juicy bits, but let me tell you, opulence would not be the right word to use. It was palatial, and probably the nicest place I'd ever been in my life, nicer than any home I'd been in, and certainly nicer than any hotel room I'd ever stayed in. I got to meet the BIG boss, and he was nice too, and Joelinton, the man who'd invited us in the first place, although not the most handsome card in the box, was very pleasant and courteous and ready and willing to assist if I needed anything at all. When we settled in, we were given a short safety briefing by the captain and watched anxiously as the anchor came up and the ropes were untied, I had this surreal feeling I was living a dream, and with Jamya standing next to me, in a kind of close up and very intimate manner, with her boobs and left side brushing mine, I knew that this trip may just end up being a lot of fun and one that I would remember for the rest of my life. When the boat left the edge of the dock, the engines began to purr and the crew assumed their regular working positions, Jamya, who was still standing beside me, turned and gave me a kiss on the lips.

"Fun times babes!" she said, as that twinkle in her eye suggested we go fuck one another before the boat had even hit the ocean. I was game, and she could see it, but manners prevailed and we followed all the other girls into the bar where alcohol was about to rain freely and sex and debauchery were about to begin.

Joelinton was kind of a dorky guy, but that first night on the ocean, Jamya fucked him on the main deck in full view of everyone else on the yacht, including the crew! What a performance it was. The two of them went at it without any care of who was watching, finishing off with a floury, as Joel pulled out of Jamya's pussy and came all over the deck to a solid round of applause from their audience. After they'd finished, she and I got into it. Firstly, we took pics of each other's boobs, and then our pussy's and then we got one of the other girls to take pictures of us both together, kissing then eating each other out. It was so erotic. While all this was going on, Jamya started what became the champagne challenge. How far could we stick a bottle of champagne up inside our pussy's? She won that hands down, every night! I think she was bi-polar, she thought she was just a party girl, but whatever she chose to be, she'd excel at it. She was hilarious. We fucked one another, we fucked the crew, we fucked the captain, several times, but best of all, we became friends. I introduced her to the world of E$corting, and not long after we got off that boat, our pussy's red raw from all the fucking and champagne bottles we'd inserted over that two-week vacation, Jamya and I sat down and came up with a plan to fuck Orange County dry and to make a fortune. That turned out to be a huge mistake, on my part at least.

We had an agreement in Orange County, whatever guy I passed on to her, she'd give me a percentage of the takings, and vice-versa. We tag teamed. She'd pick up a guy, fuck him and give me $50 and I would do the same. All good in theory, but in practice, that system lasted about 5 minutes. Jamya was completely wild.

Jamya had never been to Parker, so I took her. Our first night in Parker, she fucked 2 guys, and the second night? She vanished. She would get into all kinds of trouble and then show up a few days later with the most bizarre stories, all true and all believable, but completely outrageous. One night in Parker she was on board a boat with guys who were putting GHB into water bottles and feeding it to all the girls. I mistook a water bottle for a vodka bottle and passed out within moments of taking a swig of water. Jamya went off to party on her own, and she got into all kinds of trouble when a boat without lights on rammed into the boat that Jamya was on, throwing her into the river, where she was picked up by another boat filled with only guys, who then all decided to gang bang her, at her request, dropping her off on the CA side of the river, where she began all over again, fucking at least another 4 or 5 men, ending up with the reddest raw pussy I had ever seen. She'd then go to bed, sleep an hour, look like brand new and start fucking all over again. She was a machine, and a machine that was on auto pilot. She didn't discriminate by age creed or color. She just fucked whoever would or would not pay, and then she would come back to me, put a CD on, cry for ten minutes and be as right as rain again. Weirdo, would not sum up her personality, pure fucking mental, would! She ended up in rehab, and then got married and had two kids, one of whom nearly died in yet another boating accident she was involved in. Her and I no longer speak, thank God! Jamya, if you're reading this and you would like to pay me, I figure you still owe me around ten grand! Friends? Who needs them? I know more women who owe me money than I care to admit, all filled with promises, promises that were never fulfilled, and promises that were only there to be broken. I hope all of you feel good about yourselves! One in particular, who shall remain nameless, lives on a ranch just to the east of LA, a huge ranch, a ranch that I half paid for! Not that I am bitter, well, maybe I am just a little jealous, but one guy in particular who I recommended to this lady, the lady with the ranch, kind of paid for the whole estate, single handedly, and although my friend is very clever, obviously a lot cleverer than me, her neglect when 'forgetting' the promised kick back for the introductions I made, stands at tens of thousands of dollars, dollars that right now, I could really do with.

And then there's my friend Roz, who is a doll, and has remained a good friend. At one point in time, Roz owned a very nice apartment in Costa Mesa, and that apartment was either left unused and empty half the week, or rented out by another E$cort or two that Roz trusted and gave keys too. When empty though, it was really a 'play-pen' for me and my 'dates', dates that I picked up from this bar in Newport Beach on Sunday afternoons. This bar, not really a dive bar, but a fun place to hang out, (I won't give them a plug in my book because they are still open 25 years on from this story), and each Sunday, especially in the summer months, I would show up around 1 PM, when the Reggae or Rock band was starting to play, walk in with my tits hanging loose and ready to be fondled, watch carefully as the whole bar looked at me, at least all the men in that bar, and maybe a few women, with looks that said 'fuck me please!' and take a seat. I would never pay for a single drink after my backside hit that chair, and more often than not, I would go home with some guy, random or not, fuck him, and leave, only to repeat that performance the following Sunday with a different dude. One Sunday, however, I was sitting at the bar, drink already in hand, when Steve, a guy I knew from my weekend visits to Parker, sauntered in to this place, all cool and jacked up on cocaine! We eyeballed one another, I signaled for him to come and sit next to me, and well, the party began. The guy who'd bought me the drink I had was given the shove, and me and Steve started flirting. Steve was a complete menace when it came to touching my tits. He just loved them, and he loved to fondle them, no matter if we were in public or private. When I'd fucked him in the past, and yes, there had been a few occasions when Steve and I had executed our sexual desires in a drunk and careless manner, Steve had sucked my tits and my pussy bone dry with his over exuberant tongue motion and willingness to make my nipples feel like they were long lost relatives he'd not seen for years, and needed to make amends by providing them special affection that never seemed to end. One time when we were 'at it' in Parker, my nipples were so drained from his overly attentive mouth, that I couldn't put a top on to cover them up for more than 24 hours, so I walked around the boat we were on, a boat that had another 12 people on board, completely topless and somewhat in pain, as Steve just kept on brining the mouth to nipple action every time I walked past him. On this occasion, whilst we sat at the bar, catching up, he began the nipple twerking that he so adored and I often desired, right in front of this crowded space we were occupying at that moment in time. It was exceptionally erotic, Steve, with his hand moving gently around my areola, my nipples stiffening to attention and protruding keenly from beneath my top, while I was massaging his large cock, now expanded recklessly inside his tight-fitting jeans, and ready to pounce, like a viper, at any moment.

My phone rang. It was Roz.

"Sweetie, where are you?" she asked.

I told her.

"Listen babes, I owe you, right?" Was this a question or a statement? "You always owe me Roz" I replied.

"I owe you for Graham, from last week. Big tipper, I made more than a grand from that one"

Roz always came clean, always made it clear that she'd benefitted from my generosity or referral, and always paid me back. It was a continuous cycle, I helped her, she helped me.

"So what do I get?" I asked.

"Haley and Liz are on their way to the same bar you're at, my apartment is free, you know where the keys are, and knowing you, you have a guy already in tow?"

She knew me too well.

"Haley and Liz will take you back to my place, assist you while you fuck that guy and free of charge to you, will play their part in the 4 some about to take place on my bed!" she laughed.

Wow! This was great news, and instead of my usual fee, a fee that Steve already knew he was going to have to pay, (we had a golden rule, fuck me in Parker, fuck me for free, but fuck me anywhere else, it was $300) and he was happy to spend an afternoon with me rather than his wife and kids, but now the stakes were raised to a 4 some, Steve would have to fork out a grand, and all that cash would come to me, thanks to Roz. What a nice bonus, a bonus Steve didn't know anything about, just yet! Roz wasn't a so-called friend; Roz was a TRUE friend.

 The two girls arrived about an hour later, and by that time, Steve knew the deal, paid the cash and after buying Haley and Liz a drink, we headed out. Everyone except Steve knew where Roz lived, and I decided to join him in his car, accompanying all the way there, in case he was going to play chicken, and run off.

The valet parking attendant took his ticket to go retrieve his car, only to return 10 minutes later to tell him they couldn't find it!

"What do you mean you can't find it" Steve shouted.

The valet guy was so embarrassed, and offered no explanation, other than it might have been misplaced.

"Fucking find it!" Steve told him, now quite plainly exasperated by the who situation.

I could feel the $1000 I was about to earn drifting sadly into tomorrow as Steve began to get more and more agitated.

"Steve" I said quietly, as I tugged at his arm, "let's just go

to the apartment and come back later. Give them time to sort it"

I could tell he was frustrated and the horny look which had accompanied his erection, had long gone.

"I paid to park, where's the fucking car?" he asked me.

Again, I was insistent, and Haley and Liz were probably naked already, legs spread and willing to progress on this Sunday they were told to do me a favor and fuck for free. I just couldn't let this opportunity pass me by.

I grabbed Steve by his arm, pulling him away from the Valet guy and said "let's fuck and come back later. I am happy to drive"

He acquiesced and we left, but Steve wasn't a happy bunny.

Around 25 minutes later, we entered Roz's place, and as I mentioned, and had presumed, Haley, naked as the day she was born, greeted us at the door, while Liz, half drunk, half high, half horny, (that's a lot of halves, but that's the only way I could describe her), was lying half on and half off the huge king-sized bed Roz kept immaculately clean and fresh for occasions just like this one. Within moments, Steve was naked, I was naked, his $1000 was left lying freely on the coffee table and the fucking began. We fucked all afternoon, and Steve came multiple times, but not as many times as me and Haley. Liz turned out to be a dead loss, not caring to participate fully, (she was too drunk) and uninterested in an orgasm or two, provided by either myself, Steve or Haley. Steve though had a blast and when it was all over and done with, (I gave the other two girls $100 each for their trouble), we all left, but not before cleaning the place and restoring it to its immaculate glory. Back at the parking lot, Steve's car hadn't been found and it turned out someone had actually stolen it. They never found it, but Steve didn't care, he was rich and had two or three more cars to drive at home. My understanding was, the insurance paid out, and when I saw Steve again, about three months later, his brand-new Corvette looked fabulous as he drove past me in downtown Parker, honking the horn with his lips pursed to blow me a kiss and flip me off in a fashion only caring Steve could muster. Roz really was good to me, not only that day, but in days before and after, and I repaid her several times over, as best I could, in return for her kindness.

The Good The Bad and The Ugly

He came to see me last night, Gregory, or Greg for short. A new date, one I had been trying to see for some weeks, but because of issues with my room mates, I'd had to put him off several times.

He arrived on time, something I always appreciated with any of my dates. There is nothing worse than a late date. Someone who shows little respect for not only my time, but the energy and preparation I put into each date, is someone to be avoided in the future. There are always situations where the dude will be a no-show. It happens every week, and even though it pisses me off, I take it as just being part of the territory, and even if I've spent hours or minutes getting ready, I normally just shake my head and then block that no-show from ever being able to contact me again.

Greg arrived and what a good-looking man he was. Beautiful from his head to his waist. I usually try to chat, fully-clothed, for a few minutes, to the guy, especially if he's new, which Greg was, and then slowly make them comfortable enough to get naked and more importantly, erect. Without erect, and believe me, it happens more than you would care to believe, there is nothing, no date, no ending and certainly no fun, for either of us.

Our little chat finished and the fun began. Greg stripped off, one piece at a time, slowly. He seemed nervous, and then, just as his pants hit the floor, leaving him in his boxer's, I realized where and why the nerves were coming from. I sat, naked on the bed, ready to be fucked, when Greg's boxers finally hit the floor, and I just stared, open mouthed, probably with a look of shock written all over my face. I could tell Greg was embarrassed, I could also tell he was waiting for a comment from me, but really, from what I saw, I was left completely speechless.

You see, Greg's penis was a coke can! Not an actual Coke can, but it was shaped like a coke can, with the pee hole, not on a head, which is normal for any penis, but just sitting on the top of this can shaped ugly thick and disgusting price of flesh. It was about 3" thick all round, it didn't taper off, it didn't grow, it didn't do anything. I was about to puke, when Greg came over to the bed and sat next to me.

"What would you like me to do with that?" I asked him. "Greg, I can assure you that it's not going inside me" I was adamant.

He looked at me, and at one point I thought he was going to cry.

"Have you ever been married?" I asked

"Yes" he said meekly.

"Did your wife, I presume ex-wife?" he nodded, "well, did she fuck that?" I asked as I pointed to his stumpy dick.

"I have custom made condoms" he offered, "I'm presuming that's your issue?"

"Eh, NO Greg, that isn't my problem. My problem is, that is THE most disgusting dick I have ever seen, and I am not prepared to even remotely try to fit it in my tight vagina."

That was him told!

"Will you give me a blow-job for a lesser amount?" he asked. He was so embarrassed, and I could only imagine how much grief this ugly misshaped brick-like penis had given him throughout his entire life.

I had seen miss-shaped penis's before, but nothing like this one.

There was one time a guy got naked, fully erect and his penis bent round towards his backside, like a banana, making it impossible to fuck it. There had been a few like that, but NONE like this. Greg's special, I called it.

Blow-job? There was nothing to suck. His penis head was non-existent. I had no idea what I was going to do and the date was deteriorating rapidly into a farce.

"HAND-JOB!" He shouted loudly, as if he'd just thought of the best idea ever. I agreed, and began to toss him off, rapidly, only he couldn't get erect, or maybe he was erect and this was going to be as hard as it ever got. I just didn't know, but before I had a chance to even think about it, Greg came, paid me $200, got dressed and ran. I will never see him again, thank God! But it got me into thinking about men's members and their sizes and shapes, and with that in mind, I wanted to give you a brief insight into some of the one's I have fucked, sucked and jerked off. It's not a case of every penis is the same, oh no, the perfect penis, and yes, that does exist, is a pretty thing and something to be admired. The alternative is gross and often off-putting, but, with my insistence that no man should ever walk out unhappy, especially having paid me $400, I often have to 'bite the bullet', and fuck something that's completely gross.

And then there was Jeff, a super cool guy I met in Las Vegas. We met by accident, well, not quite by accident. I was sat in a bar at Planet Hollywood, people watching. I'd decided to work Vegas for a few nights, just for a change, but had run out of clients and wandered down to the bar, just to get a change of scenery. When you're in a hotel room for a couple of days just fucking strangers, a change of scenery is the best thing to recharge batteries and especially pussy batteries, so I'd wandered off downstairs into the casino, parked my butt at the bar and was looking out for the 'beautiful' people that normally walk the halls of every Vegas casino. My only problem on that afternoon? There were no beautiful people, none! Asians, Indians, fat Americans, but nothing worth gazing at or drooling over. Then, out of nowhere, came Jeff. A God, amongst the ugly!

As I sat gazing at this beautiful man, a man who walked alone and with a bottle of beer in his hand, obviously looking for beautiful women to pick up, I decided to take the initiative and get off my ass and approach him. I had nothing to lose and he had everything to gain.

Moving right towards him at double pace, I accidently/deliberately bumped right into him. Apologizing profusely, I looked him straight in the eye and said "Wow! At last, a man who looks like a real man!" or something like that. It brought a smile to his face and he offered to buy me a drink. That was the start of a really fun night, a night that didn't include sex, but which did include many bars, lots of food and some great laughs. Jeff, and that's wasn't his real name, lived in Hollywood and even though he'd wanted to fuck me, and he tried really hard all night to do so, bless him. I'd rebuffed all his advances in favor of perhaps seeing him again outside of what I did for a living. Jeff was super cool and after our one night of drinking and having fun, we exchanged numbers and I thought perhaps I would never see him again. You know how that goes? You pass your phone number over to your prospective date, hoping he calls, but he never does?

About three months later, I was invited to a party in Hollywood, and me and 6 ladies I knew hired a limo to chauffeur us from The OC up the 405 to the Hollywood Hills. On the way up there, and in need of some extracurricular activity, (the girls were driving me nuts), I remembered Jeff lived in Hollywood, and with that in mind and my pussy feeling rather hornier than usual, I pulled out my cell phone, found his number and dialed with hope.

"Hi Jeff, remember me?"

He did, and he agreed to meet all of us at the party we were going to. It was great, to see him again, and, as expected, his advances proved to be overwhelmingly enticing. As I'd come in the limo, I had no other transportation back to OC, (this was before Uber), and after sticking my tongue down Jeff's throat for a couple of hours, the other ladies got bored with my antics and left, leaving me and Jeff to sort out the rest of the night between the two of us.

Jeff took me back to his place, and by this time we both knew we were going to fuck. We stripped one another naked and as he took off his underwear, I looked down at his penis. It was erect, but it was erect in a downwards direction! Yes, straight down. I had to do a double take. It was as if he'd had it chopped off and sewn back on in the wrong direction. It definitely faced south, not east or west or north. It was bizarre and it looked like the good Lord had given Jeff his own personalized Pogo Stick to practice with every day. I had never seen anything quite like this and it made for the weirdest fuck I'd ever had in my life. You see, because his cock was pointing downwards, and it was hard and erect, I had to find the most uncomfortable positions to allow Jeff to insert it in my pussy. My head was kind of at his feet, and my pussy contorted to face his face, and then, when he inserted it, and I have to tell you, that was no easy task, it was like being fucked doggie style in the missionary position. Strange, strange, strange.

When I sucked him off, I had to have him stand over my head and that was the only way I could get near his cock to lace it in my mouth. It wouldn't bend, it wouldn't curl upwards, it was just like a stick at a downwards angle and a stick that wouldn't break. We managed to eventually make one another cum, but that was the end of Jeff. There was no sense in my putting up with this deformed penis when I could get any normal penis I desired. Again though, just another abomination on my list of abominable penises'.

Alfonso, oh yes, Alfonso, my little Mexican friend, or not so much a friend, but definitely a client.

We met at the health club. At first his attraction to me was so obvious and yet, he never made an approach. He wasn't attractive, but he was kind of fascinating just by the looks he gave me every day when we met. We trained at the same time, and after a while I began to think that the only reason he came in at that time of day was to look at my body, and perhaps to get lucky. When Alfonso and I began chatting one day, he asked me what I did for a living. I told him I was an E$cort and that if he wanted to fuck me it would never be an issue as long as he paid the going rate. Weeks went by, and Alfonso grew hornier by the day, until one day, foaming at the mouth, he actually came over and told me that he couldn't afford my going rate by that he had $200 on him and if I'd accept that he would love to fuck me. I felt bad for him, and by now knowing he was a bit of a loner and knowing also that he wasn't that wealthy, I agreed to his proposal and we made a date. Well, when Alfonso turned up and got naked, his penis, although average in size, was shaped like a banana, but a banana that curled downwards, not sideways. It was a complete abomination, and the curl it had on it was so severe, there was no way that thing was going to fit inside me. As I weighed up my options on how I was going to fuck it, the laws of physics took over and when trying to imagine how it would fit inside my pussy, I could see that after the head of his dick was inserted, the curve on the trunk of his banana shaped penis was the part that would be fucking me and the head would be coming back from the inside to the out. I told Alfonso, "Look sweetheart, that thing won't fit inside me, so how about a blow job instead?" His poor face went sour and he began to cry and I began to feel very sorry for him. He explained that he never got any sex, and that everyone he tried to bang ran away from his banana shaped penis. I knew I would have to swallow my pride and fuck him, rather than just swallow his dick, but the effort involved in doing so, and not only doing it for a cheap price, but doing it for situation that required mercy, wasn't going to be easy.

Alfonso took an age to get hard, and even when he was hard, he was soft. Hard to explain that, but some guys, most guys, are rock hard, like a metal pipe but with soft spots, Alfonso was hard, but his rigidity could collapse at any given moment due to confidence issues and then we'd have to begin at the very beginning and try to stiffen him up again. This whole process led to Alfonso staying with me for hours on end, paying me half my going rate and then ejaculating outside of my pussy because we could never find a way for his 'banana' to be 'peeled' correctly. This guy became a nightmare. He wouldn't leave me alone, he would only pay me $200 instead of $400 and he kept coming back, week after week after week until one day I sat him down and told him

"Pay me the going rate or don't come back"

Alfonso and his banana dick left me, and even though we kept in touch, he calls me every now and again. But even today I would not fuck him again. I had three attempts at fucking that monstrosity of a dick and all three attempts ended in failure.

There have been other dicks that I've laughed at, cried over, been disgusted with. Some bend to the right, some to the left, some up and some down, but in the most part, you cannot beat the perfect penis. The perfect penis, not found on that many men, is about 7 to 8 inches long with a large or medium sized head and the girth of a ripe cucumber. It fits, it works and it satisfies and what more could any woman want than a penis that pleases?

Famous Dicks And Not So Famous Assholes

"I've come for my boy" one of John Wayne's best ever lines, spoken in the movie True Grit, and a movie I used to watch when I was growing up. Everyone knew John Wayne came from Orange County, in fact, the airport is named after him and sports a huge statue of him right in the center of terminal B. There are many other great movie stars and their offspring, who also live in that part of the world and when I lived near the beach in Newport, I would go walking every morning on Dutch Shores, a very quiet, secluded and up-market part of Newport, right by the water. Sometimes I would see the same people and quite often, the very rich and often famous people who lived in the homes that backed directly on to the bay. Six-million-dollar homes, with the $25 million yachts. This was part of the scenery when I would pop out for a stroll and at the same time I was passing and if I saw these people once or twice and they happened to notice my perfect tits bouncing, men, but never women, would often come over and chat to me or pretend to walk with me as they gazed unconsciously towards my girls and their 'always on' headlights. My tits really were incredible back then. I know I've told you this, several times already, but even now, my tits are my best asset. They're just perky, flawless and adorned with two rosy succulent nipples that all men want to ravish. I've had clients that do nothing but suck my tits for the $400 they pay me, instead of choosing just to fuck me. I have one client who sucks on my tits for so long during his weekly visits, I need special moisturizing cream to perk them up after he leaves and I can't let anyone else touch them for 3 days until they return to normality. He's a beast, but he pays well.

Back to the beach, and one particular morning, as I was sauntering along with my iPod blaring out my favorite tunes, I was suddenly shocked when someone tapped me on my shoulder. I looked round and there stood a tall handsome gent with a black Labrador puppy on a leash, saying something I couldn't quite understand. I motioned for him to wait, raising one finger in his direction while turned off the music blaring in my ears.

"Hello, is something wrong" I asked.

"No, not at all. I see you every day walking and I wanted to introduce myself. I think you're a very attractive lady and thought that perhaps, if you were single, we might chat and go for dinner?"

"Sorry I don't do that" I replied.

"You single?" he asked

"Yes"

"Then why don't you do that?" he persisted.

I laughed and told him that "I love to play hard to get"

We ended up walking together and the man in question happened to be the, the youngest son of one of Hollywood's best-known stars. Not only was this dude tall and handsome, he was rich and a pleasure to be around. We enjoyed our walk that day and then parted under the premise that we would meet again in the same spot and walk the same route at some point in the near future. He asked for my number, which I gave him without thinking twice, and we said goodbye and walked on our two separate ways.

2 hours later, my phone rang. It was him.

"Wanna hang out tomorrow, same time?"

"You mean you want to fuck me, right?"

He laughed, I laughed and then we made a time to meet.

I showed up

"I charge you know!"

"You what?" he looked surprised

"I charge, and it's $400 per pop, you OK with that?"

"That's your job?" he inquired.

"Got a problem with what I do?"

"No"

"Then get your cash out honey"

By this time, I was inside his home. It was magnificent. The house itself was modern and clean, and I thought to myself, 'why on earth can't they all be like this?'

He came closer, we kissed, we kissed again, and then we fucked. We fucked all over his home, everywhere that is, except the bedroom. He took me on his couch, then the kitchen counter, then the bathroom and then the living room carpet. He fucked me senseless, and to his credit, he could go and go and go without stopping, until finally, without warning and just as I was about to orgasm for the umpteenth time, he pulled out of me and asked me to swallow his load, which, I did gracefully, if that's entirely possible? "Enjoy that?" he asked

With a straight face, I looked at him and said "it was OK"

"Only OK?" I think he was shocked at my expressionless face.

"$400 cash, and I don't give credit."

"Listen sweetie, I don't have cash in the house, and as I didn't expect you to charge me, would it be OK if I paid you next time, because you know there is going to be a next time"

"That's fine. Now, clean up your mess, I need to move on, I have a walk to complete."

We walked together, hand in hand for about an hour and decided to see one another the following day. This routine, fucking, walking, and fucking again, went on for about a week, until, with no cash forthcoming, I decided to put an end to this mess by giving him an ultimatum. "Either you pay me what you owe me or we are done" I never heard from him again, miserable fucker. He still owes me $1600. This rich trust fund imbecile screwed me out of what was owed, and I have never forgotten, nor will I ever forget, where he lives.

And then there was Hunter.

Oh Hunter, such a tease, such an asshole, such a great fuck.

Blythe Arizona, what a great party town. I often went there when I stayed on the river at Parker, but on this particular weekend, the weekend when a threesome became a foursome, and then just a single. Hunter had invited my girlfriend, April and her friend Renee, to party hard at his home down there. Hunter is a rich guy, unmarried, but fancies himself as a bit of a playboy. I have known him for many years now and although he likes to fuck, and pay for it, there's always a negotiation when it comes to receiving my full worth. Don't ask me why, and I'm not saying that Hunter is stingy, he's actually very generous in more ways than one, but whenever he fucks me, the $400 he's supposed to pay me, turns into $250, without any consideration for our relationship, friendship and fuckship. Hunter loves to negotiate. Doesn't matter if we're in a bar, a restaurant, a general store, negotiation to Hunter, is what it's all about. It's like a game, a game he cannot ever lose.

April and I have known each other for many years too. April shares her men with me, and I share mine with her. I also pay her a commission if she sends me over a client, and she's supposed to do the same with me, but that reciprocation rarely, if ever, happens. With that being said, I still love her to bits and our friendship has outlasted my continual angst over her nonpayment of fees owed. We always have fun together and when the occasion calls for an 'extra pussy', I always think of her and she always thinks of me.

Hunter had called April and asked her to bring a friend to his home in Blythe, and April, having already set up the trip with her other bestie, Renee, asked Hunter if it would be OK to invite me. He agreed. April and Renee had been in Blythe a week already when I received this call.

"Honey, get yourself down to Blythe. Hunter is partying, AND he's paying"

I packed a bag, not expecting to stay more than a couple of days, and on a warm Friday evening, in early May, I headed down to AZ, about a 6-hour drive, arriving there just after 1 AM on Saturday morning. I had with me, a couple of bikinis', a dress, and very little else. I knew that we'd spend most of the time naked, so there really wasn't any need for clothing other than what I'd brought with me. When I walked in the door, all three of them were on the couch watching that Showtime series Shameless.

"BLONDIE!!!" they said in unison, "you have to come watch this show, it's fantastic"

I sat on the couch and the party began.

I'm going to try to describe this as best I can, but when you're drunk, high, or both at the same time, it's often difficult to recall the exact details, and being as I don't really do drugs, alcohol was my only poison.

At first, Hunter started to feel comfortable around all 3 of us, and while the TV was blasting Shameless and then other shows, we decided to get the toys out, toys that April had purchased before leaving OC. She usually frequented a store called Wicked Chamber, in Costa Mesa, and on this occasion, she'd bought vibrators, butt plugs, pussy beads, and many other deliciously fun gizmos. Hunter was really into this toy game, finding it amusing as he tried to make us all cum by pressing vibrators on our clits for hours at a time. And I do mean hours! One session lasted more than three hours, two of which I came so many times, I was flat out exhausted, when, by the shear grace of God or Buddha, or Allah, the batteries ran out, and Hunter had no spares, so he had to fuck me instead. To say I was higher than a kite when cuming so much, would be an understatement of the facts, and Hunter, while playing with April and Renee, was popping little blue pills just to keep up. This was an orgy of the BEST kind and it was only the first night. I still had two to go.

When we all woke up, around midday on Saturday, I was served up a breakfast that included whisky, OJ and bacon. What an erotic combo that turned out to be. We all downed it in a hurry and then, the sex began once again. I was amazed that Hunter was able to pick up from where he'd left off. He was a bull. He fucked April and then me and then Renee and then he did it all over again. We really were in the process of beating all world records for fucking, one after another, we made each other cum and then a complete sense of calm and happiness descended on us for the rest of the day. That day included, more Shameless, more sex toys, a little journey down the river on Hunter's boat and then, after a small interlude for a nap, when Hunter decided he wanted one on one time with April, we hit the bars in Blythe and got wasted. Again, that night ran into the next morning and after waking up around 11.30, the bacon, OJ and whisky breakfast treats we were now becoming accustomed to, were served up for all to enjoy. This was heaven for me, and, I was supposedly getting paid to have fun.

My three-day trip ended up being a 7-day holiday. I was fed and fucked and then fed again, Hunter being the perfect host, and the other two ladies, April and Renee, my perfect companions. I don't think I have ever had more sex in one single week than I did that week and when it came time to leave, I discovered that April and Renee were going to stay on and enjoy more of the same.

"What do I owe you?" Hunter asked, as I made my move to leave after packing up my car with the few belongings I'd brought. I knew this moment was going to happen at some point and I had given the matter some thought in advance of Hunter asking. I also knew he'd fed and wined and dined me for 7 straight days, and that $2000 for getting fucked on top of being treated well, didn't, to me at least, seem that much or outrageous.

"$2000" I told him.

Hunter looked at me, and smiled and then he said

"I was thinking about $1000"

I said nothing, realizing that this wasn't going to be as easy as I'd planned.

"$1500" I said, looking right at him, without smiling.

"Nope, $1000 and that's it" he was adamant and he began to write the check, even though he knew I preferred cash.

He handed it over, I never even looked at it, then he gave me a huge hug and we said farewell. I was off, back to OC, another 6-hour drive and April and Renee were off to get another good fucking from a man whose sexual appetite was insatiable.

I arrived home later that day and unloaded everything from my car and then remembered the check. I had to cash that asap, just in case, (one never knew if a check was good in this business, that's why I only took cash), there was going to be a problem. I took the check from my purse and for the first time, since Hunter had written it, I looked at it. It was for $1500. I smiled and blessed that man for coming through after all. I'd had one of the best weeks ever and now it was time to get back to the grind and find more clients, clients who would come and go and clients, some who I cared for, and a lot that I didn't.

Sluts and Whores

My friend Lucy moved in with me. Long story, but one of my roommates, the nutcase, was eventually evicted by me and so freed up a room at my home. It took several trips to the police, a few meetings with a lawyer client I have and then an almighty effort by my other roommate and I to have this guy evicted. It's hard when three people share a lease, but the long and the short of it was, the man was threatening to expose what I did for a living, even though he'd known me for years and indeed, had sex with me on occasion. His chances of winning that battle were slim to zero and finally when the restraining order and eviction notice were served, I was so delighted to see him depart, I just stayed in my room for 2 straight days, thanking my lucky stars he was not in my life anymore and also taking time to relax from what had become the most traumatic 4 months I could ever remember. The man was a moron, filled with hate and an uncanny knack of rubbing me up the wrong way, and I was so happy to be rid of him for good.

Lucy, someone I'd known for a short period of time, was introduced to me by my long-standing friend April. April, now she's a story in herself, had made the introduction one evening when we were in this local bar having drinks with another acquaintance of mine, Terry.

"Want to meet Lucy?" April asked me, as my eyes feasted on this tall blonde firecracker who was lighting up the bar with her humor, her looks and oh yes, her tits. (Yes, it's always the tits!) Lucy has magnificent tits and a killer body. She's an ex-model, and now, at the age of 44, a complete whore! She loves to fuck, but I didn't know that when I was introduced to her. She's also a grandmother, a GILF, (Grandma I'd Like to Fuck), but you'd never believe that if you met her, she looks so young. She attracts men like a magnet, every man in that bar was lined up asking to buy her drinks, while another line formed trying even harder to get into her panties, something that she made clear would be impossible unless they had plenty cash available to guarantee some action. Again, at that point in time her business was not my business, at least not back then, but things were about to change after we were introduced by April. The evening started the way it was meant to continue. A few drinks, a few laughs, a few suggestive comments and then, a few kisses. I was kissing Lucy, she was kissing me, and we were both getting rather wound up. Stopping short of actually fucking one another, during one brief conversation I happened to mention that I had a room for rent at my apartment. Lucy, who lived about one and a half hours drive north east of where we were currently standing, asked me very nicely if she could possibly rent it? I, of course, quickly agreed, telling her what the rent would be and asking her what she planned to do in that room. I didn't know she was also an E$cort, but unbeknownst to me, Lucy already knew what I did. April had told her everything about me.

"I'm just like you" she said, "a complete slut and willing to do anything for money, lots of money." I was rather surprised but I pounced on this opportunity.

"I'll tell you what" I whispered in her left ear, "you pay me $900 per month and 20% of what you take, and we have a deal"

"You want to be my Madame?" she asked, as she laughed out loud.

"No, I am or will be your landlord, but I want a cut of your action for putting up with your clients marching in and out at all hours of the day and night."

She thought about it for 10 seconds and then agreed. We hugged and kissed and she agreed to move in one week later. She kept telling me how excited she was and how much money she was going to make, and I sat back thinking, 'if this broad is going to make half what she's suggesting, I will make a ton and be very happy!'

That particular night finished in a fairly timid fashion, with Lucy disappearing back to her place or back to the place of some guy she'd decided to fuck, and me and April went back to her place for a few more drinks and some serious discussion on whether I'd made the right deal with Lucy. I ended up spending the night there, and the following morning, around 10 AM, when I was just coming to terms with the fact that my body really couldn't party the way it used to when I was 23, with my head feeling heavier than my feet, and my mind not really knowing what I'd done to deserve such treatment, the phone rang, my work cell, not my personal cell.

"Hi, it's Lucy" the chirpy shrill voice on the other end of the line shouted.

"Good morning, how are you?"

"I am still in the OC, I bagged a client last night, he just paid me a grand, fucked the shit out of me, but it was worth it for $1000. Want to meet me for coffee?" she offered.

'$1000??' I thought, 'how the fuck did she manage that and why can't I find guys that pay that well?'

"Sure" I said, "where should we meet?"

Lucy told me where she was staying and I picked the closest Starbucks to her location, pulled on my dress, which always fit tightly over my naked self, and bid April farewell, thanking her for her hospitality, as I headed to my van, which was parked about 4 minutes' walk from April's home. I hit the road, eager to meet Lucy and ready to do a deal with her for my spare room. Lucy was already there waiting, sitting drinking her jet black, unsweetened coffee, as I pulled up waving one hand at her to get her attention while keeping my other hand on the wheel as I attempted a ridiculous parking maneuver. I entered the shop, she got up and we hugged. I liked this lady, liked her a lot, even though I didn't really yet know her that well, and we just seemed to click.

"So, I have this spare room, as I mentioned to you, and would love to rent it out" I began," I would like $900 per month and if you're up for it, I will take 20% of your takings and without question, you can bring in as many clients as you like" Straight to the point, no nonsense and right in her face. I was on song.

Lucy looked at me and laughed.

"Deal" she said, and with that one word, we agreed to become roommates, with Lucy moving in 2 days later.

Things began immediately her clothes were unpacked. The men started rolling in. It was amazing. She'd set up an account at Listcrawler.com, a new site where E$corts could advertise in relative safety and vet their clients with ease. Lucy had placed an Ad and was receiving around 200 replies a day for her services. It was incredible.

She took 8 clients the second day she'd moved in, from noon until midnight, they just kept coming. Young, old, middle-aged, she didn't care. She brought them in, fucked them, took their cash, and kicked them out, then the two of us would laugh like crazy as she counted the money and divided it between us. I was making more from her than I was on my own. It was time for change, so I also set up an account at Listcrawler.com. As soon as I did this, my luck changed, and along with Lucy, my client list began to expand. One afternoon, I came home from the swimming pool, where I'd just performed my daily routine of swimming 2 miles, (a girl has to stay in shape you know!), and there was a guy standing in the kitchen talking to Lucy. He had a really familiar face, one I knew I'd seen before, but just couldn't figure out where?

"Hi" he said, as I walked in, my hair still dripping and my nipples shining through my skimpy summer dress.

"This is Joe" Lucy said, as she introduced us.

"You look familiar" I told him.

"You too" he replied.

As Lucy and Joe were sipping on a couple of glasses of wine, and I could tell that Joe was about to go upstairs and fuck her, I decided to leave them in peace and go to my room. I was packing away my swim bag and taking my wet clothes off, when there was a knock on the door.

Joe shouted, "I know who you are now!"

"Who am I?" I replied, laughing while I said those words.

"I've seen you in the street, many times, and I always wanted to ask you out" Joe was snickering, as was Lucy, who must have been standing right next to him.

"Good for you Joe" I said, as offhandedly as I could, knowing that the two of them had had a few glasses of wine by then and were most probably drunk, or on their way to being in that state. My door was still shut, and Joe was determined.

"Come and join us, Lucy says you are into doing what she does" Joe was still laughing, and Lucy was definitely encouraging him, kind of egging him along. "I can afford both of you!" he continued, "so come on out, let's fuck"

And so, with Joe's words still ringing in my ears, and my clothes sitting in front of me, on the floor, my naked body clean and fresh after my swim, I opened the door and before I knew it, Joe, who was half naked by then, scooped me up in his arms and led by Lucy, carried me into her room. We fucked for the next three hours, and at the end of this session, not only did

I come to terms with the fact that Lucy was a complete fucking machine and a total ace when it came to getting clients to pay for 'extras', but that we'd made enough to pay rent for the next month, plus, Joe, my neighbor, was going to be a new regular client. The decision to answer Lucy's on-line Ad, had brought Joe much joy that day, and he only had to walk one block to achieve that joy, something he was extremely grateful for.

My journey with Lucy was just beginning, but oh boy, what a start it had been. She was awesome in all ways and someone I was able to both trust as a roommate and enjoy as a friend, both at the same time.

Which reminds me of the time I caused a divorce at a wedding. Vicki Dupont, who is sadly no longer with us, looked just like Lucy, my new house mate. Vicki was a stunning woman, gorgeous, classy, and ever so elegant. I had known her a few months when the two of us, through a mutual contact, were invited to go to Palm Springs. Palm Springs, commonly known as 'the desert', was somewhere we'd all go on a regular basis. Being that it's only a 2-hour drive from where I live, it's easy to get to and a very relaxing place to hang out. On this particular Friday afternoon, the invitation was to take part in the famous Harley Run. The Harley Run was an event that took place annually and back in the day, when people were definitely a lot more tolerant and chill than they are now and where freedom of expression actually meant something. That event was a killer weekend for anyone who wanted to get laid or just show up and do whatever they wanted. The streets of what really was a sleepy old desert town, Palm Springs, was a great place to relax, visit art galleries, eat good food and back then, do whatever you desired, and do it in public too. It's changed a lot now, and those freedoms have sadly vanished to make way for political correctness. No one cared back then, not the residents or the authorities, although I'm sure some of them hated it when we all showed up in our droves just to party and generally making a nuisance of ourselves, but for the most part the locals loved us and the money we brought to their town on an annual basis. When we'd drive or walk down the main road in the city of Palm Springs, mostly on the back of our boyfriends Harley Davidson's, topless and with our tits flying all over the place, no pants or shorts, just G-strings, the locals would line the streets taking pictures and loving every moment of this once-a-year spectacle. I think most of them, especially the older folk who resided permanently there, just couldn't wait for that particular weekend. It was Viagra on wheels for them, and the old guys, although trying to hide their glee as they ogled each pair of tits, probably the only pair of tits they'd seen in many years, were inwardly aroused beyond their years when all of us naked ladies came riding past in formation. We were top of their tit parade for sure! We'd all get drunk, have sex, get drunk again and generally have a fabulous 48 hours or so in a city that couldn't believe its luck, with one after another of the best looking most gorgeous women walking up and down in a never-ending parade of beauty.

Vicki, in all her stunning glory, and of course, me and some of my friends, all of whom were there to party and party hard, were standing at a bar having a drink of two when a guy called Brian, heard Vicki calling out that I was a whore. She used to say this to anyone we met, without malice of course, and with her wry sense of humor, she made it sound, in my humble opinion, quite hilarious.

"She's a hooker! A whore" Vicki would shout out to anyone who cared to listen.

And when she did this, we'd all fall about laughing. But, on this particular Friday evening in Palm Springs, Brian, a dude I'd never met before, heard Vicki and came over immediately and asked me if I wanted a drink. "Of course I want a drink!" I bawled out to all and sundry, and so Brian obliged and we got chatting.

"Are you really a hooker?" he asked.

Not wishing to disappoint, I told him quite boldly, "why yes, I am, would you like to fuck me?"

Brian was lost for words, but eventually picked up enough courage to ask if me and my friends would like to go to a wedding, the following evening. The wedding, he told us, was between 2 bikers who'd met at this event last year and decided to come back this year to tie the knot. We all agreed to attend, with Vicki, laughing as she said it, asking everyone, "Do you think they'll like a hooker being at their nuptials?" We all found it funny, but Brian, well, he just couldn't believe his luck, because that very same evening, I was going to fuck him and make his day, if not his weekend.

My night with Brian was superb, and he paid well for the fun we both had. We got up the next day and prepared for this wedding, remembering I'd no idea whatsoever who was getting married.

The party for this wedding got under way around 1 PM, when all began showing up. We didn't know anyone, they didn't know us, but everyone knew everyone else. Does that make sense? What I'm trying to say is, we were all comfortable together, all Harley riders, all ready to party, all-in for a great day! The marriage was fast and simple, the bride, dressed in her biker-chick gear, happy to be there, and the groom, well, he was drunk. The ceremony over and the pictures in full swing, Brian and I seemed to be at the forefront of all the snaps. Brian was close to the groom, friendship wise, and I, because I was Brian's date, happened to get lumped into most of the professional shots that were taken by a volunteer photographer. All throughout this photographic session, Vicki was in the background shouting as loud as her voice would carry, "There she is, the hooker!" or "That hooker fucked the groom" or "Get the hooker in the picture" while all of us were rolling around laughing. It turned out, that when the wedding was over, so was the marriage. The bride, according to Brian, who I saw one more time about two months later, really believed that her new husband had slept with a hooker and in every shot, there I was, as clear as a bell, at the forefront and often found standing next to the groom. The irony of it all was that Brian, the groom's best friend, allegedly WAS actually fucking the bride, but we didn't know that on the day of the wedding. The poor couple separated and eventually divorced and when we all showed up for the Harley Run the following year, they were both with different partners and Brian was nowhere to be seen. Palm Springs was a fun place, not so much now, back then, oh yes, we had some great times, and some times that we all would like to forget too, such as the time I went down there with my friend Terry W, and he got so drunk that he decided to climb onto the roof of the home we were renting. He then proclaimed, from the apex of that roof, that he was going to jump into the swimming pool below, where I could be found, swimming naked. After that, he suggested, he would fuck me underwater. He managed to climb to the top, which wasn't that high, maneuvering cautiously to the edge of the roof, well, as cautiously as he could being that he was blind drunk, then edging to the corner of the gutter, counting to three, jumping and missing the pool by 2 clear feet. Only problem was, he landed on concrete, and then landed in the hospital ER with a broken leg or ankle, I can't recall which was broken, but it took him six months to recover! Instead of paying me for sex, he ended up paying the hospital 10 times the amount I would have charged him, for his treatment.

Crazy days, crazy times, crazy people, all of whom I still talk to today, other than Vicki, God rest her soul, she really was a gem.

Talking of sluts and whores. I went to a party in Irvine one evening and while I was chugging down shots one after another, I overheard this guy next to me talking to another man called Willie C, who, it turned out owned a ticketing agency in Costa Mesa. Willie was a good-looking guy and he and I spent the rest of that evening getting to know one another, but at the end of the night, although we traded phone numbers, nothing much else happened. The agency he owned got tickets to all the major sporting events and concerts that were playing in the LA and OC area and I felt at some point, since I was an avid concert goer, I would be able to use Willie to score some passes for any of the events I liked, and kept in touch with him for months, hoping that one day he might come in useful. Bingo! Judas Priest announced dates at the massive arena in Irvine, and I loved Judas Priest.

Here's roughly what went down next.

"Willie, it's me, how the hell are you?"

"Good"

"If I come to your house right now, and I give you a blow job, will you guarantee me two free tickets for Judas Priest next month?"

"Yes"

"I'm on my way."

Now, Willie isn't the best-looking guy on the planet, and he's always liked me, and even today, we are good friends, but at that time, we were new to one another and he didn't know what I was really capable of, from a sex standpoint. I was, as you know, wild, and he was about to find that out.

I arrived

"Hey Dude!"

"Hi" he said, and I could see he was nervous.

"Do we have a deal?"

"Yes"

I went into his lounge and sat on this chair. His phone was ringing off the hook and one hour later, I was still waiting, playing with his dogs and looking bored out of my brains. Willie was a busy guy. Eventually he finished, took off his pants and underwear, and I got naked. I sauntered towards the chair he was now sitting in, grabbed his dick, which was tiny, and started to suck and lick it. He couldn't get hard. He was embarrassed, and I was sad. I honestly believed if I couldn't get him off, then my tickets would never materialize. I tried and I tried, every trick I knew, but nothing would make that sucker erect, and in the end, I gave up. True to his word though, he gave me two seats for the show, and we are still great friends, all those years later. He's a great guy, he just can't get hard when I blow him.

Willie introduced me at some point to a guy called Tom. Tom was in construction, building restaurants some of the country's major food chains, like PF Chang's and Cheesecake Factory, a very wealthy, likable guy, and Tom and I became great friends too.

One evening, Tom asked me if I'd like to go with him to San Jose, to a bachelor party, telling me he'd not only pay for my flight and hotel room, but that I'd get a bonus of $2000 just for going with him. No brainier, deal! We left on Southwest Airlines the next morning, arriving in San Jose and checking into a room in the same hotel that was hosting the bachelor party. Before the event, Tom took me to a late lunch, a local place, right in the heart of downtown San Jose, which, if you've never been there, is a complete waste of space. Nothing happens there unless the hockey team, The San Jose Sharks, have a game on. It's a weird place, with dozens of restaurants, most of which are empty. Tom and I entered one of those empty restaurants, and sat down to eat. At that point in time, we'd only had sex once or twice, which Tom had paid for, but we'd never been out together for a meal, so this was a first for both of us. The menu arrived, and honestly, because the place was completely empty, other than Tom and me and the rest of the staff, the whole vibe in this place was weird. I ordered asparagus. I didn't want anything else, and Tom ordered pasta. The food arrived.

"Boy, this is THE best fucking asparagus I have ever eaten!!" I blurted out at the top of my voice, after which, I laughed, until I saw the look of horror on Tom's face. 'What the fuck is wrong with you?" I asked him.

He grabbed me by one hand and escorted me out of the restaurant, where he proceeded to lecture me for 5 minutes on how to behave in front of strangers.

"What the fuck are you talking about?" I said to him, "The fucking place is empty." But he wasn't having any of it and continued to berate me in the middle of the street, asking me to tone down my behavior and language. I told him to 'get fucked' and started to walk away, when he quickly grabbed me and apologized. We re-entered the restaurant and finished our meal, then we headed back to the hotel for the bachelor party. By this time, our little encounter had been forgotten and Tom was in a much better frame of mind as we ascended inside the hotel elevator towards the top floor where the festivities were just beginning to kick off.

The deal was simple. We'd all go to dinner first, ten guys, the bachelor and me, and after dinner, all of them would fuck me. In fact, at one point they started taking wagers on who would pay the most. Tom wasn't impressed. The bidding got to over $1500, money I would have gladly accepted, until Tom intervened. It was all in good fun up to that point, and after a delicious meal, we went to this 5-star hotel, I think it was the Fairmont, where a suite had been purchased and kitted out with several crates of champagne, tequila and whiskies. It was going to be party central for the next 12 hours, at least! And then the hookers arrived, sorry, E$corts. They didn't want to be called hookers. Mainly Asian, this was San Jose after all, and all really pretty.

Tom was in his element, as were most of the others, and the fucking began. Tom was first to get naked, then he began tearing all the sheets from all the beds, then the clothes from all the girls, and before we knew it, we were 18 naked people running around a hotel suite, fucking each other as quickly as possible and then moving on to the next one. It was speed fucking at its very best. Everyone was drunk, fucked and exhausted by the time the party finished, and I was $3500 better off. A superb result, and an evening that created a life-long bond between Tom and I, a bond that exists through today.

There was also a Super Bowl party that Tom ran in Palm Springs one year. He owned a huge home down there and quite often he'd open it up to all his friends, inviting them there for the weekend and then bring in E$corts to service those guy friends of his. It was a kind of sexually charged occasion that lasted well over three days. This particular Super Bowl had the Bronco's playing, I distinctly remember that because one of the guys who I ended up fucking was a fan. I received a call from Tom that I needed to be in Palm Springs at his villa the day before the game, which was always on a Sunday, either the last Sunday in January or the first Sunday in February, depending on the year. Tom was very specific, "bring April and Lucy with you", he'd insisted. And so, I did. The three of us shot down to his home on that Saturday afternoon, arriving to a kind of 'frat house' environment, with Tom, the cheerleader of his pack of 10 guys. He was in his element as he marched us in the front door like the bunch of concubines we were about to become. Without warning our clothes were off, the cash was on the table, half the guys were naked and ready to fuck and the other half, too drunk to do anything. It was as if they'd been waiting patiently for us to show up, getting hornier and hornier as the hours went by and as they all gouged themselves on beer and porn, which was already playing full blast on Tom's 85-inch TV set. This was possibly the largest TV I had ever seen, set up beautifully on a wall in his lounge, which was also covered with expensive art and a few family pictures. The porn, true hard core, had set the guys off, and once the three of us, April, Lucy and I got naked, and were plied with a few drinks, hard cocks were being rammed into our mouths, our pussies and our drinks. Yes, drinks! Some of the guys liked me to use their cocks as stir sticks for the martinis and other cocktails they were consuming, and then they'd want me to lick their cock dry and fuck it hard. This was a wild, and mainly out of control party. I think we all, April, Lucy and I, fucked every one of the ten guys, at least once, if not more and by the end of the weekend. The party ended at Monday 4 PM, almost 24 hours after the game had finished and all three of us made over 5 grand each. A windfall by my standards. It was a fun time, for all who'd participated, but I have to tell you when I got home and put my pussy to bed it was a week before she recovered from the pounding all ten of those men gave her. This was just another reason to love Tom. He took care of all of us, even putting us in hotels at night because the ten guys took up the whole house. Fun times, hard cocks, lots of booze and incredible and often marvelous sex.

Yes, sluts and whores, that's us for sure, but we're also nice ladies and believe it or not, normal ladies too. If you met us in the street, you'd never know what we did for a living, but when you take us to bed, you'll never forget us.

No Get Out Of Jail Free Card

My biggest fear was always the possibility getting arrested. Caught red-handed by the Cops. It's the fear of all the ladies who perform 'tricks', whether it's on the street or in the comfort of a hotel room or at home. We all fear the day they put the handcuffs on us and cart us away to jail, with no get out of jail card, and the possibility that we could spend months or years behind bars, just because we fucked a horny guy. The laws in the United States for prostitution are archaic, but laws are laws and we all know beforehand what we're getting into and what precautions we need to take to stay alive and to roam free as we practice our trade. Though it's never easy, and I'm not looking for sympathy here, we are held to different standards than most criminals, and as I say to most of the guys who ask me what it's like to be an E$cort in America, "What's worse? Getting fucked or getting killed? Fucking is natural, and yet, we are castigated for providing a service most men crave. I just can't understand why the law, especially in the USA, treats us as lepers. We are not drug dealers, murderers, thieves. We just open our legs willingly, assisting lots of different men, fulfilling their fantasies, and we certainly appreciate the compensation that service provides. My dad used to tell me, "it doesn't matter how you make a living, as long as you make a living" I chose prostitution because I love sex and I love to please, but the government says I'm a criminal, no better than the guy across the street who beats his wife ten times a week, or the gun slinger who kills innocents when driving down any road in this country emptying his AK-47 into the bellies of those who were alive 1 second prior to his bullets mowing them down. Yes, we are guilty as charged. Guilty of making people happy. Guilty of enjoying someone else's body. Guilty of an orgasm or two, and obviously guilty of doing a job that most men's wives or girlfriends can't perform properly, if they did, I'd be out of business.

When I got into this profession, I was terrified of being caught by the Cops, and I really mean, terrified. It was on my mind every minute of every day that I worked, so much so that often I would mistake an innocent black Ford or Chevy parked outside a hotel or home I was going to for my outcall service, for being FBI, CIA, or just local Vice, and I'd run a mile and miss the appointment. I got so nervous, because back then, without the internet and ability to screen clients instantly, it really was a continual guessing game when you went to see a new client. But fortunately for me, when I started, I was lucky enough to meet another lady in the same business, her name escapes me right now, who knew a guy who knew a Cop, a local cop, and this lady, (E$cort), was in possession of a list of hotels, clubs and other establishments where Vice was rumored to perform their regular 'sting' jobs. That list proved invaluable, because not only did those sneaky bastard Cops call our Ad's to set up meetings and then, once we'd arrived at their hotel room, cuff us, and cart us off to jail for the night, they also had the audacity to do it in the same places, time and time again. That list, the one provided to me in my early days of E$corting, had a complete inventory of their favorite haunts, the one's we needed to avoid like the plague. Remember, the cell phones back then were like bricks, but there was no Google and no other search engines and therefore no way to verify someone's ID when they made the appointment. Now, it's so easy. You get a call, Google the number and it's either legit or not. Then it was different, and girls were being caught out nightly. Fortunately for me, I was lucky not to be caught, and I intended it to stay that way as my career progressed.

The call I received came around 6 PM one evening.

My usual protocol when I received a request for outcall was to chat with the guy for a few mins, get a feel for what he was looking for and agree that it wasn't going to be anything other than regular sex, (although I did receive many calls that required fetish requests, I didn't always agree to them), and after we'd agreed a time to meet and I was confident the guy was real and not some flake or law enforcement, I would head for the shower, wash all my bits and do my hair. Then, after making myself look delightful, I would pack up a small bag filled with all the necessities, condoms, lube, etc., Then and only then, I would head for my car. On this particular night, having just returned home after spending the afternoon on the beach, the timing wasn't ideal for me, leaving me rushed in make my hair pretty, which pissed me off no end. I decided to take a blow drier with me in the hope that the guy I was about to see wouldn't mind me doing my hair in his hotel bathroom. Once I was all packed up, my hair still wet, I got into my car and drove the 15 minutes to his hotel with my front car windows down, hoping the warm summer air would help dry my hair just a little. As per my usual routine, I parked the car about a hundred yards away from the hotel leaving me about 2 minutes to walk to the entrance and yet another guaranteed on-time arrival. I never gave it a second thought, but the name of the hotel, which was in Huntington Beach, seemed familiar to me for some reason, and I just couldn't quite think why? Eventually, as I walked into the lobby, I put all of those thoughts out of my mind, as I began to concentrate on my upcoming date. As he'd told me on the phone, I entered the lobby, turned left to the elevator, ignoring the reception desk staff, walk into the elevator and punch the button for the fourth floor. When I got to that floor, I exited and turned right, then immediately arrived at room 412. I knocked, he answered. "Handsome dude" I thought, as I made my way into the room, giving the guy a hug on my way past him.

"Mind if I take two mins to blow dry my hair hon?" I asked him, as if he had a choice in the matter, "I was at the beach when you called and didn't have time to do it after I showered"

He agreed by nodding his head in the affirmative, and I made my way into the bathroom. "How much do I owe you?" he shouted from the bedroom.

"$200" I shouted back, just leave it on the bed"

As I finished blow drying my hair, I walked back out into the bedroom, and the guy had vanished.

"Strange" I thought, 'where the fuck did he go?"

I picked up the $200 off the mattress and as I did this, the door to the room was flung wide open and 3 guys, all cops, guns out and pointed right at my face, barged into the room, shouting

"Get on the ground, get on the ground"

I nearly puked.

My date, the guy I was supposed to fuck, entered behind the three fully armed cops, and it turned out, he was their boss.

"You're under arrest for solicitation and prostitution" he said, as he smiled, and then he read me my rights.

I was about to shit my pants. I had never been arrested before and it was exactly at that moment when I realized my huge mistake. The paper, that one I had been given which listed all the hotels and other places the cops would set up stings, I hadn't reviewed it before I'd left home, something I always did like clockwork but obviously hadn't done on this occasion. And that is why the hotel sounded so familiar to me. It was on the fucking list of places to avoid. What an idiot I was.

Handcuffed, and in my skimpy little summer dress, bra-less tits bouncing freely, the cops went through my hand bag, which was filled to brimming with condoms I'd just purchased but which I hadn't had time to dump in the drawer at my home. There must have been 200 of them! They also found my car keys, and asked where I was parked, then escorted me downstairs into the lobby area, and in front of the many wide-eyed onlookers took me outside and dumped me unceremoniously into the waiting cop car. I was so embarrassed so hurt and so scared. They then went across the road to where I'd parked to search my car. It turned out that was an unlawful move by them, they didn't have a warrant and hadn't asked me for permission to do so. About 5 minutes later, one of the cops returned to the cop car, where I was sitting, holding a small bag of marijuana,

"Is this yours?" he asked.

I replied meekly, with tears, primed and ready, about to run down my face, "yes"

"Well, you're also under arrest for possession with intent to sell" "What????" I shouted as loud as I could. Marijuana wasn't legal in any US state at that point in time and the small amount I had was for my own use. I never ever sold drugs. I had no idea what they were talking about, but it made me even more upset and frightened.

The cops finished their paperwork and we began the short drive to the local police station.

Arriving at the Police station, I was fingerprinted, photographed and thrown into a cell with 25 other felons, yes, I was now a felon too, but I didn't think of myself as being 'one of them'. This whole experience seemed quite surreal and totally incomprehensible. After about two hours, I was let go with a ticket to appear in court 3 weeks later. When I got home, I knew I needed a lawyer. I started to make calls, firstly to my friends to see if they knew of anyone who could represent me, and then I started an on-line search, calling almost 25 different attorneys' until I found this guy called CL, (I am not going to reveal his real name in this book). When I spoke to CL, he made me laugh with the very first comment that came out of his mouth, which was something along the lines of, "if you were my daughter, I would bitch slap you upside your head!". CL became my lawyer instantly, and still is to this very day. Fortunately for me, he was available and willing to take my case, and after a brief get together, about 24 hours later I found myself, with some relief, waiting at home for CL to complete paperwork for the judge, which he believed would get me out of the mess I'd put myself in.

"What happens now?" I asked him.

"I need to fill in some more paper work for the court and then they will review it and sentence you, or not, as the case may be. I think I can get you off though"

CL prepared the paperwork and presented it to the court, but then called to tell me he needed to do it again because the judge had rejected it. He took his time, slowly going over everything that was required, entered the court room again and made a second attempt to get my name cleared. He'd filled out a 'Motion to Suppress' form, apparently incorrectly at first, but his second attempt was perfect, and the judge agreed. After 20 minutes of back and forth, I was given 10 hours of community service, which I would eventually spend cleaning up local freeways. He left the courthouse and called to give me the good news. I was so relieved. I thanked him profusely and made my apologies that I needed to shower. Getting ready to rinse away all my worries, I quickly disconnected the call. I showered and checked my cell phone messages. I had another client, waiting, and ready for action, all the details on where and when to meet him and how long he wanted to spend with me. I thought to myself, 'what the fuck? You only live once', and got straight back in my car and drove to the guy's home. I'd been out of jail or should I say, let off the hook, for less than a day, and I was back fucking for a living. What a strange time this was turning out to be.

My community service sentence, cleaning up freeways, was brutal. It made me sore, it made me unhappy, it made me think a lot about my life, but it also hardened me to the choices I'd made which had taken me there in the first place. I was dead set on continuing with E$cort services, but I also wanted to find a more legitimate job, perhaps one that I could do part time. These thoughts ran through my mind each night I returned from my duties on the freeway, stiff, unable to bend my arms or back and finding it impossible to do much other than go to bed to rest.

About a month went by, and I'd also found a part time job selling Pre-Paid Legal services for a law firm, just to make extra cash and supplement my income, and give me a footing back in the 'real' world, if that's where I ended up wanting to go. Anyone I met, I tried to sell them this service, and honestly, I wasn't doing too badly. It paid the bills at my new apartment, a condo I'd bought in a place called Tustin. One of my close friends, who I trusted and respected, had advised me to put money down for this brand-new apartment, and I'd listened to him intently as he'd reminded me of all the benefits of becoming a homeowner. It turned out I lost a lot of money on this purchase by selling it too early, but that's another story, maybe for later in this book, and has little to do with what happened next. The apartment was cute, comfortable and cozy and when I had clients over, they all really seemed to like it. Everyone thought I was mad for letting strange men into my home, but where else was I supposed to practice my in-call E$cort services? I didn't really have a choice. My apartment was safe, at least I felt it was safe, and it gave me that extra option of staying home to entertain my guys, rather than traipse to hotel rooms and strange homes. Being arrested at that hotel in Huntington Beach had really scared me and so staying home really was a great option at the time.

This big fat guy showed up one evening. When I say fat, he was overweight but kind of cute and sort of fit looking. He was definitely nervous when I let him in, but I figured he must be doing this for the first time, and without too much thought, I showed him into my living room. He sat down and we began conversing, the conversation turning almost immediately to my Pre-Paid Legal service job sales pitch. They guy looked like a perfect candidate for that service and perhaps a non-starter for my E$cort service. Whenever I began talking to people about this service, I found it difficult to shut up, and this seemed to be the case when, with the guy on the couch looking very bored indeed, I realized that perhaps I'd gone too far. He'd picked himself up and made an excuse to leave. I didn't lose many clients like this, there had been one or two over the years, but most men just put up with me and hung around until it was time to fuck. This guy didn't. He was off, with no turning back, leaving me alone in my apartment ruing the fact that $300 had just split on me. They are all cash to me, not really names, just numbers, numbers that added up into large amounts of money to pay my bills. There's no emotional attachment, just a financial one. It's still the same, even today.

As I sat there deciding whether to call the guy and bring him back, my mind going back and forth between the financial rewards versus the guy wasn't really into me, greed inside me called him back, although not immediately. I waited a couple of days, just to let him cool off, or calm down, or lose his nervousness. "Hey you, I am so sorry that I talked your head off the other day. I was unaware that I was boring you and I know you came to fuck me, so please come back" I pleaded with him.

He agreed to come back.

He arrived about 4 hours later at my apartment, all sweaty and asking if he could take a shower, and I agreed. There's no way ever that I would fuck any sweaty smelly guy. I offered him a towel and soap. He went into the bathroom and turned the water on. He was in there for a very long time indeed. In fact, I was beginning to wonder if he'd drowned in the shower, when suddenly he reappeared. It was so strange; he didn't look like he'd showered or attempted to wash. I was about to say something to him, when he made this stupid excuse that he needed to leave.

"Oh oh, here we go again" I thought to myself. "This one is a real tease and must be incredibly nervous and indecisive. His excuse was that something had happened to his mother and he'd just received a call from a family member telling him he needed to go to attend to her immediately. I thought, "that's weird, I never heard his phone ring while he was in the bathroom?" As he opened the door to leave, I was standing right behind him. The door was suddenly pushed in towards my face, and two cops, a man and a woman, pushed the fat guy back inside towards me, creating a kind of domino effect. Fat guy banged into me, spinning me around and then he turned to face me, this time with his police badge hanging from his neck. I'd been busted yet again. They sat me down, booked me, gave me a ticket with a court date on it and left. This time, thank goodness, I didn't go to jail, they just let me sweat it over inside my own apartment. I called CL, my attorney, and told him what had just happened. He was sympathetic, and told me that the two arrests were so close in time to one another and in two different cities, that the left won't know what the right is doing and I'd be fine. When this happens, simultaneous arrests, no more than a couple of months apart in cities that are run by different police departments and courts, one city doesn't know that the other city has made an arrest for a similar offense. It takes months and months for their systems to catch up and register multiple offences by the same person. CL believed he could push through our defense and seek a resolution for this offense before there was any record of my first arrest, 4 weeks earlier, in either of the two cities computer systems. He did.

I received another 10 days community service, no jail time and on this occasion, I was offered the opportunity to serve part of the sentence as an assistant in the Goodwill store in Tustin as part of the 10-day punishment and then the rest of the time at the Newport Club, where all the AA and sex offender meetings took place, where I would serve tea and coffee for those who attended sessions there. This was much better that cleaning the freeway, and at the time I remember thinking, if I ever got busted again, I hoped it would be in Tustin and not Huntington Beach! Twice in 4 weeks I'd been caught and CL, had lectured me and given me a piece of his mind after our Tustin court date, letting me know in no uncertain terms that if I got caught again, I'd be put in jail. But his advice and concern went in one ear and out the other, because, of course, I was caught again, and again, something I'll tell you about shortly.

In the meantime, after working 3 or 4 days at the Goodwill store, I was transferred to the Newport Club to serve food and help out by cleaning the bathrooms and kitchen. At the time different organizations, such as Alcoholics Anonymous and Drug Rehab groups, used the club to hold their meetings. The first day I was there, I met this cute guy. He was attending one of the AA meetings and I ended up fucking him in the bathroom, which, I was supposed to be cleaning! I'd locked the doors from the inside and fucked this guy in one of the stalls. He loved it, I loved it, and the Newport Club had no idea what had just happened! My community service ended up being tolerable and indeed lucrative, because I charged that guy to fuck me! I promised myself, the time served at that Club was going to be my last, but yet again my plans were rudely interrupted some 6 weeks later, and this time, I was caught completely unaware and to this day, in my opinion, I was totally innocent.

My friend Anthea, famous (if that's the right word) for dating a guy who took her to Catalina Island one afternoon on his boat, and on the way back, crashing that same boat into the rocks at Newport Beach harbor. His recklessness made all the main news broadcasts that day and left the two of them needing to be rescued by the Coast Guard. Anthea lived in Newport Beach. She and her boyfriend, not the dude who owned the crashed boat, a new guy she'd found, were party animals. They loved to entertain, they loved to have me over and I loved to go there. Their home, a lovely detached house close to the harbor, was in an ideal setting for partying. We used to get drunk, have great times diving in and jumping out of their swimming pool smoking pot and balancing on all the floaties, or just running down to the beach and jumping in the ocean naked. This one afternoon, a fabulous Orange County summers day, they decided to throw an afternoon party, bikini friendly, something I adore. There is nothing better than a bikini party, nothing! I'd been partying all day and then I received a call from Anthea that her party was definitely on. She'd asked me to pick up her boyfriend Eric on the way over, he was at some other gig, already drunk and unable to drive, which I agreed to do. After collecting him, I made my way to their home, as I mentioned already, a home nestled on the beach and in the most idyllic of locations. The party began in earnest after we arrived and about an hour into the festivities, I'd already had one or two drinks, Anthea asked me, quite casually, "Are you OK to drive?"

"Sure, what do you need?"

"Do me a huge favor and go to the store, it's only round the corner, and pick me up some salad dressing?"

I agreed, and I got in the car and went to Ralph's supermarket, which really was less than half a mile from their home. Salad dressing was an easy find, and after paying, I got back into my car and drove back to the party. Just as I was pulling up to their home to park, the blue flashing lights of a police car lit up my rearview mirror and a loud voice through an in-car tonoi, asked me to pull over.

"What the fuck?" I asked myself.

I hadn't even seen them coming, or following me, and I'd no idea what I'd done wrong. By now, the party crowd inside the house had noticed what was going on, and they all gathered at one of the front windows in anticipation of my pending arrest.

"Driver's license and insurance please" the officer said as he came up to my window, which was now wide open in anticipation of his request.

"What did I do?" I asked him. He ignored me. I handed over the documents he'd asked for.

"Please stay in the car" he directed. Then he left and went back to his car. By now, everyone at the window was laughing at me, all of them believing I was going to get a ticket, but honestly, I had no idea, even to this day, what I did that warranted them pulling me over.

The officer returned with my license and insurance in his hand.

"Please get out the car" he barked.

I did as I was asked.

He then told me to put my hands behind my back, and at this point I knew I was being arrested. As I did so, he asked me, "do you know you have a warrant out for your arrest?"

"What?" I shouted. "Sorry, but do you have the right person?" I asked.

"Yes ma'am, you have an outstanding warrant" he repeated.

"For what?" I asked

"For something we will discuss down at the station."

The crowd inside the house went nuts, some of them shouting abuse at this poor cop, though for what reason, I didn't know.

The cuffs went on my wrists and the officer escorted me back to his vehicle, where I was once again unceremoniously dumped in the back seat.

Anthea came running out of her home and asked the cop where he was taking me and for what reason. He told her.

"Don't worry sweetie", Anthea reassured me through the window of the cop car, "one of us will come and get you"

Her words of encouragement didn't help, trust me, I was shitting myself, really, I was.

"What is the warrant for?" I kept asking the officer, as he drove me back to the police station.

"I's unclear Ma'am" he told me, "All I know is that you have one, it looks like it's for possession, but we will need to clarify that when we get to the station"

"Why did you stop me?" I continued our conversation.

"You ran a Stop sign"

"I did? Oh, shoot, I am very sorry!"

"Don't worry, you seem like a nice lady, I know you've not been drinking, and I know you're not high, so we will sort it out in a few minutes after we get back to base" Little did he know that I HAD been drinking, but his casual attitude definitely put me at ease and something inside me believed this would all work out and it was just a clerical error. My optimism was to be proven correct. When we arrived at the station, and after I'd gone through all the formalities of checking in, I was let go fairly quickly, which surprised me. When I say I was let go quickly, in actual fact it took about 4 hours for that to happen, but it felt like it happened a lot sooner than that. At first, I thought the arresting officer had made a mistake, and that's the reason I was being released so quickly, but after I left the jail and seeing Anthea standing in the lobby area waiting for me, I realized quickly that she'd bailed me out. I called CL to let him know what had happened, and as gracefully as he could, remembering that this was my third arrest in as many months, he promised to sort it out. In the end, I was bailed out after the bikini party had finished, but deep inside me I was sure my luck had really run out and that I should contemplate a new direction in life. That contemplation however didn't last too long. My phone continued to ring off the hook with horny clients, potential that I would always turn into my own financial gain.

CL got the warrant, (a warrant that was genuinely active), dropped in return for more time at Newport Club, serving teas and coffee's and fucking one or two of the addicts and staff, for cash of course! It had been a whirlwind few months, and my lessons learned were soon to be ignored.

As time progressed, my little home in Tustin proved to be too much for me to maintain, in the end I sold it, and I moved into a rented apartment close to Newport Beach. I wish I'd kept that home. Now, it's worth almost ten times what I paid for it, but my immaturity at that time just wouldn't accept that I had to be disciplined with its upkeep and committed to paying all the expenses that are the responsibility of any homeowner.

My good friend Timmy, a drug dealer I fucked now and again, supplied me and my friends with weed now and again, and his supplies came nicely packaged in batches that weighed around a pound. Timmy would drop off these 'supplies' at my apartment once or twice a month. I would smoke some and sell some, but again, my habit was minimal in comparison with most of the other people I knew, and the amount I sold to friends was ten times what I actually used. One night however Timmy showed up and left a huge stash with me, about 3 kilos, telling me I should keep it even though I didn't need it. He suggested supplies may become scarce for a few months due to shortages all around the state of California, and that 3 kilos would tide me over until normal service was resumed. After putting the weed under my bed, my hiding place, we all went to a restaurant at the Triangle in Costa Mesa, me Timmy and a few other girlfriends. Timmy and I were just beginning to get a little tipsy, when, with a subtle nod of his head, he motioned over to a table on our left, asking me to take a look. I had no ideas what I was supposed to be looking at, but Timmy was annoyed, really annoyed. I knew that look well, and realized immediately that something was wrong.

"Fucking cops!" he exclaimed

"What?" I said, looking over and then quickly turning my head back towards Timmy, "Don't be crazy" I told him, "They're just two guys having a quiet drink together"

"No, you've been followed, they're cops" he insisted.

"I've been followed???" I exclaimed. "Why do you think it's me and not you?" Timmy didn't respond, but he got up and went right over to the table the two guys were sitting at and as he passed them by, he muttered under his breath, although loud enough for everyone in the restaurant to hear, "GOODBYE COPS!"

The two guys just laughed, and as they did so, Timmy left the restaurant, leaving me and my girlfriends to pick up the tab. We then all decided to leave and follow Timmy, heading back to my place with our 'take-away' food. On the way out however one of the 'supposed' cops got up, approaching me and my friends and asked me if I could get him some weed. I was surprised to say the least, thinking at that point in time because he was asking that question directly to my face, there was no way on this good earth he could be a cop. 'Timmy must have been wrong', I thought. These guys couldn't be cops, and with all my prettiness and my nipples shining right in their faces, I said, "maybe, but give me your number and I'll call and let you know for sure" I just never learn in life and am always so trusting.

"Where do you live" one of them asked.

"No too far from here" and then I offered up, "do you want to follow me?"

How could I have asked them such a stupid question? It was crazy, but I did it and when I did it, I realized how naïve I was. It was too late and before I could change my mind, they were up and ready to leave with us.

"Sure thing" the guys said, let's go.

I quickly found the courage to change my mind, and said, "just give me your number, I will call you" feeling really stupid as I did so.

And he did, but in doing so I could see him looking at me in the oddest way. We all went down to the parking lot, my group got in our car and headed back to my home. I was mulling over and over in my head if I should call the guy or not? Timmy had brought me dope, so much, and indeed I didn't really need it all. I supposed I could make a few bucks by selling some. These guys just didn't look like cops, even though Timmy had warned me, and I presumed he'd been winding me up when he'd left the restaurant whilst taunting them.

Unbeknownst to me, the fucking cops, yes, that's what they were, waited for us outside the parking lot, leaving the restaurant at the same time we had and moving their car into a position, allowing them to spot us driving off. We arrived at my place, and my friends dropped me off. I went inside, and I decided to call the guy and to sell him some weed. I needed the money and I didn't require such a huge stash of weed in my home. He answered on the first ring.

What I didn't know at the time was that he was sitting right outside my home.

"Hey it's me, from the restaurant, and OK I will sell you a couple of ounces for $200" I told him. "When can you come over?"

He agreed, telling me he'd be there shortly, so I gave him my address. As I was putting the phone down, my doorbell rang.

I went to answer. They were waiting at the door. Two of them, guns drawn. They barged in and I thought to myself, 'here we go again'.

Because I was on parole and because they'd followed me home, run my phone details and then my car registration, (the car was parked in the driveway) they knew who I was, and because I'd offered to sell them dope, I was in deep shit and they knew it too. They searched the house and sitting right there on the coffee table was the massive amount of dope that Timmy had brought round earlier that evening. I was caught red-handed and doomed.

I was cuffed and yet again, taken to the police station, where this time, I wasn't going to be so fortunate. CL came to see me, and he told me, I wasn't getting out this time.

I'd been a complete moron, and all I could hear in my stupid head was Timmy saying, "I told you so!"

Hell

Three strikes and you're out. CL, my attorney, was right. The Judge sentenced me to 3 months in prison, and gave me 4 weeks to get my affairs in order. I was ordered to show up at the penitentiary on a specific date, where my freedom would be taken for me for 90 days, without any chance of leaving earlier. I literally shit myself. Never in my wildest dreams did I ever imagine going to jail for any length of time, let alone 3 months without chance of leaving sooner. I had rent to pay, I had very little money in the bank, I had car payments to make, clients who wanted to see me, family who would now find out what I did for a living, and friends who, for the most part, I would miss terribly. When I left the courthouse sobbing, after being sentenced, my mind was in overdrive, and my body, just weak and devastated. I had 4 weeks to make everything right, especially my living accommodation, because I didn't want to lose my apartment while I was in jail. That would have been an unprecedented disaster. "What was I going to do?"

    4 weeks isn't a lot of time by anyone's standards, especially when you have a limited budget and are placed in a situation where your freedom is going to be curtailed for many months. Ensuring your life doesn't change too much while you are away, is a real challenge, and a challenge that I took head on once I'd received the exact date for my impending incarceration.

    My friends rallied round me, one in particular, my current boyfriend at the time, Kevin. He agreed to take care of my rent, and my car payment. Utilities were another matter, but I soon figured out a way to resolve that issue. I'd write Kevin several blank checks that he could use to pay the bills and keep my life on track while I was inside. This left me free for about three weeks to make as much money as I could, enough to see me through that three-month incarceration. Although my mind wasn't in it, my pussy certainly was, and for 3 straight weeks, I fucked my way into jail. I made a bunch of cash, all of which was going to pay my bills. I used to sit in front of the TV and on would come an advertisement for a new movie, "Coming Sept 12" the Ad would state, and when I saw that I would shudder, knowing that was the date my time inside would begin. I was going to jail, directly to jail, not stopping at GO and not receiving $200, but I was getting 12 weeks. Oh boy!

I decided, after I'd been sentenced, to research what it would be like inside Jail. Let me explain. Jail is different from Prison. One, Prison, is for long term criminals, and Jail, for short term. I called friends, some of whom had served short sentences in jail and one who had been to Prison. They all told me the same thing, boredom would be my biggest enemy. I suffer terribly from Allergies, and one of my main concerns was, "would I get my nose spray, eye drops and allergy pills?" The short answer would be a resounding NO. That panicked me even more, if that was entirely possible, because I was already panicked. And this was just the beginning. One of my friends told me to go out and buy several good books and have people mail them once a week. I did that. Another friend told me to take money to put into the commissary, that way I could buy extras when in jail. I did that too. My nerves were at a raw end. My heart was sinking even lower and my pussy? Well, she was on fire and fucking as if her life depended on it. I made 'mint' in those three weeks before I was incarcerated, banking all of it, enabling Kevin to pay all of my bills. Days turned into nights and with each passing hour, my freedom dwindled into desperation. Two days before I was due to turn myself in, I showed up at the Jail to finish the paper work and register. I sat around on a concrete wall, my backside just aching as each hour passed slowly, only to find out that I had showed up a day too soon. The guards and staff felt sorry for me, but they processed me nonetheless and told me to come back the following day. While I waited in that hall for 5 hours, I was surprised at how nice some of the guards and staff were to me and with that thought in mind, the apprehension I'd had about spending 12 weeks locked up with a supposed bunch of bullies, just vanished. The staff were normal people, just like me, and most of them wanted to chat to find out what I'd done to get my ass locked up in the first place.

Kev was waiting outside for me after I was done, about 5 hours later. He drove me home and dropped me off and I began the process of sterilizing my home. I had to prepare the house for its 12-week sabbatical. The fridge had to be emptied, the water shut off the bathroom left spotless, and so much more. I also had to finish my laundry, leaving everything clean and tidy for my return. I never slept at all that night. I just lay there, contemplating the next three months and wishing it over and done with. The thing was, it hadn't even begun, and when my eyes finally closed and I drifted off to sleep, I was rudely awoken by my alarm clock at 6 AM, knowing Kevin was collecting me at 7. I rose and showered and had a ten-minute spell on the toilet seat, where all my anxiety was left in the bowl. I felt good, I felt nervous, I felt ready to conquer my fears.

Arriving at the jail house, Kevin and I hugged and at precisely 8 AM on September the 12th, I entered this big old ugly building where I would spend the next 12 weeks of my life. Even though I'd been processed the day before, I sat around in that huge empty concrete room again for more than 6 hours, sometimes being called to a desk to verify my ID and other of the documents I'd signed the day before. I was then, after agreeing to everything, let into a cell, which was not to be my home cell, but just another step to entering the jailhouse proper. I was told to strip, and when I was naked, the female guard did a complete body search, and I mean COMPLETE, as I stood there fully nude shivering and feeling very humbled. The night before I'd entered the jail, I'd cut all my nails off at the suggestion of someone I knew who'd been through this process before, and after being given a blue smock, some pants, a bra (sport bra actually), and slippers, by putting on my new underwear, I got dressed in prison garb for the first time. I was told that I had to wear that bra, something you already know I would never do in the outside world, but in there, I had no choice. After being searched again, this time when fully clothed, I was asked to show my finger nails, and then complimented by the guard for having already taken care of that issue. No fingernails in jail! I was given a toothbrush, toothpaste, a blanket and a very thin mattress, a bar of soap and that was it. I was done. Led by another female guard into another cell, still not at my final destination, and left there for another hour or so, until finally I was escorted to my new home, a 12 x 12-foot cell, with two bunk beds, one already occupied by another inmate, and a metal toilet without a seat and a metal sink. This was it, paradise!

The door behind me closed, and I was left to fend for myself. My first order of business, placing all my 'goodies' on the bed, the top bunk was already taken so I had the bottom. I then introduced myself to my cellmate. To this day I cannot remember her name, but she was older than me, and had short brown hair and a few tattoos. After talking with her, and she was very nice by the way, for about an hour, she filled me in on all the daily routines I could expect. This jail in Santa Ana, was built like a Lego block. It was 3 floors deep, one cell on top of another with cells on either side of me, stretching for 200 yards to the left, about 50 to the right and then repeating front and back to form a perfect square of Lego cells. It was noisy, it was freezing cold, with A/C being pumped through vents full blast at the top right of each cell on the opposite wall from where we slept. Most of the occupants of this jail were incarcerated for issues relating to drugs, cocaine, heroin, etc, or for selling or possession of Meth, or for domestic abuse and battery. There were, it turned out, some very strange people in this place, and also some very normal people, but we will come to that shortly.

Three meals a day, after rollcall at 5 AM, began with breakfast at 8, lunch at noon and dinner at 5. The food for breakfast and for lunch wasn't too bad, prepared by inmates and served by them too. It was healthy enough to keep me going without starvation setting in. Two weird things about the food were as follows, we got bread, tons of it, with every meal, and for dinner each night we were served a basic sandwich, more often than not, bologna, which wasn't really that disgusting, just a little repetitive, and by the time I left that cell, I was sweating an odor that smelled just like all the bologna I'd eaten. But back to my first night in jail.

The lights went out at 9 PM, but the cell was so noisy. You could hear everyone, from the furthest cell, almost 200 yards away, to the cell next door. When someone farted, the jail laughed in unison. The vents above the beds kept on pumping freezing cold air. It was nonstop and eventually, about three days into my stay, I began using the excess bread they fed us to plug the vents in the grill, which kind of dampened the flow a little. Lights were also an issue. They never went off. When the main lights went out at night, they were never really out, in fact it was bright enough that we could all sit up after curfew and read with ease from the light that penetrated the cell. We were not given any pillows, and the only way to compensate for that missing necessity, was to use a book or two to rest your head on. Eventually though, I found an inflatable pillow in the commissary, which I purchased, and though it was very small, about 8 inches square, it sufficed.

My cell mate didn't snore, but she farted a lot. The smell was quite often unbearable, but where could I go? Nowhere! We were locked up for 23 hours a day, and when you had to shit, you had to do it there and then and right in front of your cellmate. We used to shout out "Courtesy Flush!", to one another as we pooed and flushed and pooed and flushed, just to keep the smell to a minimum. It really was disgusting. And then they offered us release times, one hour a day, where we would go into a huge hall and walk round the perimeter, or play basketball on a half court which was about the size of a pool table, or just sit and chat to one another. Some of the women in there were interesting to talk to, and others, well, let's just say my 5-year-old nephew had more between his ears than any of them.

I discovered we could sign up for classes, business typing, cooking, and one or two others, which got you out of the cell for more than an hour at a time. After being in there for a week, I was taking three or four classes a day, just to get out that cold cell. One old Asian woman I met used to stay in her cell, perched on the edge of her bed 24 hours a day. She was wrapped in her blanket staring into the middle of nowhere. It was very sad. There was a lot of sadness in that place, and a tremendous amount of regret too. Days passed and weeks passed and then one afternoon, my cell mate was released. I was on my own for a while and began chatting to myself. I was talking about nothing in particular, when suddenly a voice, and a voice I'd never heard before, came right through the walls, full blast. "Are you OK?"

"What the fuck?" I shouted back. I was startled. I thought at first it might be Jesus, but the voice was female.

The lady said to me "I am watching you, and you're talking to yourself" It was at that point I realized that there was really no privacy anywhere in jail. It hadn't occurred to me there were cameras in the cells too and that meant that every time I took a shit, they were watching. There seemed to be something very wrong with that vision! Every morning at 5 AM, was rollcall. We stood at the door and we had to show we had all our clothes on, including the bra's, which we demonstrated by lifting the left top side of our blue smocks, and showing the bra strap. Such a crazy routine, and one I could never understand, but God forbid, if that bra wasn't on, there was Hell to pay! A situation I didn't ever want to find myself in. Life without a cell mate was boring so thankfully, when Doris showed up and was placed in my cell, after ten minutes together, we hit it off.

It turned out she was an E$cort too. We used to sit and tell each other stories about our clients and their fetishes, and we would pass the day rolling around in laughter, discussing men's dicks, their insatiable appetite to fuck different women every day, and our abilities to charm them, fuck them and take all their hard-earned cash. Doris was hilarious and for the next 3 weeks, I was a lot happier than I'd been prior to her arrival. My first cell mate had been ok, but not great, Doris however, was fun.

There was a knock on our door one afternoon and the warden came inside. We stood, a show of respect. He told me I was being moved to 'The Farm" with immediate effect. The Farm is an outdoor facility, or should I say, open plan facility, where, although everyone sleeps in the same room, about 80 women total, all in small beds, the rules allow for a freer flowing day. I wasn't kept locked up all day. I could get my hair cut, watch TV, read in private, and all sorts of other perks. I had no idea why they'd moved me, and The Farm was only a few miles from the jail, but I appreciated everything, especially the freedom The Farm offered. The fact we all slept in the same room, pissed me off and I also missed Doris. I received some visitors during my time there, Kevin being one of them and my sister too. My stay there, well, it was short and sweet, and it seemed that just as soon as I'd arrived at The Farm, and again, without being given a reason, I was switched straight back to the Jail house, and back to another cell with another, completely different cellmate.

My 12 weeks stint was coming to an and. I'd read several books, met and chatted with many different people from all walks of life and honestly, I'd enjoyed my rest, a rest from being fucked every day, having to worry about paying bills, cleaning the house, fixing my car, and speaking to men I would often only meet once. All in all, the 12 weeks proved invigorating in many ways and debilitating in many others. Was I rehabilitated? No. Was I going to go back on the streets and sin again? Yes. Was I regretful of the fact I'd been caught? Of course, but it was time to leave, and when I finally was released, Dec 13th, I had left all those books that I'd read with friends I'd made while inside, and my sandals, the one's that had never left my feet in 12 weeks, went to my cell-mate. As I walked out that door for the final time and into the arms of Kev, who was there to pick me up, drive me home and show me what a good boyfriend he'd been, I was both relieved and very happy. Being in jail for so long surrounded by guards and locked gates, with an inability to do anything that was really 'girlie', had left my jailbird pussy with more 'barbed wire' on her than she'd had in many a year. I was so used to shaving regularly, and of course, in jail, that just didn't happen, and certainly wasn't allowed. When I got home, and after checking that Kev really had been a good boy and kept my place in tact while I'd been inside, I went straight to my shower, taking out a brand-new Venus Lady Shaver, and got to work. I remember being in that shower for more than an hour, with Kevin coming back and forth, knocking on the door, desperate for a fuck, (after all, it had been 3 months without sex for him), rushing me on by telling me that he didn't care if he was going to play on a football field or an ice-skating rink. I preferred he only skated on the flat shiny surface I was creating so diligently in that shower, and by the time I'd finished, an hour of cascading water, water which was warm and delightful as it rushed all over my body, had felt so wonderful and energizing, and I was ready to go. While I was away, I'd had time to think a lot about Kevin, and I'd decided he was a complete loser and that I was going to dump him. I couldn't actually do that straight away, after all, if it hadn't been for him, all my affairs would have been a complete mess, and my apartment, which I had found out he'd been living in, would have gone to someone else by now. With all of that in mind, I got dried and got ready for Kev, who, with his unfortunate shaped penis, began fucking me, a fucking that lasted for three straight hours, and a fucking where he managed to ejaculate at least 4 times into my well-rested pussy. When he was done, I laid back, half exhausted, partly disgusted, on my king-sized bed and thought 'Yep, I'm back, and it's time to make money again, time to perform, and time to get back in the saddle" Which is exactly what I did.

By the end of my second day of freedom, Kevin was history. Poor guy pleaded for me to reconsider, but his time was up and his weird shaped dick could go fuck someone more caring than me. He didn't deserve the 'fuck you' treatment I gave him, because without him, my time in jail would have been more stressful. I will always be grateful for what he did for me, but not for the way he tried to extend our relationship by begging me not to let him go. Kevin, if you're reading this, you're a wimp!

The Circus

The circus that has been, and still is, my life, is often unbearable, often ridiculously stupid and not surprisingly, farcical. Most of the farce is self-inflicted, and I hold my hand up taking full responsibility for my own actions.

    I used to live with two other men, in a home that is rented, but rented in my name only. Over this past year, since I began writing this book, one has gone, ejected, as I already told you, and the other? Well, he's very strange and only comes to his room once a week to pick up some clothing. I have no idea where he stays when he's not in my place. I decided, at some point in time to rent my two spare rooms. Two hard working E$corts I know and love took me up on that offer. The good news is, the two guys who are no longer with me, were driving me nuts and the bad news is, the two E$corts who are now with me, are driving me even more nuts than the two guys who I got rid of. It's like that TV show from the 70's Soap, one never knows who is coming or going, but the rent is paid and the rest is history, until history is re-written. There's always some other nonsense that happens at my place, and while we all look the other way in the hope we are all dreaming, that nonsense consumes us all. The only problem is, we are never dreaming and we are all fully aware and responsible for our own actions, actions that can often get completely out of hand and sometimes make me so crazy that I often wonder how the fuck my life ended up the way it has. I'm a true professional when it comes to worrying about my own life, and I seem to do this continuously without ever coming to any firm conclusion on how I got here in the first place. I normally just ignore my thoughts until, as planned, they resurface and drive me insane once again.

    Lucy moved in, about 4 months ago, something that at first, seemed logical to me, after I threw my crazy former roommate out the front door and then sued him and put a restraining order on his crazy ass. I was so lucky with the timing of that particular situation. Covid hit about one week after we went to court and he left. One week later, and with all the restrictions regarding eviction that our crazy Governor imposed, and that roommate would still be around. Lucy is also crazy, but a different type of crazy. Although at the time we agreed she'd rent the spare room, (I have two spare rooms), I had no idea how wild a woman she was going to become.

Lucy, as I briefly mentioned earlier, is divorced and is a grandmother, and is also dating someone, while working as an E$cort on the side! Lucy has the biggest pair of tits you've ever seen, fake of course!

Lucy and I met at a party. Lucy is a party, a walking party with boobs. I needed a roommate; she needed a place to stay and she also wanted to get involved in the E$corting business. We came to terms, with an agreement to rent the spare room, 4 days a week, and for Lucy to give me a cut, 20%, of any money she made from fucking. All seemed wonderful, with Lucy fucking her way through the whole of Orange County, and me, the rent collector, prospering and becoming more financially independent than I'd ever done before. Certainly, this was more lucrative than having my old roommate, the jerk that he was, staying with me, and contributing nothing other than grief into my life.

This past weekend however, things began to take a turn, and not for the better.

Picture the scene.

A small 3 bed condo, tucked away in a leafy lane, just on the outskirts of Costa Mesa California. The complex itself was built in the 1980's and has a very nice cozy feel to it, with around 100 condo's, 2 and 3 beds, and a communal pool, a pool that I love to frequent, especially when it's scorching hot. I have lived in this condo for two years and have made many friends, especially when I'm lying out at the pool, where no one any the wiser about my chosen career path. I respect the solitude that I get when I'm home and the complex itself is a family-oriented facility with normal people coming to and from work, looking only for peace and tranquility that this place offers.

As you know, I keep 'unusual' hours, and each day I have many strange men going in and out of my condo. In this complex, no one ever bats an eyelid or questions why or what I am doing, and I love the place for those reasons.

And then Lucy came, and chaos reigned.

I returned home one Wednesday evening. Lucy and I and all of our friends had been out to dinner. We'd had fun, but Lucy decided it was time to make money, and had arranged a 'date', a date with her geeky Asian compadre, a guy I cannot stand and one who's head does not fit his body. His head looks like an orbiting satellite on a body that is so out of proportion, it's unfortunate, but also very funny. Anyway, Wong or Wang or whatever he's called, was already pacing up and down my street when we arrived home.

"You know how pathetic that looks" I told Lucy. "The neighbors might call him is as a pedo" I continued, "and who'd blame them?" I was mad, truly mad. Lucy ignored me, jumped out of the car, gave Wong or Wang, a big hug and disappeared inside and then upstairs to start fucking. I went to bed. At 3 45 AM, but something woke me up. I think Lucy or her beau dropped a can of soup in the kitchen, which is situated right below my room, and it exploded. Whatever it was shook me from slumber and I toddled off downstairs to see what was going on. The 2 of them were standing half naked, sharing a slice of toast, begging me to get naked and join them in the jacuzzi. "Fuck off" I said, "it's nearly 4 AM, and what the fuck is he still doing in my house?" I asked as I pointed to my new Asian admirer. Wong always stared at me as if he was undressing me.

"Relax sweetie" Lucy said, just meet us in the jacuzzi.

I relented, in the hope both of them would fuck off and leave me alone. The only issue was, the pool at my complex has strict rules, one of which was the opening hours, 10 Am to 10PM. The gate was on a timer system, only opening between the aforementioned hours and there was absolutely no other way in, unless….

I had discovered on one of my own 'date nights' that it was possible to bypass the timer system using a knife, simply by wedging it in-between the lock and the gate post. Lucy wasn't aware of this trick, but she knew I'd been in the pool area having sex at 3 or 4 AM previously. She also knew I had the power to get her and Wong in there too. I just wanted to get back to sleep, something I am not good at, and normally, when I am up, I am up. I have had serious sleep issues all my life and when I am fast asleep, for someone to wake me up as stupidly as these two had done, well, it just rankled me. Irritated beyond words, I took both of them to the pool area, and, knife in hand, I split the lock in two and opened the gate. Bingo! They both ran in, got completely naked, and I left them there.

As I made my way home, I was listening to the sounds of continual moaning as Wong began fingering Lucy, or Lucy began rubbing one out for Wong. Whatever the case, I was determined to get back to sleep, if possible, even though I was totally pissed off.

6 AM. I hadn't fallen back to sleep yet, and the gruesome-twosome had finished in the jacuzzi and had made their way back into my house. Again, with the subtlety of a flying mallet in a china shop! I was livid, and I made my sentiments known, especially to Wong.

"What the fuck are you still doing here?" I asked him.

"I'm her new manager" he replied, and I could tell from the look on his face that he was being serious.

"What?" I was flabbergasted.

"She needs me" he said

"She needs her head seeing to" I told him, and as I said this, I shouted at the top of my voice, LUUUUUUCCCCCCCYYYYYYY!!!"

No response. If Lucy is one thing, it's a great sleeper. She can put her head down on the pillow or floor and fall asleep instantly, and nothing, I mean NOTHING, will wake her up. I walked upstairs, Wong in tow, and sure enough, Lucy was sparked out, fast asleep. Unreal.

Wong said, "Guess I'll just hang around until she gets up and then I'll start making bookings for her"

"You can fuck off, and fuck off now" I told him.

This was my house, and I wanted rid of this guy, this imbecile, this moron, and I wanted rid of him, and Now!

Wong cowered in the direction of my front door, which I willingly opened on his behalf, slamming it right behind his sorry ass as he left. I was dead beat, and ready for sleep, but my phone was ringing, and I figured I'd answer it in the hope I was about to get another client. As I picked up the call, I looked out my front window and there was Wong, sitting cross legged on my grass. That was the last straw for me, and to the determent of the person calling me on my cell phone, I nudged open my window and in no unlikely terms told Wong to get off the grass or I'd call the cops, something I would never do. He wasn't to know that though, and reluctantly, he got up and left. I gave up on the phone call I'd received and went to bed, passed out in seconds, although I was filled with rage and determined to set this matter right, for the good of my sanity, as well as my home and safety.

Lucy and I woke around 1 PM, and it was time to have a heart to heart with her.

"What the fuck are you doing?" I asked her. "This nonsense with Wong is pathetic. You need to come off Listcrawler.com, (the web site on which Lucy placed all of her Ad's) and get yourself on a different web site, something more up-market, something classy. You're selling yourself short" I said. "It's time to make money. Why fight with these morons for a couple of hundred bucks when you can get $500 on any other site. It's nuts."

Of course, I had my own well-being at heart too. The more Lucy made, the more I made. We had an arrangement, even if it was only verbal, and I was on a percentage.

Lucy looked up and said, "I can't be bothered and I am having fun."

I had no chance. She was stubborn and I was greedy, but she was also smart, and at the end of the day, it was her decision.

"Wong says he's going to be your manager and booker"

"Maybe"

"Well, is he, or isn't he?" I asked, "I don't want him round here anymore, he creeps me out"

"You should let him do your bookings too" Lucy suggested.

I rolled my eyes and made my way into the kitchen to make coffee, and guess who was sitting in the front yard again? Wong! Fucking Wong!

Lucy called Wong back into the house. The two of them vanished for a few minutes, then left. Next thing I knew, I received a call from another E$cort, Allison, asking me how well I knew Lucy.

"Why?" I asked

"Well, she gave me your number as a reference and she and some guy called Wong are headed to my place for a threesome, that Wong is supposedly paying for?"

"OK" I said, pausing for thought and taking in what Allison was telling me.

What I couldn't come to terms with was why would Lucy want to have a threesome with another E$cort, when she can do it with me? She'd run off to find a stranger, someone I'd heard of but didn't know, when she and Wong could have hung around my place and we could have all had fun. Hypocritical, I know, especially after me throwing him out, but hey, money is money!

I didn't give it too much more thought, deciding it was better to get on with my day than worry, and replied to Allison, "you'll be fine", as I ended the call. This was all nuts and too much for me to take in. I went to lay down in my bed and ponder what the fuck was actually going on in my life and if I liked it or not. It was all just pure madness, and my life had become farcical and was spinning completely out of control. Lucy was a loose cannon and Wong? Well, I just disliked that man intensely and couldn't figure out what was going on between him and Lucy, unless I'd missed something and Lucy was using him as a sugar daddy and hadn't told me yet. If she was, I was due a cut. I needed to rest.

I fell asleep and was rudely awoken once again when Lucy and Wong returned, making it very clear to all and sundry that by the amount of noise they were making that they didn't care less if I was around or not. This time I was too tired to get out of bed and so I just lay there, hoping their never-ending racket would eventually dissipate into the silence I so craved. It did, and within time, I managed a few hours' sleep which not only refreshed me, but gave me the impetus to book some clients of my own.

I was back down in the kitchen pouring myself some OJ, when from nowhere, Lucy completely surprised me. She trundled in, looking as though she'd been fucked from here to LA and back, 20 times. Her gruff, loud voice, scaring the shit out of me as she spoke.

"That room we have that's empty," she said, "I was thinking I'd invite Daz to come and stay, offering her the same terms you offered me? What do you think?"

"My old neighbor Daz??" I asked, and as I did, Lucy took out her phone, which was nestled inside her bra, right between her 36 DDD tits, and pulled up some images of this 32-year-old stunner. Daz was beyond gorgeous, with natural large breasts, (turned out I was wrong, and they were indeed fake, but the best fake boobs I'd ever seen), short blonde hair, a simply elegant and striking facial bone structure, on what was a stunningly beautiful face. She also had some wonderfully colorful tattoos on her tummy. She'd lived next door to me for many years, but I'd lost touch with her when she'd moved out of state. We used to be great friends and I often looked after her kids when she and her husband needed a babysitter. She and Lucy had remained friends though and Lucy had spoken to Daz while she was going through her recent divorce, suggesting she move back to CA to become an E$cort.

"Wow!" I said, with some enthusiasm. "She still looks great, if not better than when she lived here!"

"You see what I mean? We can make great money with her in this house!" exclaimed Lucy.

She was right, and without too much thought, I agreed to let her stay.

"Where is she now?" I asked

"Nashville"

"And she's interested in E$corting?"

"Yes"

"OK, one condition"

"What's the condition?" Lucy asked.

"Get rid of Wong"

She agreed and we made plans to kick Wong to the curb as soon as he woke up and to make the spare room livable for Daz, even though it would be three weeks before she actually showed up. The circus was well and truly in town, and it was about to expand, with me as it's reluctant ring leader.

Wong left the building, just like Elvis, although no one ever cared if Wong might stay alive after he'd gone. Life got back to some normality for a week or two until Daz arrived and then the chaos that was, became the chaos that is.

Air Traffic Controller

When I decided to become an E$cort, I never believed at the age of 57, I would still be as active in that business as I am today. I thought I'd do it for a couple of years, make some hard cash, then get out, get married or just get another job. After 23 plus years in the business, I'm amazed that things are about the same as they were when I began. Guys with small dicks, big dicks, unclean dicks, horny as heck, married, single, perverted, looking to fuck a blonde with great tits and a really tight pussy. All of these factors still remain, the only thing that changes? The date! I still see one or two guys a day, I still like to get fucked, but I'm now at the point in my life where a change is either going to be forced upon me, or is something I will do regardless, because at 57, I am no spring chicken, and I think that it's time to figure out what I will do for the next 25 years, well into my 80's, and we all know, it's definitely NOT this!

My home is now filled with E$corts, Lucy, Daz and on occasion, one or two others. I make money from all of them, but I am not a Madame. I love each and every one of them, but I am not in love with their intrusion on my property and on my personal time. I do enjoy seeing them occasionally, but over the past months, I have become like an air traffic controller, directing them like planes in the sky, especially Daz, into the correct spaces with the correct guys, all of whom are horny and most of whom are rich with money to burn and erections to soften. My life is changing now, as I mentioned, perhaps not for the better, but it is changing, and only time will dictate if these changes will be good or bad. I have been offered contract work selling different items for a wide variety of corporations. I have also been trying to complete this book, which, I have found extremely entertaining and fulfilling, recalling all, or at least, some of the best parts of my crazy life. I am now trying to coax some of my best friends from the E$corting business to tell their stories, and by the time we are all done, this book should contain a wide array of in-depth tales from a business that, as we all know, is the oldest profession on earth. My days are interesting at the moment. When Daz arrived, I signed her up to that site that we all advertise on, Listcrawler.com, and within moments, she had a line of 300 guys banging at her door, not literally of course, wanting to fuck her. She charges $400 per pop, with one-time orgasms only, no MSOG, Multiple Shots on Goal, allowed. My home has been jam-packed with suitors, all with cash in hand, and erections. If you added up the number of guys who've been here over these past few weeks, they would run from my home to the beach and back, a distance of 5 miles! Each guy shows up at his allotted time, displaying nervous intentions, and a willingness not only to cough up his cash for an easy lay, but most have inclinations to fall in love and take Daz away with them to live happily ever after. Some refuse to leave, they love her so much, and some cannot get it up, because they fear the inevitable anxiety of failing to perform when required, and it takes patience and coaxing to help them finally ejaculate. In general, though, my organization skills, arranging times for of all these men has proven to be a valuable asset to Daz, who is only 32 and still learning the ropes. By the time she is my age, I estimate that Daz, should she stay in this business as long as I have, would have been poked by more than 62,000 cocks, and that my friends, is a conservative estimate. I wish her nothing but success and hope that she finds a way to make and to save money more efficiently than I did, although I strongly doubt it.

My investments over the years have been futile. My life filled with bad advice and with people, mainly men, who just wanted to take advantage of me. I am not looking for sympathy, mostly it was my fault, and I take responsibility for where I was at 25 and where I am not, at 57. I made decisions that were poor and some that were good. I invested in. things I should never have gone near and divested of assets that I should have retained, but in general, I am a very happy and content human being. I don't want for anything and I am not really an extravagant lady. There are other ladies in this business, especially the 20 something stunners, who are making fortunes from guys who have more money than sense. Ladies who have sugar daddies splurging out on dreams that will never be fulfilled. These girls are clever, very clever, and spend money like it's going out of fashion, because they can! I've met ladies who earn upwards of

$1000 per hour, and some who make even more. There's been times when my own interpretation of these girls' intentions has been blinkered by an internal jealousy that I am not their age with their looks, but then, I sit and I think about things for a few minutes and really, at the end of the day, I am happy and I am content. Yes, I would love to have more in the bank, and yes, I would prefer it if my tits were still 25 years of age and my arms and legs were wrinkle free, but that ship has sailed, and I am who I have become. I have matured into a lady with experience and with patience and with a desire to move onwards to something that is bigger and better than what I have done in the past. I have made many friends in the past 30 years, some good and some better, but mostly, I have had a life to remember, a life with few regrets and a life that can rarely be rivaled in terms of excitement, and that is just the beginning folks. The next part of my life will be even better. To all the men who have fucked me, I wish you well, and nothing but happiness in your lives, because honestly, most of you have no idea what you are doing, and some of you need to learn from the poor situations you have placed yourselves in. I have been a mother, a girlfriend, a good fuck, a beacon of hope and a councilor to all of them, though rarely all at the same time. They have been an income to me, an income I have been very grateful for. My name is Blondie, and to those of you who know me, after reading my stories, I hope you will remember me as fondly as I remember most of you.

Daz
Nashville, Summer 2020

I'd had my suspicions, even though I'd pushed them to one side and decided to compartmentalize them into a part of my brain that told me, 'NO WAY, HE'D NEVER DO THAT', but I'd been wrong. There I was, looking for his 'stash', yes, he and I partook of the marvelous weed now and again. I was in the front seat of his car, rummaging around in the place he'd told me to look when he'd arrived home in one of his usual stinking moods. I was searching back and forth, and unable to locate that baggie, the baggie that would end what had become a miserable day. I just couldn't find it. The sun, unbearably hot, one of the reasons I hated Nashville, along with its incessant summer humidity, at 98% and climbing, turning any semblance and possibility of happiness, into sweat that ran like continual tears down my tattooed stomach and into my soiled panties. They'd been soiled at 8 am after I'd walked my 5-year-old son to daycare, this oppressive weather, kicking the shit out of any attempt I had of staying clean and cool, and now, some 8 hours later, soiled was the only description that I could think of to sum up my own self being and the state my clothes seemed to always end up in on hot Nashville summer's days. Yes, Nashville, two years of torment, about to be concluded by one very small bag of marijuana, a conclusion that I hadn't expected, but to be very honest, desperately desired. This day, a day that would change my life, although I was about three minutes from finding that out, would end up not only taking me back to California, a State where I grew up and a State that I loved, but would also take me down a different career path, a career I had never imagined following, but a career which was going to make me so much money, I would, at long last, be able to support myself and my 3 kids without the assistance of my, soon-to-be, shitty ex-husband.

You see, I had been married since I was 19, remaining loyal and faithful to a man who'd given me 2 beautiful kids, (I'd had one more kid with another guy, long before I'd met my husband), never being anything other than the 'doting' wife. Cooking, cleaning and bringing up the children were my forte, while he concentrated on his own career. I was happy, more or less, to put up with his faults, as he'd been putting up with mine, until, when that little baggie in the front seat of his car had seemingly gone missing, and my instincts and desperation to get a 'hit' had driven me to search the rest of the car, feeling that perhaps he'd made a mistake when he'd said 'front seat', thus leading me to open the trunk, lift up the spare wheel and hey BINGO! CONDOMS!!!!

That moment, one solitary moment, a moment in time that I will never forget. My incredible desire to scream out loud. That feeling of terror, of letdown, of disgust, of wanting to kill someone, yes, that one moment, led me to do what I am doing today. Quite how it got to that, is a little more convoluted, but as I ran back inside our home in Nashville that evening with every intent of confronting and then killing my husband, never in a million years did I ever believe that within a few short months I would become an E$cort, not just any E$cort, but an E$cort in Orange County California, and an E$cort that dozens of men would be forming a line to fuck, some multiple times a day, an E$cort who would make a fortune from doing something as simple as having sex with men who didn't know me, didn't care who I was or where I'd come from, and men who were infatuated with my tits and my pussy, two bodily items I'd not given much thought too since my husband had given up on fucking me the way he'd used to when we'd met in 2004. Yes, life changed in an instant, and this, well, this is the story that will show you how things can go from good, to bad, to worse, to incredible, without too much thought, too much effort and the help of one amazing friend.

Before we get into that, let me tell you a little about my past, a past which is only 32 years in the making, but a past that has been exciting, boring and repetitive in many ways, and a past nonetheless. It's my past, and a past that I am proud of, although if my parents and my kids knew what my past had led me to today, I don't think they'd appreciate what I am doing now and how complicated life was just to get me to this point.

My life is probably no different to anyone else's life on this planet, but now I have the opportunity to document it in detail, and so I hope you can sit back, relax and enjoy my tale.

Blondie invited me to participate in her book, The Secret E$cort, and for that gesture alone, I am eternally grateful. My story runs parallel to hers, intermingling through our clientele and our ability to be the best of friends. We've known one another for many years, and I believe our friendship, which is shared between the covers of this book, in unbreakable and everlasting. Although we never grew up together, our career choice and the way our lives have crisscrossed, have given both of us an appreciation off all that's good and bad in life. My particular life as an E$cort is relatively new in comparison to hers, but as you read through the next chapters, you'll see that we are peculiarly similar both in outlook and desire.

Early Days

I was brought up in a normal home with normal parents and normal siblings. I loved my life in California and appreciated every minute I had in the never-ending sunshine filled days that Orange County provided. It was just an abundance of great weather, good food, fun times and so much to do. Outdoors was my passion, but not an obsession. By the time I got to high school, I was still a virgin, but that would soon change, and although I never slept with that many guys, as was the norm with so many of my other girlfriends, when I was 19, I was already in love and getting married and I was also pregnant. You see, my life changed in an instant the day I found out my son was inside my belly. I was no longer that innocent young lady with big tits that every warm-blooded male around me wanted to fuck, I became a wife, a mother and had a great job with the local school district. The only thing missing in my life at that time seemed to be the travel bug, which everyone else around me enjoyed. I was destined to be a stay-at-home mom with a part time job, and really not interested in seeing all the other parts of the planet that my friends were venturing out to explore. It didn't really matter though because right after my first child, and first divorce, came my second marriage, and second child and then my third child and then came my second divorce, which, ended up in a court room brawl somewhere in Nashville Tennessee. The long and the short of it is, I am now in my early 30's and a single mother of 3 wonderful kids, and the past, at least in my own head, does not matter. It's only the future that I can count on, and that future lay in the hands of the most wonderful lady I'd ever met, Blondie, yes THE Blondie, one of the most well-known E$corts Orange County has even seen. Blondie used to live next door to me and my second husband, when we lived in OC, and has been my friend for over 14 years. My life at the time I met Blondie was chaotic, with one child running around our apartment complex creating havoc most of the time, another child in my tummy, this time from my second husband, and a realization that Blondie, who had no husband and no kids, seemed to lead this wonderful existence that I once craved. She and I were kind of inseparable, and I was the only person outside of her clients, who actually knew what she did for a living. We'd met by accident, found out we were neighbors and then we became 'party girls' on the occasion when I was able to get out and really let my hair down. Blondie took me everywhere, when she wasn't working, and we just grew closer and closer as friends, until that fateful day when my husband came into our home and told me I was moving to Nashville. I had three kids at that time, and didn't want to go, but you know how partnerships work and, in the end, I had no choice. Such a shame, but there was always an inevitability that it would end up in tears. When it did, my only outlet was to return to Orange County and a reunion with my bestie, Blondie, brokered by my other friend Lucy.

I remember when I called her and told her I was returning to the OC, she just jumped for joy. Having heard the news already from Lucy and relishing the possibility that we'd be reunited again. Finally she asked me what I was going to do to support my three kids, knowing very well that my second husband didn't really give a fuck. Yes, he'd agreed to child support, but there wasn't any way on this sweet earth I would take alimony from him because I never ever wanted to be in a situation where he could hold that as a dangling carrot over my head when issues happened with custody or other problems relating to the kids sometime in the future. I'm no fool, valuing greatly my independence, and I also realized the nature of the beast. It would be far simpler, in my humble opinion, to take larger child support payments and make my own way in life, rather than relying on him to keep me in the style I was accustomed to, which, by the way, wasn't palatial by any manner of means.

Blondie, who I'd always looked up to, had told me that being an E$cort was so much fun, and extremely lucrative. She'd been adamant that with my killer curves, I could make a fortune if I ever decided to try it. This was back in the day we'd first met and become close buddies, and long before my 3rd child popped out of my belly. I loved sex, I still do, and the thought of being fucked by different cocks every night used to keep me awake and also made me extremely horny. I'd lay next to husband number 2 dreaming of the wonderful life I believed that Blondie led, all the sex she was having, the different ways she'd experiment in bed with her clients, and I was jealous. Always interested to hear her stories, which made me wetter than heck and hornier than ever, I'd mulled it over several times in my head, that one day I would love to try doing what she did, just to see what it was like. Adventurous in bed, I felt that I would or could take to doing this E$corting thing, like a duck takes to water. But it never happened and my dreams remained only dreams until my nightmare with hubby 2 ended and then, after a few calls between Blondie and I and my impending return to the OC, opened that magical door, a door that has become my lucrative future.

"Blondie, I am getting divorced and returning home. I don't have a job and I don't have a place to stay. Can you help? Lucy says you can" I said to her, as I sat sweating my pants off in the middle of that oppressive Nashville summer. It had been so hot, and I'd been cheated on, which made everything seem just that much worse. Blondie was patient with me, taking her time to ask me what exactly had been going on and then she replied,

"I know it's what you've always wanted to do, so yes, let's set it all up and make you some money girl!"

Those words rang true in my ears. Blondie knew me, knew what I was interested in doing, that I was reliable and knew that men would go crazy for me in the OC. With all that said, it was certainly going to take some courage to actually become an E$cort. I'd slept with maybe 10 guys in my entire life, none of whom had ever paid me and none of who were one-night stands. The whole premise of fuck them and forget them, after taking cash of letting them do whatever they wanted to me, was rather curious and a little scary. And what would I tell my parents and my kids?

Three weeks, and a lot of internal anguish, later.

I arrived outside Blondie's apartment in Cost Mesa around 3 PM. My kids were with my parents, and my sanity had long ago been left in Nashville. Blondie ran outside and we embraced, just like long lost sisters. I had a great feeling when we hugged and the old times seemed to be back again.

"Girl" she said, "you look amazing! And look at those tits!" Blondie hadn't seen me since my boob job, which I'd had done a couple of months back. The surgery had taken me from a 34 C to a 36DD. I looked good, Blondie thought I looked good and boy did I feel good. Being back in the town that I'd grown up in and lived all but 2 years of my life in, this was truly home.

We marched inside her apartment, and before I had a chance to even sit down, Blondie was in my face telling me how much I was going to make, what room in her house I could have, where the condom supply was and so much more. It was totally overwhelming, but also exciting, and even though I was dreading this change of direction, I was being courted by Blondie in a manner that I just couldn't say NO to anything she was offering. The confusion inside my mind was rife, but I was dreading going back to a 9 to 5 job, so after some internal back and forth, the devil inside me agreed to move forward.

"We need to get pictures of you, we need to come up with a name, we need to make sure that you are out there girl" Blondie said, in her usual excitable manner. Eventually, we both sat down and smoked a joint together and calmed the fuck down as we got high and very silly.

After a couple of hours, we were sitting together, still slightly high, and much more relaxed. Blondie's phone suddenly sprang into action with a call requesting her services, and she began arranging a date for that evening. My thoughts turned to my own ability of following through when it actually got to the stage where I'd have to fuck a stranger. Blondie was great, so professional and I knew I could count on her for anything, but to actually perform? Well, as she was discussing money with her prospective date, I was stretched out on her sofa, contemplating sex and even more sex, all with unknown men. Kind of exciting in ways, kind of weird in other ways. I'd already made my mind up to try it, and at least if I didn't like it I could go out and do something else, right? So confusing, so utterly confusing. I needed to make a living, and my body could guarantee that the living I made would be lucrative, or so Blondie had told me. I wasn't ever going to be able to feed three kids and put any of them through college by working at the school district, so.....

My first day at Blondie's place was monumental. Blondie showed me the ropes, giving me explicit instruction on me how to behave when receiving phone calls from clients and then what was expected of me for an in-person meeting/date. She also showed me the screening process for unknown callers who wanted to make a date with me. How to act when they arrived and how to kick them out when they were finished. It was fairly simple stuff, pure common sense actually, and once I got the lie of the land, I was all set to begin. But first, pictures.

Blondie took out her phone and I got naked, semi-naked and partially naked. Yes, there is a difference. She clicked and clicked, focusing mostly on my tits, my wonderful nipples and trying hard to avoid the stretch marks from birthing three kids, which were clearly visible on my lower tummy. We had so much fun, downing several bottles of wine in the process. Then we wrote my Ad, and Ad that would be placed into one or more of the E$cort sites most OC men or men living in LA or San Diego would peruse. Blondie suggested I should be a $400 per hour fuck. I had no idea what I should be, I just wanted to make money and make it fast. My kids and I were currently living with my parents, and I needed money to get out of their home and into a rental as soon as possible, so $400 per hour sounded good to me, in fact it sounded amazing!

We got the Ad up and running, adding some pictures, listing a new phone number I'd purchased especially for the purpose of being anonymous to anyone who didn't know me. We downed another bottle of wine, and we waited.

The wait time was almost nonexistent. I kid you not, after about an hour of the Ad going live, the phone began to ring, and boy did it ring, it rang off the hook!

Blondie would be my guide, and in fact, she still is. We made an arrangement, a financial one, between the two of us, and came to terms. I needed her assistance, and she needed the cash. It was her home, it was my body, but it was also her experience that would guide me through this quagmire that was going to be the E$corting life. She was amazing, telling me what to say on the responses to messages that I sent by text, letting me know never to negotiate, looking into the history of each potential client to ensure a safe experience each time and finally, making sure that these clients knew what to expect from the moment they entered her home until the second the ejaculated and left. I couldn't have done any of this without her and was so happy she was around.

My first client arrived and it was only 1 PM on my first day. Things were moving so quickly. Blondie told me that this guy, we can call him Robert, was a level 4 on the web site where we were advertising. The site, Listcrawler.com, was the site that Blondie recommended, to get the ball rolling. On Listcrawler.com, the more E$corts a guy fucked, the higher the level he became, and the higher the level, the more secure and reliable he was supposed to be. A level 4, is the second highest level, and one that is supposedly trustworthy. No law enforcement. Each E$cort gives the guy a rating after he pays her, that way, each new E$cort he approached after that would know by his rating that he's safe to see and to be around for a sexual encounter.

Screening is easy when the man's level rating is higher, although these guys don't always live up to their billing. Sometimes ratings can be deceitful, just like in the movies! Robert however, well, he proved not only trustworthy, but reliable and on time too. One thing I'd decided before I'd even begun to perform this job was, no DATY (dining at the Y), and no DFK, (Deep French Kissing). There was absolutely no way I could bring myself to perform either of these acts, not for any money. This would be known on my profile as my NO list. I was adamant I'd never veer from that list. When Robert showed up, came into the house and up to my room, I reiterated my NO list to his face. He understood, but that didn't stop him trying. As soon as he saw my tits, he was erect and ready to go. Within a few minutes, where the struggle became real and I was fending off his advances to kiss me, the condom was on and he was inside me having the best of times. I lay back and let it happen. He came in the condom he was wearing, pulled out, tried to kiss me again, only for me to rebuff him one more time, but this time with a little more vigor, and then, when he understood that it was all over, he left and his $400 went into the drawer. Easy!

And then, just after Robert left, Chung arrived. A small, well-groomed Asian man, smiling and happy, and ready for his first experience, or so he said. Chung was not shy in coming forward. By the time we were finished, and he'd tried to kiss me for the umpteenth time, offering me wads of cash to do so. He was madly in love with me and pleading with me to let him stay and to let him take me out. I had another appointment right after him, and I told him that patience was a virtue and to come back another time when we could spend an extra hour chatting, as long as he paid for that time. Eventually, with a sulking face, he left the house, to the relief of both myself and Blondie, who by this time, was kind of ushering him out the front door.

20 minutes later, in walked my 3rd client in as many hours. This time, a Hispanic gentleman Jesus, although not he from resurrection fame.

I seemed to be fucking my way around the globe and it was only day 1. Ethnicity meant nothing to me, and as long as they paid when they entered, and then left happy after they came, I was happy and this was about all I could hope for. Jesus loved my tits, fake as they were, and he couldn't stop playing with them. He tossed me an extra $100 on the way out, impressing upon me that he'd had a blast playing with 'the girls'. We laughed and I was extremely grateful for his generosity. He promised to return.

My day was over. It was 4 PM, I'd fucked three guys, all reasonably nice, and had made over $1200 in cash, of which I had to pay Blondie for rent and fees, leaving me with just over $800. This was a great start, and a leg up to a better life, I hoped! A better life? I needed someplace to stay. My kids and I living at my parents' home, could only be a short-term arrangement, otherwise we may have ended up all killing one another. Their place was nice, but with the kids all living in the same room, and me on their couch, I needed an apartment of my own, and I needed to find it fast. My only problem was, I had shitty credit and no job, at least no job that handed out registered pay slips and proof of employment. This was a real issue for me, and an issue I wasn't sure how to resolve. It was easy to find places to live, but everyone wanted to do a credit check and see employment history. I just didn't have either. The depressing part of all of this was, I had the cash, lots of it, and was prepared to pay several months in advance if I found the right place to live, but no one wanted cash, and red-tape ruled the roost in this business of renting a home. Blondie had been calling around asking all of her contacts if they could help. But there was nothing anyone could do, which made my situation even more depressing.

Although Blondie had three bedrooms in her home, only 2 were being used. Her other room was rented out by a guy who was never around, and the room that I used was shared between myself and another E$cort, Lucy, who was as wild as any woman or man I had ever met. Lucy worked when I left, so she arrived around 4 PM and stayed all the way through to the following morning, when I'd show up again. She was amazing, making so much money, she could afford anything, and I mean ANYTHING, she wanted. We all got on, me Blondie and Lucy, just wonderfully well, and had an appreciation and respect for each other's idiosyncrasies and abilities to wind one another up the wrong way, and do it often!

Sitting around Blondie's kitchen table on day 3 of my newly formed E$cort career, the subject of my finding a place to live came up, this time with Lucy involved in the conversation. I was explaining to her what the issues were when suddenly she blurted,

"I have a client who can fix that for you"

"What do you mean?" I asked, my spirits suddenly raised.

"You need pay slips, and you need an employment address, correct?" Lucy said.

"Yep"

"Well, I know a guy, a guy I fuck all the time, who can fake it all for you"

"You do?" I was so surprised. How the heck would anyone be able to do that? After a few minutes of back-and-forth chit-chat, Lucy called her client, explained the situation and set up a meeting between us.

"You'll need to fuck him" she told me. She didn't ask, it was just a given.

"If he sorts out my problems, he can have me for free" I quipped.

'Free, honey, is something you'll never be" Lucy said, as I came back down to earth with a bump.

My first client of the day arrived, and with that, I left the kitchen, went upstairs and began fucking once again, hopeful that Lucy would be able to get her client to produce documentation that would allow me to go find a new home to rent. I fucked vigorously that day, I remember it well, my spirits raised, just like my legs, only my spirits never got tired!

The plan had been hatched. Lucy's client provided fake pay slips at an address where I was supposedly working, and armed with all the paperwork to prove it, yes, Lucy's man had come through big time, although, as yet, I hadn't fucked him to thank him, I went house hunting in Huntington Beach, hopeful that I'd qualify to rent an apartment and that I'd be able to move out of my parents' home..

It didn't take long to find a place I loved, and after sitting down with the building manager in their leasing office, I pulled out my fake pay slips to prove my income stream. Watching nervously as they went through each paper thoroughly, I walked out with the promise of a deal, pending work verification, whatever that meant. What I didn't realize at the time was they actually showed up at the address on the paperwork I'd given them, an address of a company I have never been to or even talked with, but, according to the leasing office, and this is baffling to me as it is to everyone else who was involved, they showed up, got the verification they needed and then offered me the apartment! WTF?? To this day, I have no idea how that happened, and honestly, I don't even care. All I know is that I was verified and within a week, I moved in with my kids and to date, we are still there. I ended up fucking, Tom, Lucy's friend, the guy who made it all happen, and I think he was as pleased as I was with the outcome of our meeting.

Experiences

Four of us sat on the king-sized bed, me, Blondie, our client and Julie, a friend of Blondie's who drove limousines for a living. The client, Jawbone, yes, his chin was chiseled and he was as fit as they come, had asked for a threesome. Julie had been in the house when his text had come through asking me to fuck him and with some gentle persuasion, we'd asked her if she'd like to take part is some sexual fun, to which, without hesitation, she'd readily agreed. Julie had a steady boyfriend, was not and never had been an E$cort, but her curiosity had peaked as she sat at the kitchen table listening to Blondie and I talk of our E$cort experiences. These conversations made Julie exceptionally horny, and by the time this guy had texted back and forth with Blondie confirming times for arrival, Julie's pussy juice was overflowing and she was all too keen to join in the fun. Julie is a 40 something, pretty redhead, curvaceous and with a great sense of humor. She was really up for this experience and so we renegotiated our rate with the client, telling him it would be $700, of which Julie would get $200 and Blondie and I would split the rest. He'd accepted, driven over to Blondie's home and was now lying naked, surrounded by the three of us, not knowing whether to finger us or play with our tits, or do both at the same time. Julie's demeanor was turning from serious to very silly, refusing to suck our client's cock, an act Blondie and I were both performing simultaneously. Not wanting to let him finger her at all, she'd taken cold feet and had retreated into the background. Then as suddenly as she'd vanished, she was back, taking him by his ankles and lifting his whole body into the air. Julie isn't a big girl, but after watching her perform this feat, my perception of her strength completely changed in an instant. This guy was hanging in her hands, legs and backside in midair, upper back and neck and head all on the bed, and he was not amused. He'd paid the fee in advance, but the way things were unraveling, I honestly thought he'd ask for a refund, which is something we just never do. Suddenly, and without warning, Julie dropped him back onto the bed., and at that point in time, he looked at me and while pointing to Blondie and Julie, asking, quite politely, 'can you just get rid of those two and stay on your own?'

After Julie and Blondie left, I fucked the guy in multiple positions and made him very happy indeed very happy. He got washed and dressed and then left and that's when the fight began.

Julie, "I want half of the fee"

Me "For doing what?"

Blondie "You didn't do anything Julie"

Me "You wouldn't even suck his dick, and you nearly killed him when you lifted him off the bed by his ankles!"

Julie "He loved me doing that to him"

Blondie "You get $200, take it or leave it?"

Argument over, Julie left, happy.

I vowed that never again would I share any man with anyone other than Blondie. At least she sucked dick, and helped get the guy get off.

My next client that day was from Mexico, a really good-looking man, fit and tanned, but very hairy.

He arrived, and we began.

He paid, we stripped. He sucked on my tits, I threw him down and began to suck his cock, but nothing happened. I continued to try other ticks of the trade, but still nothing happened, and he remained soft. I stopped trying.

"What's wrong sweetie?" I asked him

"Long story" he replied and then proceeded to tell me he'd had prostate cancer and surgery and he didn't know if he could get erect anymore. I told him to hang on in there, and I left the room to get Blondie. I explained what the issue was and then came back into the room.

"Would you mind if my partner joined us?" I asked

He didn't. Blondie came in, and between us, we worked this guy, all over, for 45 minutes, all of us sweating profusely because it was 100 degrees outside and the AC in Blondie's home was ineffective. Suddenly and without warning, the guy blurted out, "I have an idea! You…." And he pointed to Blondie, "will suck me off and then you will kiss her…" and he pointed to me, "and then you will swap my cum from your mouth to hers and then back to hers and then I want you to swallow it." Well, he got hard as quickly as he'd been soft. This turn on seemed to be a genius move for him, until the thrill had worn off once again, and his soft dick remained soft. At the end of the 45 minutes, a very unproductive 45 minutes, the guy got out of bed and as he did so, Blondie and I looked down at the sheets. He'd been sweating so much; he'd left a sweaty imprint of his body on our sheets! It was disgusting, but even though we'd put in all that effort, he couldn't cum. It was so sad, but he didn't seem to care, leaving the house apologizing to us, when we felt we should be apologizing to him. He said he'd be back another day to try again, but we never saw him again.

Sometimes it's just too much for men who show up full of bravado, thinking, "I am going to fuck the shit out of this bitch", only to lie there unable to get an erection, but with this guy it was different. He'd arrived filled with expectation, although not bragging about it, and he left knowing that he tried but that whatever had taken away his manhood, would not return it and that for all good purpose, he was going to have to live with this for the rest of his days. So sad, because as I mentioned, he was good-looking and fairly young.

And then, I had the worst night ever, in fact, not even a night, an afternoon, and then a night.

My favorite Asian, Chung, was adamant that he'd take me out to dinner. He told me, he'd gladly pay me for the time we just sat together chatting and then perhaps afterwards, once I'd filled my belly on food and wine, we could retire to Blondie's and to my room, my rented room, and fuck. Chung loved to fuck and it had gotten to the stage where he wanted to pay for it at least once every two days, which for me, at $400 per pop, was great. Shit, as far as I was concerned, he could fuck me 5 hours a day at $400 per hour, and sometimes he threatened to do just that! Chung had a small dick, and fucking him was a breeze. With lube as my best friend, I never really felt anything when Chung was inside me. The only thing I needed to put up with was his terrible breath and his thick pubic hair, so typical for any Asian. They just don't believe in grooming. It's like barbed wire, thick and uncomfortable to the touch. I hate it, especially when I have to go down on him or them. I know I am generalizing here, so Asian men, please don't be offended. We were sitting in this Sushi restaurant, about 15 minutes' drive from the apartment, and having a great time. I was knocking back as many sakes as he was, only I could take it and he couldn't. His eyes were becoming more and more bloodshot, and his speech was starting to slur, as was mine, but not as much as his, and his ability to do anything but devour his alcohol and sushi, well, let's just say I realized very quickly that no erection would be forthcoming. And with that in mind, after 3 hours of gorging ourselves, Chung paid ME $1000, paid for the actual lunch, which had turned into an early dinner, and then decided to get an Uber back to his home in Irvine. He'd left me with my cash in a half drunken stupor in a parking lot in Newport Beach, willing myself on to get behind the wheel of a car I should not have been anywhere close too.

Chung had driven off and I was staggering, not quite on my last legs, but fairly 'happy', towards my car when I noticed it looked like it was kind of lopsided and sitting at a very strange angle. My initial reaction was to blame the intake of sake on my poor vision, but as I got closer, I realized with some dismay I might add, that the left front tire of my car was completely flat. I sauntered up, taking a second drunken look, prodding it with both my right foot and left hand, willing it to inflate and to carry me home safely. It's amazing how your emotions can be influenced after a few sakes. Nothing happened, nothing was going to happen, and that tire remained deflated, and my car, remained inoperable.

I had a AAA membership, so I called them, and they told me they would be there in about an hour. There was no way I could change or was going to change the tire myself, and as I paid $65 a year for the AAA membership, it was their problem to sort it out. At least that's what I was telling myself. I called Blondie for emotional support.

"Ummm I'm truly fucked. My tire is flat and AAA won't be here for another hour, so if I have any clients this evening, please cancel them." Blondie was perplexed, but understood and asked if she could come over to where I was stranded, and pick me up. I didn't see any point in inconveniencing her, so I refused the offer of help, with my appreciation for the fact that she'd cared enough to offer.

There I was, surrounded by cars that worked, and sitting uncomfortably in the front seat of mine, praying that AAA would show up sooner rather than later.

As I puffed on my menthol Vape, the AAA truck pulled in. He saw me and I saw him and after a few hand signals back and forth, all polite and with the intention of guiding him towards me, he parked up and got out the truck. The conversation began.

AAA, "Good evening ma'am, flat tire?"

Me "Yes" as I pointed to the front of the car.

AAA, "Can I see your membership card please?

Me, "Yes, here it is" and I passed it over to his outstretched hand.

AAA, "Have you been drinking?"

Me," What?"

AAA, "It's a simple question"

Me, "And why is that any concern of yours?"

He stared me down, big time. I became instantly aware that this was going to be a problem, and I panicked. AAA man went back to his truck and I could see him picking up his cell phone. I picked up mine and I dialed Blondie.

"This fucker from AAA is calling the cops because he says I am drunk" Blondie told me not to move and that she was on her way over.

AAA, "Ma'am I believe you are drunk and with that in mind I have called the cops. I cannot assist you until they arrive"

Me, "What is my physical state got to do with you and why on earth would you do that?"

AAA guy walked back to his truck again.

Within, what seemed like seconds, a black and white OC cop car was pulling into the parking lot. Two cops got out the vehicle.

Cop 1 "Ma'am is this your vehicle?"

Cop 2 was making his way over to the AAA truck.

Me, "Yes, it is, but as you can see, I cannot drive it"

Cop 1 "License and registration please"

Me, "Yes sir" I said and I took out both.

Cop 1, "Please wait there" and he walked back to his car, where Cop 2 was now standing.

AAA guy was still by his truck and had a huge grin on his face. Fuckwad! Cop 1 came back.

Cop 1, "Have you been drinking?"

Me, "A little, but I have not been driving. I came out of that restaurant" and I pointed to the Sushi place, "and got to my car and the front tire was flat, so I called AAA. AAA showed up and he called you, although I don't know why, because I barely said two words to that man and what business is it of his to decide if I am drunk or not, especially if I am not driving?" I was becoming more and more agitated and Cop 1 could tell this.

Cop 1 "I am going to have to ask you to take a sobriety test"

Me," For what reason?"

"Intoxication with intent to drive" he said, as he asked me to put down my Vape and place all my belongings on my car hood.

He then began the protocol that's offered to all intoxicated drivers, and that protocol, as seen many times on the TV show COPS, Innocent until proven Guilty, began with him shining his flashlight directly into my eyes. As he did this, I could see Blondie pull up into the parking lot and get out of her car and make her way towards Cop 2, who basically tossed her to one side and told her to stay away from the scene until Cop 1 had finished.

Cop 1 continued by asking me to do several different movements, one of which is walking in a straight line placing one foot directly in front of the other. After I completed these tasks, he said," I have reason to believe you are intoxicated and above the legal limit for alcohol consumption to drive. Are you willing to take a breathalyzer test?" Me, "Yes, but why would you ask me to, when, clearly I am not and have not been driving?"

Cop 2 was now in the back of their cop car searching for the test I was about to take, and Cop 1 remained silent.

The test arrived and Cop 1 took out the sterilized mouth piece that covers the front of the breathalyzer gadget, then came over to me and said, "Blow please"

I did, and we all waited.

The test didn't work, so they did it again, and yet again, it didn't work. Cop 1 was now looking to Cop 2 for direction, and Cop 2 was shrugging his shoulders in complete disbelief that 2 tests had failed to work. By now, a small crowd had gathered right by Blondie, and everyone, including AAA man, was watching this scene unfold, a scene which could have been written as a Seinfeld episode. The whole crowd looked on with great anticipation, ready and waiting for my imminent arrest.

Cop 1, "We will try this one last time, and if it doesn't work, I will ask you to come to the Police station and take a blood test"

They tried again, and yes, it failed again!

They cuffed me, took me to their car, and as my head was being assisted as the last body part to enter their vehicle, I looked up and saw the AAA guy flip me the bird. What an idiot!

At the Police station, I was processed and booked, and put into a holding cell. I had consented to a blood test already and within moments the man with the needle arrived, and withdrew one vile of blood. They kept me in that cell until 2 AM, which was about 5 hours after I'd arrived, and then, poof! I was out. Blondie picked me up and we drove home. My kids had been with my parents that day, so I was fortunate that I didn't have to explain myself to them or to anyone else, but now I was determined to get my name cleared. How could they arrest me and book me for a DUI when I wasn't even driving? And that idiot from AAA, well, I swore if I ever saw him again….

Blondie was amazing, and suggested we call one of her clients, an attorney called Paco. Paco listened to what happened as we spoke on the phone. He counselled that he had an immediate solution where he'd present to the court some evidence that could lead to immediate dismissal of all charges against me. It was all legal mumbo-jumbo to me, and it went in one ear and out the other. "Just do whatever it takes" I told Paco.

But first? Negotiation.

Paco, "You'll need to pay me $300 an hour"

Me, "Well I charge $400 and I am willing to pay in kind"

Paco, "Done deal"

Paco had zero hesitation in accepting the barter deal. One fuck for every hour he had to put into my case. He was on a win-win.

As I write this, my case is still pending, but Paco's cock is a lot happier than it was a few days before my transgression. My efforts to resolve this problem by bartering sex for legal work? Genius! Let's hope Paco's legal brain is as fruitful as his Cock's membrane!

In the meantime, without wasting too much time, Blondie set up more appointments for me. My brief spell in jail had given me the impetus to enjoy my freedom and to fuck like a bunny again. I have to tell you, I am a tough cookie, but sitting there, in a cell with 3 brick walls accompanied by other felons I'd never met before, scared the crap out of me. I have had some tough situations to overcome in my life, but that one, the 5 hours behind bars, well, that was not at all pleasant, and I only hope that it never happens again. Yes, I was stupid, but in my eyes, maybe not in the eyes of the law, although that has yet to be proven, I did nothing wrong. I will tell you though, that if I ever see that guy from AAA again, I will not hesitate to seek revenge. Mark my words, he is a wanted man in my eyes.

Trotting Along Nicely

That day in the limo, yes, THAT day. One to never forget, nor possibly to remember, unless I want to torture myself. Blondie and her friend Terry, a nice man, and fairly wealthy too, made a point of renting this limo once a year to go to Dana point for the Thanksgiving Turkey Trot and festival. Terry had a fetish for fucking more than one of either Blondie or Lucy or any of Blondie's friends at a time. A nice man, but sexually, a real fuck head. This particular year, Blondie and Lucy invited me to join them, and although none of us was going to participate in the fun run, an event where thousands show up and run 5 miles to raise cash for charity and possibly meet the partner of their dreams while jogging through the sunny streets of Dana Point, we were showing no interest in joining them. We had our sights set on a limo pub crawl, hoping to get very drunk and then expecting Terry to fuck us all in the back of that limo. He paid Blondie a small fortune each year to do this, and Blondie had warned me, "things can get out of hand, so be prepared'

The day started quite civilly, the limo arriving to collect all three of us around 11 AM. Terry was already in the front seat next to the driver and directing proceedings as we meandered down Pacific Coast Highway for the short 6-mile journey to Dana Point. I personally hate limos, and sitting in the back of that elongated tube, which, for some unknown reason always made me feel sick. That particular day was no exception. The driver had to pull over twice, even though the journey time was less than 30 minutes. I needed to get out to catch a breath of air, while Blondie and Lucy remained in the back seat, devouring champagne and tequila. I just couldn't take it. Once we arrived at our destination, I felt not only relieved, but horny too. That's another thing limo's do to me. The rock'n roll movement that the back seat of any limo makes, turns my pussy into a waterfall. I have no idea why this happens, but it does, and when we got there, I felt that my jeans were already showing pussy juice stains, which I excrete abundantly from a real good fucking. When I cum, I cum like a waterfall, the remnants of which, seep through my clothes as a clear give-away to all my wrong doings! I looked down at my crotch and there seemed to be nothing. My little kitty had managed to keep herself in the good books, at least for now. We all headed for lunch and then bar hopped for the next few hours, and then went to dinner. It was non-stop alcohol and food, something that I just wasn't into, and I kept asking Blondie, 'when's he going to fuck us all so I can head home?' Blondie was too far gone and too far under the influence to really care. At around 10 PM, we all bundled into the limo for the last time, but this time, Terry decided to sit with us in the backseat as we headed back to Newport Beach. When we got on the road, after zig-zagging out of the harbor, Terry was horny and began fondling all of us. He took a keen interest in me, not Blondie or Lucy, something that pissed Lucy off, but which had little or no effect on Blondie at all. As we exited Laguna, Terry suddenly ordered the driver to take this little dirt road, which only he could see and which the driver reluctantly agreed to do. The limo went off the main drag, PCH, and down this small dirt road for about a half mile and then stopped. The driver got out and walked towards the beach, where Terry had asked him to 'hang out' for about an hour. This is when all hell broke loose and things got really out of hand. Blondie was so drunk that her head was almost in her lap as she contemplated sleep. Lucy, well, she was annoyed, and wanted to be fucked by Terry, but Terry wanted nothing to do with Lucy and wanted only to fuck me. Lucy, sensing she'd been jilted, started to smack my bottom really hard, as I started to give Terry a blow job. Lucy found this hilarious, I found it excruciatingly painful, but as my mouth was devouring Terry's cock, and her hand was hitting my backside, I just couldn't stop. There was something quite erotic about the whole scene. Lucy found it all hilarious and each time she hit me, she burst into fits of laughter. I, on the other hand, had a backside that was beginning to blister and a mouth that was about to be filled with cum.

Terry jumped up.

"Right!" he commanded, and pointed at Lucy and Blondie, who was now awake and ready to join in. She'd rallied!

"You two, get out and go find the driver, YOU!" he bellowed, as he pointed to me, "stay here and finish the job"

It was like God had appeared from heaven and was directing his flock. Blondie got out, followed by Lucy, who, on her way out, slapped my naked bum one last time, and they both slammed the car door, and made off towards the beach to find our driver. Meanwhile, Terry just pointed to his dick, and commanded me to return to the blow job I'd been rudely interrupted from. I did as I was told, he came, I swallowed, and he passed out. Blondie and Lucy came back with the driver, we took off back to Newport and I had to stand up inside the Limo most of the way back, because my backside was so sore from the beating that Lucy had given it, I was convinced I would not be able to sit for a month.

Arriving back at our house, Terry took out his cash, asked to come in so he could fuck me again, told Lucy she wasn't getting fucked and Blondie that she was in charge of the cash. We stomped into the apartment, Lucy went to her room in the huff, Blondie went to her room to sleep, and Terry fucked me in all my holes for the next hour before getting back into the limo and heading home. All in all, a lucrative day and evening, with free food, free drink, and $1000 in cash in my pocket. It took Lucy 3 days to talk to me again, even though she'd made just as much as I had, but after she realized the damage she'd done to my poor tosh, she was very apologetic and we remained besties, just like all girls should. As for Terry, well, he became a regular client, and still is to this day. The most incredible thing about what I was doing now, and who I was becoming, was that when I thought back to my married days and who my husband was, when I'd actually found the condoms in the trunk of his car, our car, I hadn't given much thought to who he'd been fucking, and at the time, I didn't really care. I honestly believed that he'd been screwing one of my friends at first, a lady called Irene, but those thoughts soon evaporated when I found some E$cort sites imbedded into the search engine of his computer and then on his phone. After doing some research and snooping, I found out that he'd been meeting E$corts on the side, some local and some in Mexico, where he'd been a couple of times on business. These E$corts were sending him messages, texts, and emails, and I also found a few calls and voice mails from the Mexican ladies, some of which were astoundingly vile.

Anyway, at the end of the relationship, when everything exploded and I kicked him into touch, one of the first things that came to mind when I called Blondie to get myself lined up as an E$cort, was the complete irony of it all. There I was with zero tolerance for the things that my ex-husband was doing and now here I am, practicing all of the things I was dead against at that time. Oh, how I longed to call him up one day and say something like, "Hey, fucker, look at me now. I'm at the other end of the phone if you want to pay for it!" Yes, fuck him and fuck all of the women he slept with. He had something special going with me, and he lost it all in favor of paying for sex with strangers and now I was doing the same thing, only I was the recipient of all of the cash. This made me laugh out loud on many occasions after I'd started offering my body for money, but that day out with Terry in the limo, well, that kind of brought it all back to me because I knew that my husband wasn't being taken out in limousines, and I also knew the women he was fucking weren't in my league and were probably charging him double my going rate. How life changes, and how it comes around in full circles!

And still on the subject of cars. I'm not sure what it is with men and their superchargers or their limo's, but Blondie's friend Hunter, you already read about him in earlier chapters, well, he arrived at Blondie's place about three weeks after I moved in there, and he fell in love with me in an instant. I'm not being big headed here, but most men seem to do that when they meet me. It must be the fake tits or my tight ass. Anyway, after a brief negotiation and the realization that my pussy was for rent, he and Blondie agreed terms and we all fucked like crazy for a couple of hours that afternoon. Then, Hunter became a regular, so much so, that he's been fucking me at least twice a week ever since. The system we have is interesting. Sometimes I will go to his office in the middle of the day and we will fuck behind lock doors, and other times, he will arrive at Blondie's and we will fuck in my room there. He doesn't care if I fuck other men, and he really doesn't mind if he fucks me when I am having my period. He always lets me know, "I have earned my Red Wings!" He just wants to fuck and he loves every minute of every fucking session, declaring loudly and proudly at the end of each momentous orgasm, for him at least, that 'this is the best sex I have ever had!'

Well, I wish it was for me too!

He called up one afternoon and invited me to spend the weekend in Parker Arizona, Blondie's old haunt, where he keeps and boat and RV. I wasn't sure if this was something I wanted to do, because I normally look after my 3 kids at the weekend and we spend family time doing something together, like exploring the countryside or going to eat with my parents, so getting away for three days, Friday to Sunday, is not always easy. After he made the offer, I discussed it with Blondie.

"Go" she said, "you'll have a blast and make tons of money"

Hunter also intimated that he would require me to drive another car back from Parker, one that he owned and had left there over the summer, but as Fall was now upon us, he wanted to drive it back. This meant that although we would go down there together, I would be on my own driving back. I wasn't too fussed to do that, but after talking to Blondie, she'd told me that Hunter would need to pay me extra to do this. Blondie and I discussed the whole proposition and although I wasn't necessarily frightened to call Hunter and discuss the 'business' side of this deal, Blondie had suggested that it might be better if she did it for me since she knew him well and believed she would get more money out of him that I ever could. I agreed.

Blondie "Hunter, we need to talk money, and I am acting on behalf of Daz"

Hunter "Nothing to discuss, I will give her $1000 for the weekend"

Blondie "Let me sit down while I laugh Hunter. It's 48 hours at $400 per hour, so you do the math"

Hunter "No way, I will give her $1000, final offer"

Blondie "Then she's not going with you"

Silence.

Blondie already knew Hunter was truly desperate to spend a weekend with me and she also knew that his offer, miserly offer, of $1000 was only a starting point.

Hunter "How about I pay her $1500?"

Blondie "How about you go fuck yourself. It's $6000 minimum or she doesn't go"

Hunter "3 grand max, and $750 for you"

Blondie "Deal, but I want all my $750 and half of her $3000 in advance"

With the business side of our weekend out of the way, (something I hate is negotiating, and I am always grateful when Blondie jumps in and takes over for me), her experience in these matters was invaluable to me and I was now free to sit back and contemplate what was hopefully going to be a wonderful weekend away in Parker Arizona. No kids, no worries, and oh yes, I had a few days to sort out child care for my 3 beauties, something I was hopeful my parents would take care of, oh and by the way, I just happened to have started my period the same morning that invitation came through and so it was going to be a very bloody weekend for one of us at least!

Before I left with Hunter, I received a legal update from Paco, my DUI attorney.

"Here's what's going to happen" he told me on the phone, "I will be doing all of your paper work, but my colleague, Mr. Lee, (I now call him Lee the Lawyer or Lawyer Lee), will do all the court work. There will be a requirement to include different court appearances at differing times, and Lee will attend to them, you don't need to go, but that means our total cost will be $5000. Lee and I have checked you out on the web, and obviously I have known Blondie for years, so we understand what your rate is. We figure you can fuck both of us 6 times each and that will cover the fees. Do we have a deal?" Did I have a choice? Lee would be my first experience of a legal fuck and rather than me telling a lawyer to go fuck himself, I would be fucking a lawyer to go help myself! He showed up the night before I left for Parker, and bearing in mind I had just fucked Hunter at his office, also for free, Lee was the next freebie that very same day, but hey, if he got me off and I saved $5000, did I care? From the moment he came inside his extra small condom, Lawyer Lee was in love with me. Yet again, another man who just fucked me once and then wouldn't leave me alone.

Hunter picked me up around 10 AM on Friday morning and we headed East on the 10 freeway. From the moment we were together until the second we arrived at his RV in Parker, he had one hand on the wheel and one hand on my tits. I'd tried to blow him twice on the freeway, both attempts ending in failure, his failure not mine. His mind just couldn't come to terms with the fact that when he told me he loved me, I just laughed. "I will marry you in January" he'd said, quite nonchalantly, and each time he'd repeated that, I had laughed and laughed, telling him to go fuck himself and that I was no man's bitch. We eventually arrived at his place, we unpacked and then fucked for two hours, non-stop, and ate dinner, while we both lay naked on the floor of his so-called lounge. We watched TV, porn of course, and then, around 9 PM, Hunter suggested we have a 'toy' session.

"What the fuck is that?" I asked, knowing all too well what was about to happen.

The sex toys miraculously appeared from underneath his bed, and believe me, I knew I wasn't the first lady to see or to use them. I asked him,

"I hope you've cleaned these since the last time you used them?"

He laughed, gathering them all up in his hands and headed towards the bathroom, where I immediately heard the sound of running hot water and Hunter's attempt to 'polish' up his toys using soap and water. I was glad that I'd asked.

He returned a few minutes later, and the show began. I think if we'd filmed this, we would have made a fortune selling it on the internet. But we didn't, so the opportunity to cash in was lost. His selection of toys was, let's say, eclectic? There was black one's, brown one's, mechanical one's, battery operated ones, and toys that I had never seen before. And so it began, in earnest, and with the biggest black dildo I had ever seen, which Hunter, bless his soul, believed would fit into my someone tight pussy. I know I'd had three kids, but his attempt at stuffing it into me, while we both drank tequila and listened to rock music blaring from two of the world's largest speakers, well it just got too much, and even though he managed to get the tip of the dildo into my pussy, the rest of it wasn't going anywhere. In the end he sized down and we settled on a nice comfortable white dildo, more my size and certainly more pleasurable.

"The last lady I had in here managed the black one" he told me.

"Yes" I replied, "but when you fucked her did you feel anything?"

We laughed and the show continued, with me utilizing cock rings and a battery U shaped vibrator on his penis, something he told me would not only stimulate his erection, but also make him cum harder, and Hunter going through a multitude of different toys, using some on my clit, some on my nipples and some in my mouth. It was midnight when we finished, at least I think it was midnight, I was so exhausted, I didn't really know or care. We retired for the night, but not before I made him clean up all the blood from the floor. Remember, I was on my period, but thankfully it was its last day so the mess wasn't too much to clear and Hunter made a point of cleaning it with vigor!

One of the things that Hunter loves to do when he's in Parker is to go off-roading on dirt bikes and other interesting 4-wheel vehicles that mean nothing to me, but a lot to him. When we got up on Saturday morning, after sleeping until almost noon, Hunter jumped out of bed, filled with excitement, bragging that this was the best day I was ever going to have in my entire life. He got in the shower and I joined him, a tight squeeze for sure, and we fucked standing up. After he came, we washed one another from head to toe, and then got dressed and drove to the local diner for bacon and eggs, and guess what? Yes, more tequila. Hunter insisted that each day in Parker had to begin the way it was meant to continue. After breakfast, out came the dirt bikes, loaded with care onto the back of a trailer, and then he loaded two more vehicles emblazoned with Honda logos, and off we went. We drove an hour, into the middle of nowhere, in fact, it was so desolate, I thought Clint Eastwood was going to ride out of nowhere, and shoot some bad guys hiding behind the brush! After setting up a camp, we offloaded the vehicles and went exploring in them. I have to tell you; I had never had such a great time. It was fabulous entertainment, and so much fun. About 3 hours later, we were exhausted and hungry, and we loaded the truck up yet again, then Hunter asked me to give him a blow job in the front seat of his Ford F150. I did this with some speed, because the 35 calories he ejaculated into my mouth were never going to satisfy the hunger I felt at that point. We drove the hour back to town and we stopped off at one of the bars in Parker, drinking and eating until about 8 PM and after that, once back at his place, we began fucking again. I found it hard to believe that this man could fuck so much. He was a complete animal in that sense. After all was said and done, I think we had sex about 4 times that night, and that was AFTER the blow job in the desert! Hunter was amazing, but there was no way I could let him off the hook that easily. I suggested we got the toys out again, only this time, I was going to fuck his ass and make him scream, and that monster black dildo was my weapon of choice. Hunter, I have to say, played along like the trooper he is, and we had fun for a couple of hours before crashing and sleeping for at least 10 more. Sunday, we fell out of bed, literally, and neither of us could barely move.

"I got my money's worth I suppose!" Hunter laughed.

I was so sore, and so happy to be going home.

"Hunter" I said, as I smiled and pouted my lips, "The BMW that you want me to drive home. Who is it for?" I asked him.

"Spare car" he replied

"If I fucked you again right now, and then told you how much of a doll you are, would you let me keep it?" my heart was in my throat, not knowing how he would react to my question.

"Yes dear, it's yours to borrow for as long as I say. I have 9 more cars, so I won't miss this one, and when we get married in January…" he laughed, I balked! "… it's going to be your wedding present." "Yeah right!" I said, as I rolled my eyes towards the back of my head.

After another sex session, this one only lasted 30 mins, we were ready to get out of there and drive home. It was after 2 PM and with a 5-hour drive in front of me, and my kids already calling to see where I was, I was ready to be back home. I was given the keys to the BMW and we rolled off his lot in Parker around 2.30. All the way home, every 2 or three minutes, Hunter would text me something like, 'Let's stop and fuck' or 'Pull over, I want to suck on your tits.' This became tiresome and tedious and also dangerous as the hours went by and the roads got busier and busier. It was the end of a great weekend, but I was dying to get back to normality and as I called Blondie from the road, she reminded me that I had a bunch of guys lined up for Monday morning, all of whom were desperate to get inside my incredible, well fucked, pussy. Oh boy, this was some life, but the 3 grand that was now in my purse, reminded me that things were only going to get better and more lucrative as time rolled on.

Bedtime Story

The bed story. Wow, when I think of this story, I'm also blown away with how erotic it became and how turned on I am when someone, especially a tattooed man, grabs me by the neck and tells me forcefully that he wants to fuck the shit out of me. I am so in tune with that type of male aggression and it brings my pussy to the boil whenever it happens, which is not too often.

I'd moved into my apartment, the one I'd managed to finagle with the fake pay receipts, and I'd made a few holes in the walls when moving in. This was nothing too serious and something I was able to repair myself, if I put my mind to it. However, I'd also purchased a new king-sized bed with a bed frame and that bed frame was proving too much for me to handle, and every time I'd tried to assemble it, I'd given up in a fit of anger. It was impossible to put together and it frustrated the fuck out of me, turning me into a complete bitch filled with anger, something my kids didn't appreciate.

Blondie suggested that I put on my Listcrawler.com Ad that I needed to trade DIY assembly skills for some sex. Great idea! And so, we placed the Ad, suggesting that any man willing to assist me with my home repair issues and also assemble my bedframe, could look forward to a free fuck, on the house, gratis, in honor of completing tasks that had so far eluded me. The Ad was up and live on the site for about ten minutes and I'd received over 45 calls from willing participants, none of which I liked the look of. I called my ex-husband and asked him to assist, he refused, and so I took myself off to Target to buy a tool kit, knowing I would have to take care of this myself. As I walked into Target, my phone blew up with messages from Blondie, but I didn't hear them or see them. My phone was on silent-mode for some reason. I purchased the tool kit and I was about to leave the store, when I decided to check my phone. Pictures of my 'dream' guy, the guy I was sure I would one day settle down with, adorned my screen, courtesy of Blondie. A 6 ft tall, full tattooed hunk, offering to come over that evening to fix all my home repair issues. I called Blondie, and we both went crazy! "This is him!" I shouted, right in the middle of Target. "Yes" she said, "I know it is"

I returned my new tool kit, knowing that in all probability I would never use it, and then I called the tattooed man.

"This is …." And before I could finish, he said, "Yes, I know who it is. I can get to you this evening, but not until 10 PM, will that work?"

Stupid question! Of course, it was going to work, and I told him just that.

At 10 PM that night, he showed up right on time. He was getting his tool kit from the back of his Dodge RAM truck, and I was peering from behind the curtains in the living room, eyeing him up as he tried to get organized. My kids were in bed, hopefully asleep. Not only did he have tat's all over, he had a pierced nose and a gold front tooth, another huge turn on for me. He came inside, I almost came inside!

We got cracking and he put the bedframe together in less than an hour and by midnight, he'd finished almost everything that needed doing. I was really impressed. During the time he'd spent fixing my shit, he'd been flirting with me on and off, and telling me how sexy I was, knowing that he was about to receive a 'freebie.' I could tell he had a huge penis, just from the bulge under his shorts and I was getting quite wet just thinking about what he was about to do to me when we got naked.

When he'd packed up his tool bag and we were sitting in my kitchen chatting quietly so the kids couldn't hear us, he suddenly jumped out of his seat, came over to me, grabbed me gently by the throat, and said, "I want to fuck the shit out of you!" My biggest turn on in life had just been fulfilled. I politely told him, "Sweetie, the kids are here, it ain't happening tonight."

I decided to play hard to get.

He was annoyed, but understood, and we made plans for me to drive to his place the following morning to repay him for his work, in kind.

With all of that happening, the freebie, and seeing some of my newest clients that same day, I began to get a slight sharpish pain in my back. I believed it had begun after messing around with that stupid bed frame. I decided a trip to the chiropractor would be the order of the morning. I made the appointment, and drove over to the west side of Irvine. As I parked up, and usually I am early for all my appointments, so I sit in my car and surf the internet, my phone rang. It was a call from my Ad on Listcrawler.com. I answered.

"Hi"

"Hi" came the response.

"What can I do for you?" I asked

"Can you give me some road head?" he asked.

I paused. I had never heard that term before, ever!

"Road Head?" I replied, not knowing exactly what this guy wanted.

"Yes, a blow job in my truck please?"

Ah! He wanted me to suck him off while he was driving.

"Where are you?"

He gave me an approximate location, and it turned out he was about 5 minutes away from where I was. I gave him directions, telling him to get to me in a hurry and that the cost would be $100, one pop only.

Terms agreed, I called the chiro and made my apologies, saying I was stuck in traffic and would be 15 minutes late.

A large Ford F150, a red one, pulled into the parking lot. I presumed this was him, flashing my lights in his direction. He drove over towards me, gesturing that I should get out of my car and join him in the front seat of his truck, which I gladly did. He was a nice-looking guy, clean cut and obviously slightly embarrassed as he thought about what we were about to do. I told him to pay up and drive down towards the beach. I knew a quiet spot where I could happily perform without interruption. Out came the $100 and off we went down Irvine Center Dr, which meandered for many miles before hitting the beach, but we weren't going to go that far. About a mile down that road, I told him to turn off to the right, which he did, and then park up in a very quiet parking lot, where I'd fucked several guys in the past. Remember now, this was a Ford F150 and the barrier between both the drivers and passengers' seats was blocked by a rather large central glove box, which I, and my lips, were about to navigate. I suggested we move to the back seat, but that was filled already with a baby seat, anchored and which couldn't be moved.

"Got kids?" I asked

"2" he said, "but I haven't seen them in months because me and the wife are separated and with Covid, it's just hard"

I understood.

I moved my body into the middle of the glove box, inching slowly towards him. If you can imagine the scene, I was perched just slightly above him, and his cock, which was now out and very erect, was kind of standing to attention, facing towards my mouth. I had to maneuver into a position where he was stimulated and I was able to suck and then swallow whatever he ejaculated. He'd made it clear I needed to swallow the lot and that there could be no residue on his precious seats. Off I went, and within moments, he came, I swallowed and leaving nothing but happiness on his face, we drove back to the chiro where I walked in, and took my seat for my appointment. Road head accomplished, $100 to the good, I was very pleased with my morning's efforts, but Golden Tooth, tattooed man, was the only real thing I was thinking about and I needed to make that deal happen. We were supposed to meet up that morning, but for one reason or another, it didn't happen. I was determined to pay him back sexually for all his assembly efforts at my home, and pay him back in a manner neither of us would ever forget.

This guy emailed me out of the blue, another guy I'd never seen before. Simple text message, and one that put me on the floor rolling in laughter.

'MILF You want to fuck?' Was all it said, accompanied by a picture of his dick, and no word of a lie, his dick was long and thin and he'd put three toilet rolls by the side of it, to show its length and I promise you, again, no word of a lie, it went from the top of the first roll to the bottom of the 3rd. It must have been 13 inches long. No thanks!

Goat breath showed up a few days ago. I call him Goat Breath, (GB from now on), because as soon as he walked into my room, I could smell his halitosis from 15 feet. It was vile. The guy was in his early 60's and a guy I had never seen before, but, although reasonably handsome, the stench from his mouth was just too horrible to tolerate. I took the $400 from him and he tried to kiss me, but I resisted, telling him I preferred him to go down on me, in the hope that his breath killed all the bacteria in my pussy. He agreed, but after slobbering all over my cunt for about 5 minutes and with his slobber running down my butt crack, something I really detest, I pulled him up and told him straight, I's so sorry, I just can't do this"

I had tears running down my face, and honestly, I was quite upset with myself, but his breath along with my newly-formed butt crack slobber, had been a real turn off. I ejected the poor guy, who by now had some sympathy for me from my openly outwards, show of emotion. He left without having cum and without asking for a refund. Oh, the trials and tribulations of an E$cort. After he left, I disinfected my whole room, which took me all night.

    Hunter was back on the scene and we were off to AZ again for the weekend. This time, on the way down to Parker he was pleading his undying love for me from the minute we jumped into his car, until the second we arrived, confirming in every sentence he spouted that he would marry me by the new year. I'd heard all of this before of course, but something in his voice was so sincere and I was starting to believe every word he said. We both got along nicely and we had fun together, so it might not be a bad marriage, I thought, but in the meantime, I was more interested in the $6000 he was paying me every month, yes, this was something we'd negotiated and so far, he'd been paying up like the good man he was, on time, and on the first of every month. For that $6000 I spent 2 days every week with him, fucking of course, and one weekend in Parker. He'd also insured me to drive any of the 8 cars he owned and instead of the used BMW he'd loaned to me on our first trip to the river, he'd now upgraded me to a New Toyota, which in my opinion was far more practical for me and my three kids and all the gear I carried around for each of their activities. Hunter was turning out to be a real find, thanks of course to Blondie. Everything I wanted in a sugar-daddy; Hunter fulfilled. He was great in bed, but of course, so was I! He was nice to me, all of the time, even when I wasn't my usual self, he always understood. When we were on our way back from this particular trip to Parker, I felt sick to my stomach, and he was good enough to pull over, then turn back and stay another night, just to let me get over my sickness. We'd driven about 45 minutes outside of Parker and I got this knot in my stomach followed by an undeniable urge to puke. Hunter stopped the car, took care of me for about an hour and then agreed to turn back to Parker so we could spend one more night and I could relax and get over whatever it was that was making me fell ill. I really believe it was just nerves, knowing that we'd had such a wonderful weekend and that the following day I was going to go back to fucking strangers' again, when all I really wanted was some stability with Hunter. My mind though, always changed once I got back into the swing of things and when that first client walked through our front door, even after those fun times with Hunter, the sight of their greenbacks helped me put all my sentiment to one side and charged my pussy with enough energy to realize she was keeping me and my kids in the style to which we were accustomed. I wasn't sure where my relationship with Hunter was going at that time, but I did know he wanted to invite me to meet his parents and to spend Thanksgiving with him, so with some confidence, I could tell I had him wrapped around my clit like puppy dog penis he'd become.

There's this guy called Tyson, a very handsome dude. He works for a huge well-known cosmetic products corporation and every time he comes to see me, he brings me lots of free stuff. Anyway, couple of days after I got back from one of my river trips with Hunter, Tyson called to set up a date with me knowing that under no circumstances do I ever let any client go down on me. I am adamant about this, except for a few special people, some of whom we have discussed in this book, halitosis man, for one. Tyson is very handsome, very chic and extremely sexy, and if I was single and had no kids, I would fuck the shit out of him for free in the hope that we would really date on a regular basis. Anyway, he showed up, his hands filled with samples, some of which were very expensive, and as he crossed the threshold and marched into my room, the words from his rather loud voice rang out all around the house.

"D!" he exclaimed, "I am going down on your beautiful pussy today, or you'll getting none of these wonderful products I brought!" Boy, was he a stud!

I took a quick look at what he'd brought with him, noticing that a lot of the stuff he had was, not only expensive, but stuff that I actually used! "Deal" I told him, "But I want $100 more"

He agreed.

We began, and after I'd let him fuck me twice, he said, "OK, spread 'em, I'm going in full throttle."

His tongue began working on my clit when suddenly his cell phone began to ring. He popped up for air, looked at the caller ID on the screen, and said to me, "I need to take this, please keep quiet while I talk."

The conversation began, and as he spoke, he motioned for me to lie back on the bed and spread my legs, which I did.

As he spoke, he would say a few words and then carry on licking my clit as he listened to the other person speaking to him, and then he would stop licking me and say a few more words and go on licking my clit while the other party continued to talk. This went on for about 3 minutes, and just as I was about to cum, and cum really hard, knowing I was a screamer, Tyson motioned for me to grab a pillow and cover my mouth and then scream into the pillow while he finished his conversation. No joke, he spoke and licked and spoke and licked and I came.

We were done, he was done, and we lay laughing our heads off on the bed. "Who was that?" I asked.

"My boss. He wanted to know why there was so much noise on the line, in fact he kept asking me that."

"Are you going to get into any trouble?"

"No, he thinks I was driving" he replied. And, technically he was. He was driving me into a fabulous orgasm. I do like Tyson, but I like all the free product he brings me even more.

Paco the attorney was next. 2 sessions down, 4 to go, and perhaps my DUI will be expunged. What a day!

I just had to add this one last story, a story which is kind of sad, yet kind of funny.

I had this guy contact me through my Ad. We went back and forth for hours, him wanting to get to know me, and me, wanting to know why he wanted to get to know me through an Ad? In the end, he gave up on me, but because Blondie's profile and my profile are linked, and we also have some pictures we've shot together, especially for men who would like a threesome, he'd started texting Blondie, telling her that I looked just like this porn star, Bonnie Rotten. Google her, I look nothing like her. She has totally different hair to me, she has tattoos all over and she has obviously more money in the bank than me and would never place any Ad's on the sites where I am advertising. Anyway, he wouldn't take no for an answer, pestering Blondie, asking her to set up a meeting between me and him, which, after about 5 hours back and forth, I agreed to, even though I'd said no earlier on.

 The guy showed up, looking suave and sophisticated, and obviously desperate to impress. We hugged briefly and went into my room. I got naked, he got naked and as he walked slowly across my room, which is only 10 ft or so, his body goes into a state of convulsion, as he's walking, not falling! I thought at first, it was an act to make me laugh, but I was wrong. This was like watching the Terminator re-form his body, in slow motion. Frightening! As he was having this fit, and by this time he'd managed to get on top of me, (I have no idea how he'd done that, but he did), he came, all over my tits. I hadn't even touched him. His mess was everywhere, and honestly, the guy had ejaculated from over 6 ft away. While walking, while having this seizure, or whatever it was. He'd absolutely ruined my bedsheets, and as suddenly as he'd cum, he collected himself, apologizing profusely to me and suggesting he'd had an allergic reaction to my perfume, which had caused this seizure. This was impossible, because I didn't wear perfume! After sitting on the edge of the bed for a few minutes, the look of disbelief so evident on my own face, he turned around and asked, quite casually, and as if nothing had happened,

"OK, that was the first time, so how much for twice more and once up your ass?"

We negotiated to $650, and he went for it, fucking me hard for about an hour, without having any further seizures, and managing to cum twice more, filling two more condoms to the brim, then quite innocently asking me if he could go one last time, to which I said, "NO I am exhausted. Get the fuck out before I throw you out!" I was joking of course, and he knew that, but like the little puppy dog he was, he did as he was told, and he left.

Took me 20 minutes to get the condoms to flush, and another hour to clean the bed sheets.

My Ex

I told you my ex-husband is a jerk? Right?

His name is Gordon, and he's a moron. He's a jealous prick, an asshole, a cheater and a man I should never have married, but at the time, I was pregnant, so, life sucks, you make the most of it, and you move on. We have two kids together, and a lot of history, some good, most of it bad. We fought all the time, he would refuse to admit he was cheating, even though, as I already told you, I found out he was, and he was insistent and instrumental on our move to Nashville, something I never wanted to do. I am a Cali girl, born and bred, and leaving here to go to Tennessee, was a heartbreaker for me and my parents. They missed their grandchildren, and I missed the climate in Cali, and my friends. Nashville is an OK city, don't get me wrong, but when you grow up in the most perfect climate in the world and then leave for a city where, in the summertime sweat just runs down every crack in your body, well, it's time to have a re-think and ponder what on earth led you to agree to moving there in the first place. In any event, once I was certain Gordon had cheated and once I'd ratted him out face to face, I was literally on the first plane back to California, accompanied by my three kids of course. Gordon soon followed, and after losing his stupid court case against me in Tennessee, he really had no will or impetus to stay there. Not thinking clearly, something he's renowned for, he quit his job, and very shortly afterwards the two of us were living as a separated couple in different homes in different streets but in the same city. I ended up earning a shitload of cash for getting fucked 5 times a day, and him, unemployed and desperate to reunite with me and his children, something I swore would never happen. My motto, Once you're out, you're out!

He did have his good points, but thinking back to when we were at our happiest, I can't quite recall what those points really were. In fact, I've no idea why I agreed to marry him. Oh, wait! I was pregnant, that's why!

My relationship with Hunter was getting very interesting. We were seeing each other several times a week and each time, his exclamation of his undying love for me got louder and louder. I was touched, and he wanted to be touched! He'd been interested to see where this relationship was going from my standpoint, and each time he told me he wanted to marry me, I kept reminding him that I wasn't divorced yet. That didn't seem to deter him, and Jan 1st looked like a good time, again, in his opinion, not mine, to announce our engagement, something that was too impossible for me to even contemplate.

One afternoon, I was summoned to his home, yes, he wanted to fuck, and with the huge amounts of cash and all the gifts he was sending my way, who was I to refuse. I decided to Uber to Newport Beach, where Hunter lived, so that I could enjoy a few drinks with him, get him all horny and then fuck him for the rest of the evening. Then I'd Uber back home and put the kids to bed. I'd asked Gordon to come over to look after the two youngest when they got home from school, leaving them under his care for dinner. I left the new Toyota Hunter had given me, in my driveway, but what I forgot to do, was lock the damn car. This would prove to be a problem, as you're about to find out, but unknowingly, a problem I should never have had. Gordon arrived after I'd left, and he would be gone before I got home. This however would just exaccrbate the issue that was about to occur.

I arrived at Hunter's and he took my hand as I came into his hallway. Before I could get my shoes off, something that Hunter always preferred I do when I came into his home, and something he liked everyone else to do as well, his hand was already on top of my breasts and his tongue was aiming directly for the center of my throat.

"You're such a fucking turn on" he insisted, as his mechanical right arm, removed my bra and his far from limp penis grew in length beneath his shorts. His left hand reached under my dress and began fingering my clit. I was so wet, and he and I knew that he'd be inside me before his front door had actually closed. My panties were removed and he inserted his cock into my pussy. Wow, this was so erotic, and so incredibly sensual, and the front door was still wide open.

As Hunter thrust his cock in and out, building up stream and sweat, he'd become more and more turned on by what was happening. The crescendo was coming. I could feel the hardness of his cock throbbing inside me, building up to yet another momentous ejaculation. Then, suddenly and without warning, he stopped and withdrew.

"What the fuck babe?" I exclaimed.

By now, pussy juice was just running down my legs, like a waterfall does in summertime after the ice pack melts. I couldn't stop, I didn't want to stop, but Hunter was kind of insistent and anyway, without him inside me, the party had ground to a sudden halt, albeit temporarily.

He lifted me off his hallway floor, where our fucking had been in full swing, raising me to my feet, and ushering me with one hand, into his garage. I was undecided if he wanted to start using car tools on my clit, or just wanted to fuck me on his garage floor. As we walked into the garage, there, right in front of me, was a brand-new white Toyota Tundra truck, all clean and shiny. I presumed Hunter had just purchased it and wanted to fuck me in the flat bed of the truck to christen it. I was wrong.

"Sweetie" he began, "this is your new truck"

"My new truck???"

"Yes, I want to Corolla back, and in return, I bought you this" he said, quite casually.

"Seriously???" I yelled.

This was unbelievable. A brand-new truck with all the extras and rails on the roof for my kid's surf boards, and satellite radio and so much more. I just couldn't believe it.

"Are you shittin me?" I asked

"Nope" he replied

"For fucks sake Hunter, what were you thinking?"

"I told you I loved you" and as he said this he smiled, "and you deserve it"

At that precise moment, my phone began to continuously vibrate. It was a text message, followed by another, then another and then another.

Hunter looked at me, and I looked at him, and we just hugged. My phone was in the hallway, yes, that hallway, where our fucking had begun in earnest ten minutes earlier, and I could hear the damn thing going off all the way inside his garage, where we were both standing butt naked and in complete admiration of my new ride.

"I hope that's not a needy client" Hunter said

"Probably one of my kids. Clients don't send that many texts" I walked back into the hallway, picked up my bag and then removed my phone from my purse. I was shocked to see 14 messages from Gordon.

This is how it went.

YOU LEFT YOUR NEW CAR OPEN BITCH.

I KNOW HIS NAME IS HUNTER.

OH AND NOW I HAVE HIS ADDRESS

WELL I DON'T GIVE A FUCK

YOU'RE SUCH A CUNT

FUCK YOU AND YOUR BOYFRIEND

MY NEW LADY IS STUNNING

YOU LOST OUT WHEN YOU LEFT ME

FUCKING BITCH.

I AM GOING TO SORT YOUR NEW MAN OUT

BEWARE BITCH

WHY WOULD ANYONE LIKE YOU

DON'T CALL ME AGAIN

Well, if that wasn't enough, he signed off with

BTW, I THINK I WILL JUST DRIVE THIS PIECE OF SHIT CAR TO THE BEACH AND LEAVE IT THERE.

Hunter, at this time, was standing right next to me.

"Is everything OK?" he asked

"Fine and dandy" I said, as I nonchalantly slipped back into my bag.

I wasn't going to let my fucked-up ex-husband ruin this moment. He was a jealous prick and he didn't deserve the attention a response would certainly give him. Instead, I grabbed hold of Hunter's penis and stuck it into my mouth, and began to blow him like he'd never been blown before.

Hunter and I had an early dinner and a couple of drinks together that afternoon and by the time I got back to my home, Gordon was gone, and the Corolla was still in my driveway. He'd left a note on the front seat though, and all it said was BITCH!

My new truck was going to be so much fun to drive and my intentions were to drive it to Gordon's home one night, park it in his driveway and honk the horn continuously, annoying not only him, but all his neighbors too, in the hope that he would get the message. I AM NEVER COMING BACK DUDE!

I got a call from a man who told me that he liked to take it in his ass with a dildo and asked if I was interested in coming over to his hotel, the Crown Plaza, for a little fun? He told me that I needed to wear fishnet stockings and he only wanted me for 15 minutes total. Yes, I often get the strangest of requests, but with everything going on in life with my ex, and Hunter, this sounded like a refreshing break to me.

I told the guy he'd have to pay me $300 for 15 minutes, and he agreed. He was insistent that I wear fishnet stockings only, repeating this request several times. Nothing else would be acceptable, he'd said. I kept telling him, $300 buddy, nothing else will be acceptable for me! 45 minutes later, I arrived in the lobby of the Crown Plaza. I texted him and he texted back his room number. I looked like the whore that I am, as I entered the elevator, dressed in fishnets, a bra and nothing much else, all covered up with a long coat. Outside of his room I made myself presentable by adjusting a few straps as I knocked on his door, quite softly at first and, after hearing no movement from inside his room, I increased my knocking volume, so much so, I was sure the neighbors in the next two rooms would decide to come and see who was knocking on their doors. Before that happened though, his door cracked open. He stood there, looking at me, briefly studying the way I was dressed. I opened the bottom half of the long coat I was wearing and said to him, "fishnets as promised", with a quick smile, allowing him to open the door fully and let me inside his room. Well, the next few minutes became some of the weirdest moments I have ever had in my life. This guy was dressed in pink fishnets, a full garter belt with two clips holding the fishnets up to his thighs, his penis, dangling like a hooked fish on the end of a rod, and his bare hairy chest, pouted and covered in disgustingly grey hair. The size of his beer belly, which protruded more than 12 inches from the rest of his body, almost blocked my passage into his room. I didn't know whether to laugh or cry, having said that, he was extremely gracious and welcoming, and once the initial shock had passed, the shock of the pink fishnets, he took out the $300, gave it to me, along with this huge back strap on he wanted me to use on his ass, suggesting that we get right down to it. With the noise of gay porn blasting from his TV set, it began in earnest. Within seconds, he'd tied the strap on around my waste, put all fours, his fours, on the bed, ready for doggie style sex, dragging me towards him by the tip of the strap on. He then inserted the end of the dildo in his well-lubricated ass hole, shouting out, "Fuck me bitch, fuck my ass into submission" Which I duly did. I ripped that mother-fucker a sore one, pounding him as he masturbated to gay porn, and eventually, as he came all over the bed sheets, and collapsed in joy at his ability to ejaculate in such a crude manner, he pulled the dildo from his ass and laughed out loud. It had taken 10 minutes, and although those 10 minutes felt like an entire lifetime, it was over before I knew it. He was spent, and I was undoing the strap on and readjusting my clothing so I could leave the hotel looking graceful and tidy at least.

"Yo!" he said, breathless and sweating, "I have a double strap on here, want to fuck my ass while I fuck yours?"

Well, I really love anal sex, so I doubled down on this guy.

"Sure, but I want $400 more before we start and I'll only stay 5 more minutes."

"Deal" he said, without thinking too much about it. He pulled another $400 from his wallet and proceeded to bring out the most incredible sex toy I'd ever seen. This double strap on, if you could call it that, had two huge dildos', one on each end, that were taller than my 4-year-old daughter. They were enormous!

"What the fuck is that?" I asked.

"Come on" he said, "You'll love it"

These things must have been 30 inches long and just as soon as he'd strapped on his end, he started inserting my end into his ass. I was about 4 feet away from him, that's how large this thing was, and I was fucking him and he was fucking me, to the point that I thought my ass was going to bleed. It didn't, and as agreed, five minutes later, he finished, I finished and I left, this time for good. It took me days to be able to sit down properly. That thing destroyed my ass hole, ripping me apart like no cock could ever do, and I swore on the Holly Bible, that I would never do that again, not with anyone. $700 for 25 minutes work though? Not to be laughed at, unless you value your ass hole that is!

And talking about assholes, and not the kind that torment me daily.

This guy came to me through one of my friends. He was recommended as a great handyman, and, as I needed things put together in my home, yet again, I thought I would explore the possibility of letting him quote. Before that happened however, I was informed by this mutual friend, after he'd seen my picture and learned what I did for a living, that he'd prefer to fuck me first, then hang my pictures later. I was now a total pro at bartering sex for the services I required. I was extremely happy to fuck the guy first, take his money and then employ him on a fuck for home services basis. We arranged a date, his name was Jack. I hadn't seen pictures of him, but I didn't care. When I needed something done, it didn't matter, just like my DUI court case, where I promised to fuck both attorneys' in lieu of services rendered. By the way, I was now half way through my part of that bargain, having fucked both of them twice already. I was still waiting to hear back from the courts on what the outcome of my case had been. My fate hung in the backlog of cases the OC court system was synonymous for. Like the sex with the two attorneys', it was slowly, very slowly.

The date with Jack was going to be at my place, not my home, Blondie's place, and about two hours before he was due to arrive, I noticed that one of my finger nails had broken. This to me, was a complete disaster, and I may be many things, but I cannot tolerate a broken nail, especially when the other 9 are perfect. Yes, I am a true princess. My attention to detail and presentation, is exemplary, always has been, always will be. Blondie suggested I put the date off for an hour and go get a manicure, but I hate doing that to anyone, especially new clients, and decided to try and fix the nail myself. After a few failed attempts, I finally got it right, and my two hands looked spick and span as the clock ticked down for the arrival of Jack.

Tattoos, I love tattoos, and you all know that now, and when Jack arrived, tattooed from top to bottom, looking all clean and handsome, my heart just skipped a beat. He was about 33 years old, short, maybe 5'7", but very attractive and very clean cut. I could tell from the minute he walked in and hugged me that this was going to be a date to remember.

"So, you got the cash big boy?" I asked Jack as he made himself comfortable at the end of my bed.

"Just want to tell you that you are so sexy, and even better in person. The pictures Julie showed me don't do you justice" he said as he took $400 from a back pocket on his jeans and laid the cash it on my bed.

"Why thank you sir" I said, blushing.

"Can I ask you a question" he said

I nodded.

"When we are fucking, can you finger my asshole?
 just love that and it makes me cum really hard"

I agreed to honor his fetish, and the sex began. Before we were completely undressed, his bulge was prominent, and by the time his underwear came off, he was erect and standing up hard, just like a toy soldier, only his penis was large and bloated, just like a Gatorade bottle. This I thought, was going to be a blast.

We fucked like it was going out of fashion for a good 30 minutes, and Jack wasn't even close to cumming. We fucked some more, and while he was inside me, doggie style, with his balls bouncing off my ass, he asked me to turn around so I could finger his ass while he fucked me missionary.

I was laying with my legs spread, he was inside me banging away and my right hand was on his backside with my index finger up his anus. He was in heaven, and I have to tell you, so was I. He came, and I came, and we both just lay gasping for air. It has been incredible, he knew it, and I knew it. Amazing sex is hard to come by, but this sex with Jack, had been more than amazing. I looked at him, he looked at me, and we both knew there was going to be more.

I asked Jack if he wanted to shower, and he asked me in return, to join him in the shower. I agreed, and together, we held hands and moved into the bathroom, where Jack started kissing me on my neck.

"Hold on there buddy, you only paid me for one time, not multiple" I scalded him.

He looked at me in the eyes as if to say, "Come to me now and I'll make you so happy", and kind of begged me not to be so business-like and just to take the moment and fuck him again.

I couldn't help myself, those tattoos, that cock, that smile, and his childish features. I was in love. We went at it in the shower, and as hot water cascaded against both of our naked bodies, he inserted his swollen cock once again into my wetness, and the fucking began, this time, without a condom. He pounded me, and was about to cum again, when his signal came for me to stick my finger into his ass. I instinctively looked down at my right hand, and I noticed the nail I'd fixed earlier was no longer there, immediately realizing it must have fallen off either in Jack's ass or on the bed when I pulled my finger out of his bum after he'd cum.

Jack was thrusting in and out and pleading for my finger to go inside him. I, on the other hand, was searching endlessly in my own mind for a place that missing nail could be?

He came, without my finger, looking at me angrily, as if to say, "you let me down bitch, you didn't finger me"

I was stunned into laughter; laughter Jack couldn't understand.

"Was it that bad?" he asked me.

"Emmm, I think you should look up your own backside, there may be a surprise lodged in there."

He looked at me quizzically, thinking that I was completely nuts, but at the same time, reaching in towards, and then up inside his own asshole and retrieving what we would later call, my 'bum nail', giving it the double entendre, it deserved. We both fell about the room laughing. Jack couldn't believe it, I couldn't believe it and the poor nail, which had taken me more than an hour to attach before our date, was going to be flushed down the toilet to its demise. We both agreed it had been one of the funniest sexual episodes either of us had experienced and we also agreed that we liked one another enough to do this again, no charge of course, on the understanding Jack would come over to my real home and fix my 'to do' list of broken items that I'd been putting off for months.

This would the start of a tumultuous relationship between us, and one that would run in tandem with the relationship I was having with Hunter. Hunter was for now, my sugar daddy, paying me upwards of 6 grand a month, based on 4 dates a month a one weekend at his place on the river. Jack wasn't ever going to be my sugar daddy, he was going to be my fuck buddy, because the sex with him, which I will describe in a moment, was going to be some of the best uninhibited sex I have ever had in my entire life.

Hunter and Jack

Hunter and Jack began to make my life very comfortable, financially and physically that is, but very uncomfortable, emotionally.

It was quite a strange situation. Of course, it was strange. How many women get to fuck two great guys, one who pays and one who fucks like a prince?

On the one hand, I had Hunter, who'd given me everything, including great sex, a couple of cars, a regular income, trips away from home and so much more. Jack, on the other hand, had come into my life as a paying client, and unlike Hunter, was now receiving sex for free because he was so damn good in bed and also great at fixing up my home. I was more attracted to Jack, physically that is, but of course, money talks, and the fact that 6 grand a month was covering all my expenses and more, made it hard to follow my heart and not my wallet. Jack began by coming over to my house, just after the episode with the nail in his bum. He fixed my broken shower and then my walls and then my garage door and then he continued by fixing my pussy with his amazing cock. That boy could fuck. He loved anal sex, I loved anal sex, and together, we made a mess in several hotel rooms, on many sets of clean sheets and also the back seat of the truck Hunter had bought for me. Jack was a fucking animal in bed, a real go getter, with stamina I had never experienced before. (I thought Hunter had stamina, but after I met Jack, I realized Hunter was in division 2 on the fuck league). He made me feel alive, and as I mentioned, he was now getting it for free. Hunter, well, the cash just kept on coming, along with marriage proposals that never seemed to cease. Every day he told me he loved me, whereas Jack, just fucked me, with a schlong that never got tired. I was shagging Hunter twice a week, and sometimes all weekend, and Jack 4 nights a week, and sometimes on alternate Saturdays when my kids were away at their dad's house. Remembering also that I had my regular clients and newbies, probably 4 a day, 4 days a week, well, my poor kitty was going to be completely fatigued by the time I got to 40! I had never had so much great sex in all my life. I'd been fucked, abused, cared for, spoiled and made love to, but oh my goodness, this was just amazing, and it was happening each and every day, AND I was getting paid to do it. Heaven!

There were several other women in Hunter's life too, all of them E$corts, and all of them vying for his attention.

April, Lucy, Shirley, Clarice and Dina, to name but a few, and all of whom had dated Hunter in the past.

I didn't care about any of them, because I knew I was the mainstay of his attention, but I did know that there was serious jealousy coming from their side, and that they knew very little about me as a human being. The one thing about Hunter that never waned, was his generosity. Spread across all of the women in his life, all of them trying hard to get what they could from this man of means. I, on the other hand, wanted nothing, yet I'd received the most, without asking for anything. The other women just received payment for sex, nothing more than that, no cars, no jewelry, nothing along the lines I'd been gifted. I had it all, and that's when the trouble began. Hunter can be a real asshole sometimes, and he can be that way quite often. I love assholes. I don't know why that is, but the more of an asshole the guy is, the more attracted I am to that man. I have always been that way. Treat me like shit, I will give you the earth, treat me nice, I will run a mile. With Hunter, the moment I met him I realized he was an asshole, there's no other word that describes him, other than perhaps, generous. Hunter is a generous asshole, but he's treated me like a queen, the other E$corts, well, he treats them like dirt, yet, because of his generous ways, they keep coming back for more, hoping to score big, but never succeeding. That brings me back to this situation I encountered, a situation that I didn't count on, but unfortunately was involved in anyways. April, (another E$cort, and also a friend of me and Blondie), and Hunter were having a date, and I believe that Hunter, in his capacity as an asshole, must have picked up April's cell phone at some point in their evening together, and, after scrolling through her appointments, noticed that April and I were scheduled to have a double date with Alfred the Asian. Alfred is a guy that we've all fucked. He's another one with money and a small cock, but a generous guy nonetheless.

As you can now tell, if April or Blondie fuck some guy, he then tends to be passed around to all of us, especially if he has money, and that way we all share in the benefit. It's kind of a trick of the trade. One fuck deserves more and these guys want to pay and conquer as it seems. Fuck one, then fuck 21. It's all part of their game, the fucking game. Anyway, Hunter must have seen the entry in April's diary on her phone, and knowing how he felt about me, he wasn't happy. When I spoke to Hunter, he was as livid as I've ever seen him and frankly, that was just a turn on for me.

"What the fuck are you doing?" he asked me, when we spoke on the phone, "I don't want you seeing Alfred the Asian, and I certainly don't want you seeing April anymore. Got it?"

Wait" I asked him, "how do you know about that?"

He remained silent, a sure sign to me that he'd been snooping.

He was so mad, so upset and so jealous.

With my loyalty, and I use that word kind of loosely, in Hunter's court, I thought about what he'd said, and I called April and told her I couldn't make it for our double date. I felt bad doing this, not only because I was letting April down, but I felt bad for Alfred, who was expecting a threesome, and April had little time left to rearrange it by finding another girl. Then things got really silly. April called Shirley, to see if she would substitute for me, telling Shirley the reason why she needed a third. Shirley went ballistic when April told her the whole story and confirming that I was now in a very serious relationship with Hunter and that he wanted to marry me, so that was the reason I was pulling out of the threesome with Alfred. Shirley and Hunter had also been an item at one point in time, and Shirley was in love with the money Hunter was paying her. But then it ended, because Hunter moved on to, guess who? Me! When Shirley heard this story, she went nuts, telling April that she was totally pissed, that she was in love with Hunter, even though she had a steady boyfriend and was fucking Hunter and many others on the side. You following all of this? It was pure drama, and remember, I didn't really know these ladies that well, they were all long-term friends of Blondie's. I felt really bad. Dina then found out that Hunter was in love with me, and she too went ballistic. She'd been trying for over a year to get Hunter to buy her a car, and when all of this blew up, Dina found out from April that Hunter bought me a car after only knowing me two weeks! A fucking soap opera, real time, with all of these women/E$corts fighting over Hunter, his riches and his adoration of me. And I, well I was the only innocent party in all of this nonsense. I made it clear to all involved that they needed to leave me out of this drama, and that I wasn't in the least bit interested in any of their gripes. This whole scene went down, believe it or not, while I was at South Coast Plaza (a huge indoor mall), one afternoon just before Christmas. My phone was ringing off the hook while I was inside Tiffany's trying to buy Hunter a money clip for Christmas, and you can imagine, as I'm there attempting to shop with my phone continually ringing and all this drama unfolding, the other customers in the stores I was shopping at must have thought they were watching a TV show live!. It was pure mayhem. I had 20 calls from all of them in the space of 10 minutes. Pure Hell and so unnecessary. After I purchased the clip and left the store, I was starved and headed out to Micky D's in the food hall, for respite and sustenance.

Hunter called

"Where are you?" he asked

"Micky D's at SCP, hungry and frustrated"

"I'm at SCP too!" he shouted.

We met up, and Hunter bought me McNuggets and a drink. We chatted for a few minutes, and I replayed the whole story from the past 15 minutes of drama which had just unfolded before my very ears. I went into minute detail, imploring Hunter to talk to all of these women and get them off my back. I also explained that his refusal to let me go on a double date with April and Alfred the Asian, was the sole reason the drama had blown up in my face and now, I was being touted as the 'bad' one in a group of women I could hardly call friends.

Hunter didn't say much in response to all of my woes, but after we'd eaten, and he'd given me a necklace and bracelet from Tiffany's, which was why he'd been in the mall in the first place, I decided to give him the money clip I'd bought for him as a Christmas present, but thought it was more apt to give him it there and then rather than wait until Christmas day. We walked back into the mall and Hunter, taking me by the hand, marched me into a store that I'd never been in before, Channel.

We walked inside

"Why are we in here?" I asked

"You'll see" he replied.

Hunter sauntered over towards a sales assistant, while he simultaneously pointed at a beautiful green and black handbag hanging on the wall. I was a few steps behind him but heard him asking her if she had that bag in all black and not the green and black which was on display. She nodded in the affirmative and went into the back of the store, returning almost immediately with the all-black version.

"There are only 2 of these on the whole planet" she boasted, "and at $5000, I would suggest it's a great investment." She smiled.

"You like it?" Hunter asked me.

"Like it?" I said, bemused by what was going on. "I LOVE IT"

"We'll take it" Hunter told the assistant.

"WTF" I muttered. "Is that for me?"

"Of course. And that's for being the best lady in my life"

He paid and we walked out, me with my handbag and a huge smile from ear to ear, Hunter, with his lady, and a promise from me to stay away from the other women, all of whom he was fucking.

I got home and all I wanted to do was frame that bag. $5000? It all seemed so crazy, and all over some drama that began with a double date.

 thought to myself, I should do this more often!

Hunter's demeanor however, didn't change. He really had a bone up his butt about April and her loose tongue, set on vengeance of some kind. He didn't realize at any point in time that he'd actually been the instigator of the whole problem. He'd had me in tears more than once in our short past, but at that point in time, with all the 'goodies' he was buying for me, those tears soon evaporated and became smiles, even though the smiles were formed from superficial gifting. My contentment for rough sex and crazy dudes, overlapped my abilities to break free and find someone normal, although, to me Hunter was normal. I was always attracted to douche bags. He'd come over one night and told me that he and I had to be exclusive, and he'd done that after I'd told him he could sleep with whoever he wanted. He was adamant, "if you want the goodies, then toe the line" he'd told me. The goodies were nice, but his desire for exclusivity, wasn't. I was still hurting from my divorce and the fact that my ex had cheated on me, and so, with Hunter's words fresh in my mind, I decided to take action.

"You want to be exclusive?" I'd asked him, 'then give up all the other women you're fucking, and I'll do the same with the men"

No sooner than he'd agreed to do so, I found out, almost instantly, he was fucking Dina, and not only was he fucking Dina, he was fucking April again, something I didn't mind, because April is a great person and I love her to bits, but honestly, if Hunter wasn't going to stick to his word, he could go fuck himself. I cried and cried after finding out that he'd broken his promise, but again, what was I supposed to do?

I arranged a date with a guy I'd never met before. He came round to Blondie's home and told me all that he wanted was a blow job. He insisted, without embarrassment of any kind, that he had ED and the only way he could cum was if we found a chair with no arms and I sat on it and then he sat on top of one of my naked legs, the pressure from that leg on his prostate. I'd never heard such BS, but, for the cash, I decided to play along. We had to do all of this with the two of us facing a long mirror in my bedroom, though for what reason, I never found out. I agreed and the fun began. When his weight nearly broke my left leg and my right hand went numb from jerking him off, having gone through 20 minutes of continual movement, up and down, round and round, the fucker wouldn't cum or couldn't cum. In the end, we switched legs and hands, and eventually, after about an hour, he spluttered across the finish line, to the relief of my legs and hands and the poor chair, which had been rocked more than an audience at a Rolling Stones concert!

He gave me $100 for an hour's work, and left, telling me it was our first time and that next time, now that he knew me, it would happen quicker. Yeah, right, I thought to myself, and for $100 I swore he would never come back to visit. I was done.

Remember tattoo guy? He was also back on the scene, again, not paying me enough and sharing me with Blondie, but the tatts and the gold tooth, well, they were just a turn on, so I didn't care. Hunter would have been livid if he knew what was happening behind his back, but he never found out, or he chose to ignore it, in favor of telling me daily that he loved me and weekly, that I was the 'fuck of his life'. I was the fuck of everyone's life, but only Hunter splurged so much cash on me.

The truck he'd bought me was still in his name, and I'd found out that it had cost him $55,000, a small fortune to me. Even though I knew it was really his, I was still enjoying driving it and occasionally fucking Hunter in the back seat of that vehicle, hoping that one day he'd also put my name on the title. My instinct had reminded me that all of these luxuries would eventually vanish,

Hunter would find someone else to splash out on, someone younger, prettier, and in his mind, more deserving, but until that actually happened, I was going to keep taking what he decided to give, in the hope that I not only built-up cash reserves I could eventually live on, but also that I serviced Hunter in a way that would make him hang around for as long as possible. This was a life I'd never imagined, but it was a life I was living, and living it in real time, even though it seemed quite surreal.

Narcissistic Prick

Definition of a narcissist as pulled from the Oxford English dictionary:
A person who is overly self-involved and often selfish.

This is Hunter, and this is exactly why I love the guy. I am attracted to this personality type. Don't ask me why, I just am, although it seems always to be to my detriment!

Hunter picked me up, it was a lovely bright January morning. He's agreed with Blondie to pay me $1100 extra, on top of his usual $6000, to spend the day with him on a whim, and we'd decided to go on a drive. At first, I was rather skeptical, knowing that we'd probably end up fucking in the back of his car all morning, which was the normal routine when Hunter came to collect me, but this time turned out to be slightly different. We fought, regularly, and then made up, even more vigorously than we'd fought, again, a regular occurrence. This particular morning however, Hunter arrived in his '65 Chevy truck, a truck I absolutely hated because of its lack of seat belts, but actually loved, because of the incredible sex we'd had in its flat bed. I reckoned I'd cum more in the flat bed of that Chevy in the 5 months Hunter had known me, than I'd cum in total in the 14 years I'd been married! There was just something about that truck that turned me on, and it wasn't just the way Hunter fingered my pussy when we lay naked on a towel on the bed of that truck, watching the stars and pretending we cared about one another. It was more the smell of the old beast, the truck, not Hunter! The diesel, the metal, the whole magical aroma of the truck's history, which turned me on and made my pussy as loose and as wet as she had ever been. My juices just flowed when Hunter took me into the back of that truck and fucked me, and with that in mind, even though the seat belts were missing, a perfectly legal scenario since the truck dated pre-1970, I was happy in many ways to accompany him on that morning's journey to wherever life was going to take us to. He pulled up, and I got in. As soon as I got in, I could tell he was wasted, not on cocaine, his drug of choice, but on beer, the empty cans, about 5 or 6 of them, strewn on the floor of the passenger side of that truck. Conclusive evidence of a binge filled morning. For Hunter, even this was a low blow. He'd normally entertain his cravings by snorting lines of coke, but when alcohol became his passion, something that happened a little too often for my liking, well, even I didn't know what was going to happen. Because I knew him better than most, the fact that even I didn't know, was frightening.

"You seriously going to drive me in the drunken state you're in?" I asked.

"Get in bitch" he replied.

Now, even though him addressing me in that manner was derogatory, I'd become used to it and ignored it most of the time, only because I knew he cared about me and never really meant it. It was Hunter's way of being falsely macho.

I got in, and we drove off. From the moment his foot hit the accelerator, our fight began. Our fights were always over nothing in particular, but that didn't stop the verbal onslaught that both of us pretended to enjoy. Hunter, the fucking narcissist that he is, was never in the wrong, and on this particular morning, his ability to always be in the right, was violently enhanced by his demeanor and his drunk driving. He was so out of control, driving erratically while he verbally assaulted me. Part of me prayed that a cop, any cop, would come out of nowhere and pull him over. We'd just driven through Huntington Beach on PCH and we were headed south, towards Newport Beach, when suddenly, and deliberately, at 55MPH, Hunter jerked his foot on and off the brake pedal, quickly and precisely, sending my face careering into the dashboard and my body onto the floor of the passenger side of the car. The shock at what had just happened, was only surpassed by the amount of blood that appeared to be running down my chin. Hunter though, kept on driving. He didn't care.

With all the power I had in my lungs, and with an amazing amount of pent-up anger building, I shouted out, "STOP THIS FUCKING TRUCK NOW YOU STUID BASTARD!!!!!!"

He did, but he did it right in the middle of a three-lane highway. There were cars flying past on both sides, all agitated and amazed that we'd pulled up in the middle lane of a 60MPH highway. Hunter didn't seem to care. My lip was burst wide open, there was blood everywhere and people were honking like crazy as they swerved to get past us. It was like something out of those Fast and Furious movies.

"What the fuck is wrong with you?" I asked him.

He just smiled, told me to get back on my seat and began driving again as if nothing had happened.

We drove for another ten minutes, both of us in complete silence, me, with blood all over my clothes, Hunter, with this smile, and evil smile, and a drunken gaze, all over his. We arrived in Newport Beach, he made a right onto a side street and stopped the truck.

"What is your problem?" I asked him.

It was at this point he became remorseful, so much so, that I thought he was about to cry.

Apologizing profusely, and still very much in a drunken state, he leaned over, taking out a wet wipe from the center console of the truck, and began to clean me up. Before he'd finished cleaning me up, we began kissing, then fondling one another and then…..

We fucked in this side street, in full view of anyone who cared to look. He was hard, and apologetic, I was wet, and encouraging. He came, I came, we both came, and all of the previous 30 minutes were instantly forgotten.

'Another typical day with Hunter', I thought to myself, as he pulled his cock out of my pussy and I helped him clean up the mess. It was at this point that Hunter decided to let his emotions out.

Hunter began.

"Your ex-husband knows a friend of mine, Kenny, and Kenny has told him we are dating"

So, my ex had found out from Kenny and not from looking in my car that night? It all began to make sense, or did it?

Hunter's cash kept arriving, along with more gifts and great sex. The sex became better and better, anal in particular, became a favorite. His dick, when it penetrated my ass, would make me cum and squirt from my pussy. It was exhilaration in its fullest and totally orgasmic. Every time Hunter banged me in my ass, I lay in bed, or wherever we were doing it, for a very long time, enjoying what had just happened and relishing the thought that it might not be too long until it happened again. If Hunter hadn't been such a big-headed prick, on one of those occasions when he'd asked me to marry him, and they were becoming a regular occurrence, I might just have said yes. But then, then there was his past.

Hunter always paid for pussy, always had done, and I feared he always would, married or not. He's not a bad looking guy, and why he has to pay to fuck, I just don't get it, but it's probably the inner narcissist that continues to drive him in that direction. His need to control, to judge, to overwhelm and to dominate. His past is littered with E$corts who I now know. All of them are friends with Blondie and all have their own stories to tell, Hunter stories, and all very much centered around money and a requirement to get Hunter to pay for all their needs, which is something I never asked for, but yet receive with gratitude. All of the other woman have begged, cajoled, and influenced him to give up his cash to favor them. I've never done that, because I don't give a fuck about money, especially his money. Yes, the money he gives me is great, the gifts too, but in the long run, no one asked him to do this, especially the gifts. I firmly believe it's just his way of gaining, in his mind, total control over each woman he fucks. After spending months going out with Hunter, I was soon to realize that there wasn't just one or two of these women in his past, there were dozens. Everywhere he took me, dancing, drinking, to the river, to go boating, we would meet or bump into an ex of his, all E$corts. It became silly culminating at a Superbowl party we attended one February. A party I would never forget.

They were all there, seemingly all. I arrived, having spent the weekend at my sister's 28th birthday party in Vegas. That weekend in itself, is a story, a story of drinking, drugs and strip joints. As I said, I arrived, and I was awake, but exhausted from my time in Vegas, and really not in the mood for any form of confrontation. In fact, my only purpose in being there was to make sure Hunter, who was paying me $6000 a month, got his monies' worth, our verbal contract clearly stating I should spend every 3rd Sunday with him, of which, this would be one. Normally we would just go to his place, after a meal or drinks, and fuck for a few hours or until he ran out of sperm, but this party, held at the home of one of his good friends, was, so he'd told me, a mandatory 'must attend' event, because he'd wanted to 'show me off' to the other whores he'd fucked in the past. I had no issue with that, knowing that I was his current favorite, no matter how long or short a time that would be for, and the other women all knew that Hunter was paying me and giving me much more than any of them had been given in the past. Jealousy has a way of hitting the gossip rounds and spreading like an out-of-control wildfire, especially when that fire was burning between 6 or 8 ex's who all wanted more from a man who was giving me his all.

My immediate reaction, having just got out of the car after my 4-hour drive back from Vegas, was to play it all very cool and to not get involved. I didn't have to wait too long for things to start spiraling downhill, and downhill with such a rapid decent that it took even me by surprise.

Shirley was first, accompanied by her 'boyfriend', who, honestly speaking, was a real douche Bag. Hunter was standing right next to me as she approached and out the side of his mouth he whispered, "here comes trouble".

"Hi Hunter" Shirley said, and then as she looked at me, she said sarcastically,

"oh, and how is your fiancée?"

Fiancée?? What the fuck was she talking about?

"Of course" she continued, "you know me and Hunter fucked just last week?"

Well, firstly, she was spouting all of this right in front of her 'boyfriend', and also Hunter, who was standing there with his drink in one hand and with his other hand holding mine, unable to take the smile of his face, and unable to deny what she'd just told me.

Quite nonchalantly, I said, "Do I really give a fuck what Hunter did with you last week?" And honestly, I really didn't! I was determined not to be dragged into any kind of cat-fight with this silly bitch, and decided to unhinge my hand from Hunter's and walk away. As I did this, Shirley became agitated, as she did so her verbiage, none of it very pleasant, began to spew, two of Hunter's other ex-lovers walked over and joined in to what was about to become, a melee!

I wasn't having any of it. I departed, not giving one solitary fuck what Hunter had done, either in his past, present or future, but these stupid women refused to believe I didn't care and continued with their disgusting mouthy barrage, probably in the hope I would take the bait and begin some kind of fight with the three of them. No chance. Not only would I have taken all three of them out in a fist fight, I would have drawn so much blood, we'd have all been swimming in it for weeks to come. These were 3 vicious and neglected women who hated the fact that I was now enjoying the benefit of their demise. From the opposite side of the room, I turned back and surveyed the situation. Hunter was standing there, irate that he'd ended up in the middle, and I could see from the look in his eyes that all control was about to be lost. An explosion of temper, his uncontrollable temper, was about to emerge. The three women were wallowing in their own self-inflicted glory, while their partners were just looking around like spare pricks at a hippie's wedding. There was, in my humble opinion, nothing to lose.

I stood up quietly, but quickly, on a chair, and, at the top of my lungs, I shouted out for all 100 people to hear,

"I am sure you all know that Hunter over there" I said, while pointing directly at him, "has fucked almost every woman in this room, including me." There was complete silence, and it seemed that even the noise from the music and TVs had disappeared into oblivion as my voice echoed around the room, and I continued on my rant.

"Well," I said, now lowering my voice just a little, in order for my planned grand finale to sound incredibly loud and intimidating, something I had planned in my own mind, and was about to execute with perfection. "Well, I, as his current beau, DO NOT GIVE A FUCK WHAT HUNTER DOES, OR WHAT HE'S DONE IN HIS PAST. DO I MAKE MYSELF CLEAR? I DO NOT GIVE A FUCK!" So, with that said," my voice now returning to its normal tone, "let's all watch the game and have some fun"

People started to chat again, and laugh, and then applaud. There were shouts of 'you go girl', and several people, none of the three moronic woman who'd started this mess, came over and gave me a hug. It was over, I hoped for good, and we were all about to enjoy the party, but not before Hunter in all his narcissistic glory sauntered over towards me and said, quite calmly, "babe, you were awesome, and I need to fuck you right now, in the car, the bathroom or right here on the floor in front of everyone. I am soooooo turned on" he said. I took him by the hand, making sure to show the three bitches who was boss, led him across the room, into the bathroom and fucked his brains out, twice! I made sure to scream loud enough to satisfy Hunter's ego and to piss off royally, all three woman who'd tried to wind me up earlier. Either way, it worked a treat, and that was the last time any of those women every tried to pick a fight with me. Yes, Hunter is a narcissist, I know it, he knows it, although he'd never admit it, and the rest of the world knows it, but for that period of time, he was my narcissist and no one else's. It would be his way or the highway, and his way suited me down to the ground, including the way he just kept filling up my bank account, and knowing that I emptied it just as fast as he'd fill it, then filling it up again. Maybe this really was love? Or maybe just infatuation.

Periods

A red flag to a bull is how Jack behaved when he fucked me while I was on my period. Sex between us was free and easy. It was also magnificent. I have no idea why some men turn me on so much, but Jack was one of those men. Whenever he touched me, it set off internal light bulbs that flickered into sensational, orgasmic, climaxes, topped only by the size of his penis, which was not only long, it was thick too. I loved our gratuitous sex, and never regretted for one moment that Jack always fucked me for free. Our intimacy have me so much, physically and mentally, and it never really mattered that I was opening my legs for free. Jack was special and although Hunter, amongst others, paid regularly to keep me in the style I was surely accustomed to, Jack made me happy, at least sexually. He wasn't wealthy by any means, but his cock in my pussy made me feel like a billionairess. The feeling was so different, and I know I've said that Hunter was great sex too, but Jack was just different.

We fucked at least once a week, and we fucked for hours and hours. Time flew by when we were together, and whenever Jack left me, it was as if my heart stopped, pondering the time, counting down every second until he returned to do it all over again. If I was going to marry again, it would be Jack and not Hunter. But thinking hard about this made me sad because with Jack, I would be poor, and knowing that sex never lasts forever….

Jack came over to my home one morning to fix a few loose light fittings. He'd done a great job and done it well within the time he'd said it would take. We decided, to enact early morning glory. He raped me, kindly of course, thrusting my legs apart as he ripped off my panties, the ones Hunter had bought for me, and panties that Hunter normally kept. Did I tell you that? Hunter bought lingerie for me, fucked me in it and then kept it as a souvenir. No clue what he did with it, but I never saw it again, and then a new set of something or other would appear, until that too was soiled and laid to rest in one of Hunter's drawers. Hey, everyone has some kind of fetish, and who am I to judge?

After the panties came of, and with Jack as hard as I'd ever seen him, he'd obviously looked down towards my crack and realized that I had a tampon inside me. My period had begun the day before, and although this never bothered Hunter, as I have mentioned before, this was a first for me and Jack. Without much warning, he pulled it out and inserted his huge hard cock inside me.

"You don't care about the blood?" I asked him, as I gasped for breath when the head of his cock hit my cervix.

He said very little, thrusting up and in and all around, as if his life depended on it. It was marvelous, sensational, and often overwhelming, as my juices, accompanied by a few spots of blood, began to roll down my pussy and into my crack and then onto my legs. Jack was a man possessed, pushing as far up inside my vagina as his cock would go, and bringing me to orgasm several times in a row, before withdrawing, teasing me by holding his cock in his right hand and banging its head of my clit, like a drum, until I came again, and again. Then, as he was about to re-insert it inside me, he spoke for the first time since we'd become engrossed in passion.

"Bet you $100 you wouldn't suck my cock now?" he laughed

"Why not?" I asked him

"It's all bloody"

"It's my blood"

"You wouldn't?"

"I would!"

And I did. I took his cock in my hand, and I licked it from top to bottom and then I inserted it in my mouth, moving up and down on it, just the way he liked me to, until he couldn't hold it any longer and came in my mouth.

"Swallow it bitch" he laughed, and I did, slowly and deliberately, sensing not only his intense admiration and appreciation for what I just did, but also his disgust.

"Now," I said, after swallowing his load plus the blood, "kiss me with your tongue!"

Jack jumped off the bed, went over to where his clothes lay and took $100 out of his wallet. He threw it at me and said,

"You win, I can't do that!"

I felt triumphant and fully satisfied. I felt at ease with myself, and most of all, I felt content. Jack couldn't believe what I'd done, and frankly, neither could I, but however disgusting it might sound, I enjoyed every moment of it, because it was with Jack, and if I had to do it again, I would do it in a heartbeat.

Obviously my three kids and my parents have no clue what I do for a living, if you can call this a real living, and if they ever found out, God only knows how'd they would feel about it. For years I've led this double life and on one occasion, it almost blew up in my face, completely by accident.

There's a shop in OC called Wicked Ways. It's a sex shop, selling everything from toys to lingerie to porno movies, which, by the way, I fail to understand how or why anyone buys, because you can see anything you want on line, for free! Anyway, Hunter wanted me to dress up in all red lingerie for Valentine's Day. He wanted red bra and panties, red garter belt, red stockings, red shoes and he wanted me to put on red lipstick and have red, strawberry flavored condoms, not that we ever used them anymore. Hunter was riding me bareback most of the time. For those of you who are unfamiliar with the term 'bareback', what it means is straight sex, no condoms, cum inside me and then clean up the mess. Birth control optional, but certainly essential, especially at my young age. No more babies for me, thank you! For Hunter, when he asks, I provide, after he provides the cash of course. I was off to Wicked Ways to spend, spend, spend!

When I walked into the store, late one Wednesday morning, I decided it would be best to look around and then seek the help of a sales associate, when I wanted to start trying things on. Normally I wouldn't bother, but Hunter was splashing the cash and I wanted everything to look perfect, including me!

After about 25 mins of shopping around, I had accumulated a huge pile of items, some of which were beautiful silky lingerie items and other's that were red whips, hand cuffs and bottles of flavored lube. I had decided to go above and beyond what Hunter had asked me to do and to put on a real show for him. I took all of the items I'd picked up around the store to the front desk and was about to ask the lady at the cash register for assistance, when suddenly I received a tap on my shoulder. Without thinking, I looked around and when I saw who it was, I nearly died. My step son, yes, my step son, Gordon's oldest boy, a boy he'd had with his first wife, long before we'd met. He now standing next to me, with a very pretty young lady, probably his girlfriend, looking me up and down, and looking all of my future purchases up and down too. This was a nightmare waiting to happen. The thoughts that ran through my head at that moment in time were

"Oh Fuck I am dead"

"Shit, now Gordon will know"

"Jesus Christ, what the fuck is Cody doing here?"

"Hello" Cody said to me with a huge grin on his face. He knew that his dad and I were no longer together, but he had no idea what I did to make money.

"I see you have plans tonight?" he suggested. The cheeky bastard was making assumptions, and as I have a mouth that most people could swim in, it didn't take me more than a nano second to bite back. "Fuck you Cody, what I buy is my business, not yours, now what the fuck are you doing in here?" I spat back. "And who's your friend?" I asked, pointing at the skinny brunette with the tattoos who stood next to him.

He was extremely embarrassed and realized his mistake. He'd always been scared of me, even though our age differential was minimal, and our relationship fairly close. I think it's because I can be very aggressive, if not on the outside, certainly from within, and I hate BS, which at that moment, seemed prevalent.

"This is Martha" he said, introducing me to the brunette. "We are going to a Valentine's party this week and wanted to get dressed to impress"

Cody was blushing now.

He continued, "you won't tell dad, will you?"

"Fuck that C." I said to him, "your father and I hardly talk and it's none of his business how you waste your money!"

The look of relief on his face said it all. Very quickly he said to me, "OK great, I'll just carry on with shopping then, enjoy the day" And fasted then he'd appeared, Cody and the brunette, vanished, filled with either embarrassment or dread, but either way, I realized at that point in time, the world was a very small place and I was going to have to be more careful if I wanted to keep my E$corting ways a complete secret. I'd always wondered what would happen if someone I knew booked me for a date, by mistake. I don't show my face in my Ad's, but so far that has never happened, and right now, my secret life, the life of an E$cort, remains buried where only I can find it, hopefully never to be uncovered.

That last story about dressing up in Red, reminds me of a date I once had in Nashville, with one of the Tennessee Titan football team players.

I'd just split up from my husband and I wanted sex. I'd already spoken to Blondie in California and decided to go back there, to my home town, and become an E$cort. This particular night, after talking to Blondie for over an hour on the phone, she'd encouraged me to go out and have some fun in Nashville before I returning to Cali.

"Go out and enjoy yourself" she'd said, "find a guy and fuck him, and see if you like it or not?"

I hadn't had sex in months, Gordon was fucking E$corts at that point in our marriage, and I was really horny, but to go out, just pick someone up and fuck them? Well, Blondie was right. If I couldn't do that, how could I be an E$cort?

Me, and two of my girlfriends, hit the bars of Nashville that same night, a Friday night in June, where the weather was warm, the bars were hot and the men even hotter. I had on my favorite low-cut red dress, a dress that enhanced my 36D boobs like no other dress could, and I thought to myself, 'if I can't get fucked tonight wearing this dress, then I can't get fucked at all'

Downtown Nashville, on Broadway, is just amazing. One whole street of restaurants and bars, all right next to one another, each one serving better BBQ then the next, and all playing live music, some with five floors and a different band on each floor. It's amazing and I can understand why it's now getting the nickname, Nash-Vegas, because everyone wants to party there. According to recent articles I've read, there are now more bachelor and bachelorette parties in Nashville, than there are in any other city in the USA. It's a fun place, with music and food that caters to anyone's taste, no matter how young or how old. Although my time in Nashville hadn't been great, on this particular night, I was determined to have fun because I knew I was about to go back West and this would probably be my last hoorah in the city I'd lived for the past two years.

We took an Uber downtown from the suburb I lived in, a journey of about 15 minutes, but by the time we were dropped off, all three of us had already downed a bottle of Skyy vodka, and we were ready to raise hell. We exited the car, which had dropped us off one block from Broadway, and we decided to go eat before we drank any more. Jacks on Broadway, a great place for incredible BBQ, was our intended destination. The sun was just setting, so as I recall, it was around 8.45 PM and we were all starving. The thing I hated most about living in Nashville were the bugs that just enveloped the city in the summer. I seemed to feel under constant attack by a multitude of varying insects, 24 hours a day, 7 days a week, for months on end, and I just hated it. Walking in the downtown area, my body seemed less susceptible to being bitten, but just as we came to the stop light opposite Jacks BBQ, I felt this crawling sensation on the back of my neck, a sensation that really freaked me out. I was about to pull my right hand up to swat whatever it was that was crawling on me, when suddenly and out of nowhere, another hand was on my neck, ridding my flesh of that unwanted and utterly disliked beastie. I presumed at first that it was one of my girlfriends who'd spotted the intruder, but as I turned around to thank her, I was confronted by this stunning tall, blue-eyed, blond, surfer looking dude, a total God. I was shocked at first to find his hand held high, still holding the bug that he'd removed from my neck.

"I think this belongs to you?" he said, smiling and exposing a set of perfectly white teeth, the likes of which I'd not seen since sitting in row two of the Donny and Marie show in Las Vegas some years back.

This guy, after I'd looked him up and down, was huge. Not just huge, but massive. One of the largest guys I had ever met, and with the body of a God. He wore a sleeveless vest and a pair of tight-fitting jeans and his 'guns' were definitely out and on show for the world to admire.

"Lost for words?" he asked me, "or are you just scared shitless I'll put it back where it wants to belong?" he laughed, and so did I.

'Thanks" I said, while I continued to gawk at his body.

"Where are you off to?" he asked

"BBQ, over there, at Jacks" I said, as I pointed across the street to our proposed final destination.

"You with anyone in particular?" was his next question.

I introduced him to my two friends.

"Would you two ladies mind if I took this gorgeous lady in red here out for a drink or three?" he was talking now to Carol and Jody, my buddies.

They giggled and said they had no problem with that at all.

"You going to ask me or tell me I am going somewhere with you?" I said to his face.

"You, sweetheart, are coming with me!"

"Oh" I said, jokingly," I love it when a man forces me to do anything!"

"Later darling, that comes much later" he replied, and with that, he grabbed my hand and whisked me away, leaving Carol and Jody for dust. In fact, I never saw either of them again for about a week. But again, that's another story.

We will call this guy Dan, for the sake of his privacy, but I can tell you, it turned out that Dan, was traded from an NFL team on the west coast to the Tennessee Titans, and had arrived in Nashville just three weeks earlier. He was still finding his way about town when he'd met me, and boy, did that chance encounter turn into a fun 24 hours.

The first place he took me to was a bar, with country music blaring. He told me his name. the second, a BBQ place, not Jacks, and he told me his age, then on the 3rd stop, another bar, but this time with rock music playing louder than anyone could bare, he told me he wanted to fuck me.

We left, almost immediately, grabbing an Uber to some large home outside of Nashville, in a place I could never imagine living, due to my lack of wealth. We entered the home by the rear door, because Mr. Football, wanted to show me his expansive pool and jacuzzi, and before we made it through his back door and upstairs to his extremely large bed, something that would happen shortly after, we were stripping each other naked on his patio, and fondling all the parts that required fondling, before diving into the pool and fucking underwater. This was something I'd never done before, but had dreamt of doing for many years. Mr. Football was huge, in fact he'd probably got the largest cock I'd ever seen, along with muscles to match, muscles everywhere. But it was his cock I wanted, and once he entered me, even though I'd had three kids, he took up the whole of my vagina and more, making me squirt right into his pool and orgasm before he'd even begun to thrust. When the thrusting began, it never ceased, at least not for hours, as he pummeled my pussy until she was exhausted. After the pool, came the jacuzzi, then the couch then the bed, then complete fatigue. It was then 2 AM and I'd been fucked so hard, I just didn't want to leave. He suggested we rest then try again. I suggested we try again and then rest. We compromised. I sucked him dry and then, after swallowing his load, his second load, I conked out and fell asleep. We woke around 9Am, me first, and then a restless Mr. Football.

"Horny?" he asked.

"Duh!" I replied

So, we fucked again, this time for an hour, and then he made me breakfast. I had time to spare, it was Saturday morning and my ex had the kids, I asked him if we could swim. He agreed. We swam and then fucked in his pool again, only this time, when he was done, I came off his huge cock and released his mess, into the pool water.

"Guess the pool man will have his work cut out this week?" I told him, while winking and suggesting he fuck me again. He though, had had enough, and with some kind words, suggested I get dressed and leave. I had no issue with this and complied with his wishes. After calling another Uber and departing, I was on my way home when I realized I'd left the red belt to my red dress at his home.

"Turn around" I informed the driver, "I left my belt at that home. Like Magnum PI, the Uber driver did a quick U-turn in the middle of a busy road and we headed back to Mr. Football's home.

The Uber parked, I got out and rang the bell. Mr. Football came to the door.

"Listen" I said, "I'm not stalking your dick, I just forgot my belt, can I please come in and get it?"

He allowed me back in and I retrieved the belt.

"Come back again soon" he told me, as I exited the home once again and got back into the Uber.

I never saw him again, but I've watched him on TV many times. Oh, my, the size of that cock still makes me salivate, even today, 3 years later.

My mind was made up. I could fuck anyone, especially if I was being paid to do so, and the moral of the story was, wear red when possible, because that color brought out the Devil in me for sure.

Trust Issues

Sometimes, when you think you can trust someone, well, not trust, but you feel they have a certain respect for you, a respect that is undeniable, perhaps fragile, but certainly undeniable, and that respect is suddenly blown away but some stupid act that the other party enact, that respect then vanishes and all-out war prevails.

Valentine's weekend. One of my favorites, not that I loved it when I was married because my ex-husband just wanted sex without all the romance, but now, after becoming single, that particular day turned out to be a smorgasbord of gifts and great sex, and a day I looked forward to all year. I had men buying me rings, necklaces, chocolates, adding $200 to $300 as tips, pleading their love for me, and each year I remained single, I loved Valentine's Day even more.

Hunter called, a week prior to this particular Feb 14, asking if he could spend that day with me, the whole day, and that he would pay me $1500 for my time and buy me 'the gift of a lifetime!'

How could I refuse? Only Jack had also called, asking for exactly the same thing and but promising to make me the 'the greatest meal' I'd ever eaten and fuck me for 5 straight hours, unfortunately for me though, without paying.

No choice, Hunter won out. I made plans. Money talks.

2 days before, this would be the evening of February 12th, I received a call from Lucy. I was with Hunter at the time, we'd just fucked and I was cleaning up his mess from the wooden desk that had become our regular bed in his sparce, but clean, office.

"Honey," Lucy asked, "want to do a double with me tonight?"

"How much?" I asked her. Hunter was right beside me, and he whispered, "are you going to fuck someone else after just fucking me?" I waved him away, acting like an empress on her throne. Be gone with you! I motioned.

Remembering that Hunter and Lucy used to bang one another, and remembering Hunter knew most of what I did, for money, but not for free, I told Lucy I'd be happy too, after she informed me, I'd get $900 for 2 hours work. Hunter offered to drive me to Lucy's home.

We arrived, my pussy still dripping wet from its 'Hunter fuck" and I got out of the car, telling Hunter to come back and collect me after I'd finished. He agreed.

I entered Lucy's home and her client was already there, waiting patiently for me to arrive to join in the party. He was a slim, older guy, grey beard, puffy tired eyes and glasses and a set of the yellowest teeth I had ever seen. With me in my own little world, where nothing is sacred, I took one look at this dude and shouted out, "No way I am kissing you dude!" The look on Lucy's face was priceless, and I honestly believed she was about to clock me on my chin. Bam!! Kapow! $900 down the drain.

She held her temper, ushering 'yellow teeth', into the bedroom, where we quickly undressed him, bathed him and then fucked him. It didn't take too long, the guy came in moments, and after asking very nicely if he could cum again, at which point I was already walking out the bedroom door, pulling my panties up as I exited, Lucy told him she'd be delighted to accommodate all his needs for another $500. The guy bailed immediately, leaving the $2000 on her dresser, $900 of that was for me. I called Hunter.

"Come on back" I told him, and believe it or not, he was there in moments. I don't think he ever left. Jealous prick!

Hunter came inside Lucy's home and they hugged, like the long-lost friends they were not! I could tell he had something else on his mind, something that wasn't about collecting me and taking me home. "You guys want to fuck me?" he suggested.

Lucy took the lead.

"$500 each, no negotiation" Ah, she knew him well. He took out the cash, I got naked yet again, and it all kicked off. Or did it? For someone who did nothing but talk badly about her ex, Lucy was so into Hunter, it was frightening. Hunter, who also spoke nothing but trash about Lucy, was into her like they were long lost lovers with a flame to rekindle and no time to do it. I, on the other hand, felt like a spare pussy at a wedding. I was sidelined, blindsided, left out, tossed, and as I watched them go at each other like two rabid dogs in heat, I wondered what the heck I was doing there in the first place. Occasionally Hunter would come over to me and finger me, but his main thrust, so to speak, was definitely with Lucy. There was no disputing their chemistry and eventually, after poking her vagina with his cock for about 45 minutes, Hunter came all over my tits, laughing as he did so and saying to me, "at least you're good for something bitch!" I was gutted, in fact, I was so hurt, I told him, "Stick your fucking cash up your ass you cunt!" as I stormed out the room, once again, picking up my panties as I left.

Hunter and Lucy went at it again. Was there no stopping this man? I waited in her kitchen until they were done, and when the two of them appeared, Lucy's hand, flush with Hunter's cash, she marched right over to me, whispered in my right ear, 'don't be jealous bitch," and thrust 5 crisp $100 bills into my pocket. Again, Hunter just laughed. I was fuming.

"Take me home" I demanded. And he did, not saying a single word to me all the way back to my house. As I exited his car, I heard the faint sound of his voice saying 'see you on Valentine's Day sexy", which just wound me up even more, so I slammed his car door and stormed off. "He pays me well" I kept telling myself, but it didn't matter. I was jealous, and when I am jealous, there's no getting over it quickly, unless…..

Jack!

Thoughts were always going through my head about getting together with Jack. Although we had gratuitous sex, and my mind set was only to make money, the sex we did have was so good and so powerful, it seemed to always kick me out any negativity that surrounded me when Hunter was on the scene. With that in mind, I picked up the phone when I got home and called Jack, making it clear I had one thing, and only one thing, on my mind. His attendance, was not requested, but demanded. It never failed with him. He got in his car, came over and stayed for 24 hours. All we did was fuck, and all that happened was, yes, you guessed it, my mood shifted from the negative to the positive, in a very short space of time. I don't know why it happened that way, and why Jack did to me what no other man could do, but he did, and that was all I wanted. Relief, pure relief and 100% satisfaction. I made a mental note, never marry anyone who was anyone other than Jack, if he ever offered.

Valentine's day arrived and it was date day with Hunter. I was reasonably excited, knowing that he was going to pay me extra, since it fell on a weekend and that a gift was sure to be something, he'd gone out of his way to procure, making certain his narcissistic ego entertained spending no less than 5-grand on whatever it was going to be.

After one or two calls back and forth making plans, Hunter asked me to meet him at Huntington Beach, at a resort hotel, which was quite close to my house. He'd booked a room, organized room service and specified that I should not only bring my bikini, but also as much booze as I thought we'd consume. I took the bikini, some makeup, in a small case, and 6 bottles of wine, and champagne. Party time!

It all began so well. We hugged, he said sorry for what he'd done with Lucy, and we opened our first bottle. The room was massive, in fact, it was a suite that was almost larger than my apartment. It had two bedrooms, and a private veranda with a small dipping pool and jacuzzi. The TV was about 100 inches wide, more like a cinema screen and the bed was round, not oblong, all quite amazing really. I had never seen anything quite like it, and I thought I'd seen it all.

We partied all afternoon, and into the night. Food arrived, and we ate, then more food arrived and we ate again, all sandwiched by sex, some good and some bad, but nothing like the sex with Jack. Nighttime came, Hunter paid me, $3000, as agreed, and we settled down and went to sleep. I was quite drunk, reasonably content, and very well taken care of in the pussy department. As I was about to doze off, Hunter brought out my Valentine's gift. It was a beautiful ruby ring, which unfortunately didn't fit, but he told me he'd have it refitted as soon as possible so I could wear it and enjoy it. Not too shabby a day after all.

I slept about 8 hours, something I didn't normally do, but when I awoke, Hunter was nowhere to be seen. And then I heard noise coming from the other bedroom, presumably it was him, so I relaxed, and looked for my phone, something I did, first thing every morning, to make sure there were no emergencies, and to see what else was going on around the planet. It was no place to be seen. I could have sworn I'd left it on the nightstand next to the bed. Sometimes when you misplace something, you lose your bearings slightly and, in this instance, that's exactly what happened. It took me a few minutes to remember where I was, and what I was doing there, and then that noise from the other room began again. It sounded like someone or something was breaking. I got out of bed, naked of course, "Hunter?" I shouted.

As I walked out of the bedroom, into the lounge area, what I saw was quite unbelievable.

Hunter was standing by a window, there was glass all over the floor, he had my cell phone in his hands and he too, was naked.

"You fuck" he began, "you fucking bitch!", he continued, "Fucking guys for free, fucking more than one I see, and not only that, you keep tabs?" Hunter had taken my phone, while I was asleep, and gone through it, one screen at a time, picking out all of my carefully edited notes, and deciding in his own mind, what was upsetting for him and what wasn't.

"That's nice, taking my phone and going through it while I'm asleep, you fucking bastard!"

I was in no mood for this, but I retaliated anyway. The battle had begun, in fact, this wasn't a battle, it was a full out war.

Hunter, in his anger, and after reading some of my messages and texts, had become so insanely violent, that he'd smashed 4 or 5 glasses on the tiled floor. There was no way I could walk across the room to him nor he to me, fearing I would cut my naked feet to shreds on the broken glass. This ended up being a good thing I suppose, otherwise we would have probably killed one another.

My phone, as Hunter had now seen, was arranged beautifully. I had lists of clients, the amounts they paid me, when I'd met them, what we'd done, how many times I'd seen them and a star rating based on their performance and my willingness to see them again. This list, Hunter didn't care about. He knew what I did and he accepted it. However, there was another list, and that list had driven him to the brink of insanity. My list of freebies. When he'd found that list, a list with 4 or 5 guys on it that I'd fucked for free, and often without condoms, all written clearly and concisely so even a fool could understand its meaning, well that list had put him over the top. He screamed and shouted and made accusations, all the time threatening to withdraw all financial support and to take back the car he'd given me, saying that I was nothing but a 'whore bitch slut' and that he never wanted to see me again. I really believed this was the end of our relationship and even though he'd been wrong to take my phone and go through it, I had been stupid to make these lists and not password protect them from the beginning.

Hunter threw my phone across the room and over the broken glass, so that it landed on the carpet where the bedroom met the lounge. It landed with a bump, after which, he stormed out of the room, with his case, having fumbled his way to getting dressed as we argued. As he left, he told me in no uncertain terms, "you can pay the hotel bill and for the damages too" And with that, he was gone.

Perhaps some of you reading this book will judge me, and my behavior, especially those of you will limited sexual experience. I'm sure there are many of you who think I'm a slut, a whore, a hooker, or whatever other derogatory term you would like to find, that might sum up my incredible sexual appetite. The true fact of the matter is, I am a horny bitch, driven by sexual desire and a wanton thirst to taste and experience as many men as I can, before I become old and withered and then drop dead. I flatly refuse to die as a frustrated spinster. That would be the worst of all nightmares for me and it's why I never really believed I would live to a ripe old age, nor would I really want to. If I can't be desired, if I can't turn a man on, even when I get into my 60's and 70's, then I just don't see the point in living. I need sex, I crave sex, I am a true sex addict, and boy, am I proud of being that way! As I have told you in previous chapters, there are some guys I fuck for free, just because I want to, and there are many guys I charge, Hunter, of course, my number one love, at this moment in time. But with all the exposure I receive, the situations I put myself in, and the magnificent body I have, I've found that when I am being 'courted' by any man who has tattoo's all over his body, even if it's just a few words he's said to me in a bar, or a nightclub, not even pick-up lines, just words, like "Hi Sexy", "Wow, nice to meet you", simple stuff like that, if the tattoo's shine, I am smitten, and that's why I have what I call my 'posse' of guys who I fuck for free. They are all covered in tatts, top to bottom, all of them are younger than me, and none of them pay for the infrequent pleasure of fucking me. I love it, they love it and when feelings are mutual, all is well in my world. Jack, of course, was my favorite, and so he's the one I've talked the most about when recounting all my memoires. He's also the one with the craziest of sex drives, the cutest of smiles and the very best tattoos.

Jack collected me for lunch, just after I'd paid the hotel bill Hunter lumbered me with. I was in a foul mood, but after being taken to a local Mexican joint, a drive-through, not a sit-down place, Jack and I were munching away at some amazing tacos in the parking lot of this restaurant, when suddenly, he took out his cock, sandwiched it in between his taco shell and invited me to "go for it"!

When it comes to Jack, and sex, there is rarely, if ever, any need for a second invitation. We shut the car windows, I threw the rest of my lunch in the back seat and began to 'munch' on Jack's taco. Within moments, I was sucking up all the guacamole and salsa spilling down his erection, while Jack, lay back on the car seat, relaxed, erect and in heaven. When it came to the chicken pieces, I gobbled them up, as I stroked his trunk. And before I could finish up, he came, but not in my mouth. By this time, I had my hand around his cock, so his cum was all over my fingers, looking just like a spider's web.

"Lick it all off" Jack challenged me

I did, every drop, mixing it boldly with bits of chicken and lettuce and cheese. It tasted amazingly good, so I offered him a bite! He cowered in the opposite direction, his face suggesting that I was a disgusting bitch, which, was probably true, and telling me he wanted no part of this 'feast'. I laughed out loud, spitting little bits of this concoction onto his face, which made him even more disgusted. After he'd cleaned off and I'd finished eating, we drove off, noticing that our swift sexual encounter had been witnessed in part by some of the regular lunch crowd that this restaurant, who, in their appreciation of our performance, began to applaud as our vehicle left the parking lot. Nothing like making a mark on people's days? Right?

This whole episode revived me, and made the situation with Hunter, the broken glass, the hotel bill etc, just vanish from my mind, cheering me up no end. And that, folks, is why I often fuck for free and keep one or two 'nice boys', on the side. It's just in case of emergencies! That day was more than just an emergency, it was a necessity too.

If you are one of those people who've decided to judge me, and you wonder what I do with my kids when I am working, let me tell you, you do not have to worry. My kids are just fine. In fact, my relationship with my kids is as strong as it's ever been, but their relationship with their father is awful. My youngest dislikes him more than anyone else on the planet, which is sad, but true. She hates going to stay with him, something that is mandated by the courts, and something she has to do, every 2 weeks. There have been many occasions when I've received calls asking me to come and collect her, just hours into her weekend visits. She and her father simply don't get along, and she insists that he talks nothing but crap about me to all of them, and that crap is very off-putting for a 10-year-old who just adores her mother. My ex calls me a whore in front of them. I might be a whore, but my daughter doesn't need to know that. I am in the process of finding a way to make their stays with him shorter or non-existent. That takes time and money and a good attorney. Talking of which, my DUI attorneys, remember them? Well, I have now fucked them both 5 times, and I am still awaiting the court date to resolve my situation. My debt to them is fully paid, but my debt to society has yet to be determined. I also fuck my weed guy for free. He's a hoot. He's short, podgy and smells like marijuana, constantly. In my life though, it matters not, and he brings me a never-ending supply of the magic leaf in return for gratuitous sex. It's not that bad, but for him, it's amazingly good because he's not getting it anywhere else. God help that man if I decide to stop smoking it!

THE ORGY

Listcrawler, the web site that I use to advertise my services, brings me more than some occasionally interesting offers. Some I like to read, and some I just ignore. One sunny afternoon, when things were really slow, I received an email from a guy with a handle, Thor1.

"Interested in meeting you. I host an Orgy once a month. You come highly recommended, so if you would like to earn big bucks, message me back and we can discuss"

Well, I'd never been invited to an orgy before, and I'd been very curious to maybe try one out. I'd heard from other E$cort girls that orgies were quite fun and very erotic. I emailed him back accepting his offer, and within moments he called me. The deal was simple.

Thursday February 27 at a home in Westminster CA, one that Thor1 had rented, 18 guys, 10 girls. $800 total to me, 1 PM to 4 PM. All the girls came from the same web site that I advertised and the guys were all members of that site, so they were classed and vetted as being 'safe'. I talked it over with Blondie and then decided to accept.

Two weeks later, and after several phone calls between me and Thor1, the deal was set. He would come to Blondie's home to meet me, pay me in advance and I would give him a blow job, his way of 'sealing the deal'. I was looking forward to performing on his cock, but Thor1 flaked and didn't show up. The question then was, what to do? Blondie suggested I call him again and tell him my rate just went up to $1000, but I didn't want to rock the boat, hoping that if I did actually make it to the orgy that it would open up the door to so many more new clients. My intention was to perform like a demon and gain the confidence of at least half of the guys who were attending, bringing them into my client portfolio at $400 per hour.

"Thor" I said, as he answered the phone with a very softly spoken tone, "What the fuck dude? You never showed up, and I ain't coming until you pay me" I was so abrupt, so aggressive and yet, so amiable, all at the same time. I can be good in that sense. Always getting what I want or need, with aggression and love, all wrapped up in one sexy little voice.

"Sorry, I got waylaid, if you come an hour early on Thursday, park outside and then call me, I'll bring the cash out to you and then you can come in after. I don't want any of the other girls to see you get paid before they do. None of them are being paid in advance"

"Listen dude, if I don't get my shit, you don't get to fuck me? Understand?"

He did.

Thursday came around and I was nervous. I drove to Blondie's place and she helped me get ready. I was in two minds what to wear, even though I knew I would be naked for three whole hours, in my own mind, first impressions are what count the most, I put on tight leather pants and a skimpy cut off top, with no bra. I looked 'da bomb!' and Blondie reinforced that by telling me that she'd fuck me if I came in to her home dressed like that. With my little 'whore' purse over my shoulder, I drove ten miles to the house that Thor1 had rented for the afternoon. Excited as heck, I pulled up to this massive house in a quiet neighborhood, just off the main drag in Westminster. In fact, it was eerily quiet, which kind of spooked me out. It was noon on a Thursday, and it seemed that no one was around, not even the local cats and dogs. I texted Thor1. He came out, took one look at me, all dressed up, sitting in the front seat of my car, and immediately got hard. I could just tell he was desperate to jump me there and then. Thor1 was short, fit, kind of bulky, and reasonably good looking. He was in his late 30's or early 40's and definitely Hispanic.

"Got my cash babe?" I asked him.

He reached in through the driver's window, which I'd cracked open just a little, pushed in $800, and then said, "You fuck me first, understand?"

I did. He was getting it before anyone else, and he'd made that very clear. He was paying me, so who was I to argue. Thor1 told me to wait in my car for 25 minutes and then to park in his driveway, and come inside the house. He said that by that time, most of the guys would be there and all of the girls would have arrived. I waited.

While I was waiting, my nerves tingling, I took a shot or two of vodka from a flask I stashed in the glove box of my car. This inevitably calmed me down. I waited.

I called Blondie, telling her I was doing fine and that I'd been paid. I waited.

I surfed the internet for five minutes, on my iPhone, to kill time. I waited.

25 minutes dragged by, and I hated every single one of them. And then it was time. I drove into his driveway, got out of my car, my 'whore' purse dangling over my right shoulder, and I made my entrance.

This house was amazing. The downstairs was huge, with the most fantastic kitchen I'd ever seen. The lounge, beautifully decorated and open plan to a massive dining area that led to the back yard, which, in itself, was about a half-acre. In the kitchen Thor1 had laid on a spread that consisted of beers, wines, gins and vodkas and soft drinks, accompanied by an array of sandwiches, chips, and nuts, chocolates and a few nice-looking cakes. Everything seemed more than perfect, other than the 'bimbo' girls he'd invited. None of them seemed to care that they were surrounded by 15 horny guys just hanging around waiting to fuck them. They were more interested in chatting in their little cliques, smoking pot and helping themselves to food and drink. All in their 20's and much younger than me, I balked when I saw my 'competition'. Then out of the blue, I got a tap on my shoulder.

"Carew, what the fuck are you doing here?"

One of my regular clients appeared out of nowhere. We hugged. I was so happy to see him.

"I'm a voyeur" he told me. "I paid less than the other guys who are here to fuck all of them." he continued, as he pointed to the ladies who were spread across the room, "but I just want to watch"

"How much did you pay?" I asked.

"$140, but all the other guys, the one's you're going to fuck, they paid $400" I quickly did the math. Thor1 was losing money. The math was not in his favor, and it didn't add up. Why was he losing money? As I arrived at this conclusion, Thor1 stepped up onto the main stairwell of the home, which, led to three other bedrooms, each one with two queen beds, the fourth bedroom was situated on the lower floor, also with two queen beds. Next to each bed was a tray. On the tray, a supply of condoms, lube, sanitizer and mints.

"People" he began, "Here are our rules. Any violation of these rules will lead to ejection. I hope you understand that while we are on a strict time limit of three hours, these rules are not subject to interpretation. What I am about to tell you is serious and sacrosanct, so don't even think about breaking any of them."

As I looked around the room, I noticed there were two black guys, one of whom was a total hunk, three Asians, two Hispanics and the rest were old white guys, some in their 50's, some older, with maybe one or two in their 40's. Quite the rogues gallery. Thor1 continued.

"Rule 1, no fucking without condoms. Rule 2, no cell phones. Rule 3, no one can get drunk. Now if we are all clear on these rules, I want to let you know that there is one last rule, a very important one, and that rule is, if you finger any of the girls, for any amount of time, and by that, I mean, 1 second or 10 minutes, you MUST, and I will reiterate this again, YOU MUST, wipe or wash your hands before fingering any of the other girls. Do I make myself clear?"

Everyone in the room nodded in agreement.

"OK, it's 1.10 PM, and it's time to fuck" as he finished his little speech, he pointed to me with one finger, and he mouthed in silence while summoning me with that very same finger, 'you, follow me"

We went upstairs, Thor1 leading me by my outstretched arm. We entered the first bedroom, and before he could say one word to me, I stripped naked, took off his pants and underwear, and I blew him. He came in less than 20 seconds, something I would have never guessed would have happened. I believed, rightly or wrongly that since Thor1 was the orgy organizer, that he'd be a to be a true pro at this and I was shocked he'd cum so fast. He just couldn't hold it. What an amateur.

"What now, Big Boy?" I laughed as I looked at his dick. It was still hard and he was wiping up the mess. "You taking the little blue pills?" His face went pure red, but I figured all the guys would be taking them, otherwise how were they going to fuck all the girls?

The party was on. As Thor1 zipped up his pants to move on to the next girl, three guys came into the room. I was still completely naked and now spread eagled on the bed. One took me by the neck and shoved his cock in my throat, one of the other two went deep into my pussy with his erect cock, while the third had his cock in my right hand, urging me to rub him hard. This went on for 20 minutes. One of the 3 then left and the other two fucked me, one at a time.

While they were fucking me, another guy came in and decided to take a liking to my asshole while I was being fucked in all my other holes. Number 2 then came, screaming hard as he filled his condom, then number 3 took over fucking my pussy, and although his dick was very small, and I couldn't really feel it, he seemed to be having a great time and eventually came and left. This circus, this stream of guys coming and going went on for an hour. I think I fucked more than 10 of them, at which point, I needed a break. Carew, my client, was watching most of the time I was being fucked, but when I went downstairs to have a break and a libation, I noticed that very few of the other girls were fucking. Maybe 3 of the 8 were at it, while the rest just sat around getting high. I thought to myself, 'why are they even getting paid, I should be getting more money than the $800 I received.'

Carew came and sat next to me. We sat on bar stools, me in my bra and panties, Carew, fully dressed, but obviously horny. I knew him well and I could tell from his eyes that he was desperate to fuck me. He kept his gaze on my pussy, knowing that I just loved to be fingered, and then, after looking around the kitchen to make sure the coast was clear, inserted two fingers deep inside me, bringing me to climax almost immediately. He just had a magic touch most women crave but seldom got to experience, and then, like pulling the trigger on a pistol, he made me squirt so violently that a stream appeared and then exploded, all over the kitchen counter and then the floor. There was no hiding this now. I grabbed him by the hand, rushed him into the bathroom, took out his cock and fucked him bareback, something I'd never allowed him to do before. He was in heaven, and honestly, so was I. I was so horny. He came inside me, I wiped up, opened the bathroom door, exited back into the lounge area and began fucking another of the paying guests. By the time the three hours were over, I was completely exhausted. Thor1 announced at 4 PM that we had 6 minutes left. One guy, a guy who'd fucked me already, and who'd followed me around like a puppy dog for the final hour we were there, came over and said to me, "we have 6 minutes, let's do it again"

We did it, after which, he tipped me $100. He was the second guy to do that. The first, a very well-hung black man, the one I'd had my eye on when I'd arrived, had also tipped me and given me his number. 6 other guys wanted to add me to their 'list' as they called it, guaranteeing they'd come and fuck me as regular clients sometime in the future. The final whistle sounded, Thor1 called an end to proceedings, and we all left, just as quickly as we'd arrived. What a day, what an experience, what a sore pussy.

I headed to Carl's Jnr to eat. I was famished. Thor1 texted me while I was driving, asking me if I'd come back to his next orgy in April. I told him I'd think about it but that I wanted more money because I was the only one doing all the work. Well, me and two other ladies, but really me. He told me that all the guys thought I was a Rockstar and they would all be calling me to become regular clientele. I thanked him while I consumed two Big Carl burgers, which didn't seem enough and I could have probably guzzled down two more, but with all the cum I had rolling around in my tummy, two was enough for that particular moment in time. I got back to Blondie's house, sat down, poured myself a huge glass of tequila and told Blondie, scene by scene, everything that had just happened to me. In most people's world this orgy would have been a surreal experience, but in my world, it just seemed to be another day in paradise!

And as suddenly as this high came, it vanished, pouring itself down that inevitable drain that seemed to transform my life from a sunny day to a rainy mess, without any meaning and without any notice. I will let Blondie continue my story because it's just too hard for me to relate to you.

Back to Blondie

This is Blondie again, speaking to you from the front garden of the house where Daz resides. When you think things are running smoothly and that nothing can possibly go wrong, shit happens, and there's never any good reason why it happens. One phone call, one conversation, one little mistake, and your world can be torn apart, and all normality thrown into complete chaos.

Daz has always been a heavy drinker. I believe she's an alcoholic, and her problem is swept under her own carpet by her inability to admit that she has a problem. No matter where we go, whether it's for breakfast, lunch, dinner, or even if we're just hanging around at my place, Daz always has a drink, or two, in her hand, along with her Vape. When, in the past, I have been to her place, her fridge is filled up with beers, and then the next time I'm there, perhaps only 24 hours later, that same fridge is empty. Now, I know she has three kids and that none of them are old enough to consume alcohol legally, and I also know she has many friends, who I've met, but who rarely, if ever drink, and that leaves one mouth and one mouth only for the consumption of 24 beers per night, plus whatever else she drinks when she's at my place and when she's out with clients. Yes, Daz clearly has issues, issues I have tried to approach her with, face to face, but issues that have been left to fester for quite some time now. In my humble opinion, and also by her own admission, Daz is a time bomb waiting to explode. She lives for the moment, and describes herself as, and I quote, "A functioning alcoholic."

What the fuck is a functioning alcoholic? An alcoholic is an alcoholic, functioning or not, so I know that she knows, she has a problem. My problem now, is how to approach her issues without scaring her into doing something completely off the wall or really stupid. She's a real tightly wound spring, waiting to uncoil, and I just don't want her to explode on my watch.

"Blondie, this is Hunter" the voice at the other end of my phone said, one Sunday afternoon. "Daz been kidnapped, raped and robbed and you need to come to her place right now to take care of her. She's a mess"

How does anyone respond to a message like that? As it happened, I was about 5 minutes away from her home when that call came through, and as soon as I put the phone down, I drove like crazy to Daz's home, anxious to ensure that she was safe and that anything which needed to be taken care of, such as reporting the rape and robbery, was done in a timely manner to the correct authorities. My mind was going around in circles. I couldn't figure out how she could possibly have been raped, because she'd been out for lunch with Jack, and he wasn't going to rape her, or rob her for that matter. They'd planned a quiet lunch in Newport Beach, and I knew that after lunch they were going to go to his place to fuck. They did the same thing on most Sundays, when Daz was able to arrange child care for her two kids and wasn't seeing Hunter. It was almost a given with the two of them, Daz and Jack, they ate, drank and fucked their way through any given Sunday! So, in my own mind, which was severely impaired by the thought of my girl being raped, I couldn't figure out what on earth could have happened, and how anyone as street wise as Daz would ever let that happen to her in the first place. My car pulled up outside her front door.

Hunter had left.

Daz was on her front porch, crying her eyes out, and although seated, as soon as she saw me pull up, she jumped up and ran towards me for a hug, which I provided immediately, and a hug that lasted several minutes. We then went inside and the story began.

Daz began,

"Jack and I went to lunch. I had beers, several of them, then tequila and then some wine and more beers, and then we ate. Jack was pissed because I was wasted, and after we'd finished lunch and had a couple of more cold ones, he and I got into a fight. I told him I wanted to drive, he told me no chance, and that I was drunk. Our fight just escalated, and having insisted on driving me home, Jack got into my car, told me he would drive it to my house, he'd park it, and Uber back, pick me up and drive me home in his truck. It all made sense. I wanted my car at my place, he was willing to oblige. He parked me, unceremoniously, in the back seat of his truck, I gave him the keys to my car, and he drove off. I fell asleep. Suddenly, I was awoken, rather rudely too, by this Asian guy, who was knocking on the back window of the truck. I was startled, thinking it must be the Cops. He just laughed at me and he was mouthing something through the closed window, something I couldn't understand, so I opened the door. Before I could say anything, the Asian guy and a friend of his, bundled me out of the truck, and into their car, which was parked next to the truck. They kidnapped me, taking me to another place, but I don't know where that place was, raped me, and then took my purse with my money and ID and car keys and left me for dead."

I sat there listening to this incredible story, all the time looking at Daz, searching for bruises, scars, blood, anything that suggested any of this had been true. I found nothing. Then Hunter returned, carrying a six pack of beer, something Daz had ordered him to go and fetch. She did not need any more alcohol at this point. She just reeked of booze.

"So" I said to her, quite calmly and with much skepticism, "where did they take you? How much did they steal? What else was in your purse? And where is Jack now?" As I said this, Hunter, who by now was standing next to me, looked at me as if to say 'leave her alone and come over here to chat to me' I did, leaving Daz fighting her tears with a beer and her own thoughts.

"You know she's lying?" he said, "this is all BS and attention seeking crap" Daz couldn't hear this. I was rather surprised, but not shocked.

"You sure?" I asked him

"Yep, I have her car keys, handbag, ID, money and there's nothing missing"

"What about being raped?" I asked

"Does she look like she's been raped?" he replied

"I don't know, what does a rape victim look like Hunter?" I was getting annoyed.

Hunter said, "Look Blondie, her story makes no sense. She says she was kidnapped, raped and robbed. Nothing is missing and if she was kidnapped, how did she get home? The kidnapper would never bring her back here, right?" He had a point.

"Then there's the alcohol and lunch date. Where's her date, Jack?" He brought her car back, but where is he? If he was going to go back and collect her, wouldn't he have found her missing from the back of her truck and reported it to the Cops?"

All valid points.

Daz, who'd sensed we were talking about her, came over to join us.

"Look" I said to her, "you need to go inside, sober up, then look after your kids, at which time you and I can have another conversation."

That just set her off again, and she began displaying all the edicts of an addict, self-pity, anger, ignorance, and had all the hallmarks of being a victim without having been victimized. But who knew what the reality of this situation actually was, and with that in mind, I decided to temper my desire to question and berate her, and I backed off, letting her play the victim until she'd decided to calmed down? Unfortunately, two days later, she still hadn't come around, and was madder than a bull in a china shop. This was going to be an episode that would run and run and run.

After asking Daz to shower and clean herself up and look after her kids, at the time being harassed by Hunter, who wanted to get her and the kids out of the house and into a hotel room, just in case the 'kidnappers' returned, I'd given up, and I'd gone home and put the whole episode to the back of my head, knowing that Daz would arrive to work again the following day, as if nothing had ever happened. I was proved right and wrong, both at the same time. Yes, she arrived to work on Monday morning. At first, she told me that she had three clients booked in to fuck her before lunch time, after which, she stormed into her room, shut the door, probably had a few beers and never surfaced again until 5 or 6 guys had come and gone that day and it was time for her to go pick up her kids. Same thing happened on the April morning, and this time, I know she'd consumed more than 12 beers during that day, because I ended up cleaning the trash from her room, something I detested, but did anyway, just to keep the place clean. There was no doubt in my mind that Daz was a raging alcoholic, the issue I had was how to confront her, how to intervene, or perhaps just leave her to wallow in her own grief and take a step back and let her suffer. Thursday arrived and I decided it was time to act. I was just too old for all this crap.

"Daz, you and I need to have a discussion" I told her, as she walked in my front door, headed to her room and shut the door in my face. I walked in after her, and boy, was I fuming.

"Listen to me!" my voice was raised and my mood was foul, "either you and I talk, or you leave. It's your choice"

She looked and me and began to cry and I knew there and then that this might be the only opportunity I got to make things better between us and to try to make her see the error of her ways and perhaps get her to cut down on her alcohol consumption.

"I want you to tell me one more time what happened last weekend. I know you've told me already, but tell me again" I was more than insistent.

Daz sat back on the chair in her room and began. She related word for word the same story that she'd told Hunter and I three days previous, only this time, she left out one part of the tale that I found to be very interesting. She omitted the part on how she'd managed to get back from where the 'kidnappers' had raped her, to her home. It was at that point I kind of realized that she was perhaps making most of the story up and that what this had become was a cry for help from an alcoholic who was in desperate need of assistance. What she really needed was a real friend to help her with an addiction that was now tearing her apart. Thank goodness I had foresight to understand this and to take matters into my own hands and begin the process of helping Daz to get professional help as soon as possible and to understand that she was just a lost soul staggering through the ordeal of daily life, trying hard to wash away her issues with alcohol. And believe me, Daz had so many issues. She had issues with her ex, her kids, her friends, her parents, but alcohol was her biggest issue, the issue that would kill her if I didn't intervene, and that issue wasn't going away, it was only getting worse.

"What do I need to do to help you realize that you're killing yourself?" I asked her

More tears, more anguish, more cuddles and more discussion followed.

We spent that whole day lying next to one another on her bed. She'd canceled all her clients and listened intently to what I had to say, promising me that things were going to change for the better and that she would do her best to clean up her act. She insisted that she indeed had been kidnapped and raped, assuring me that this story wasn't made up and had happened in real time, refusing to budge from her side of that tale. I didn't argue with her, knowing that to do so would only exacerbate the situation and probably drive our relationship into a state of complete disrepair. At 3 PM, she left to get her kids, and I went to bed for a week. I was exhausted. This was a full-time job, babysitting Daz and the other ladies who came and left my home, all with issues, all with ambitions, but all in need of counseling. This business, the E$cort business, where I'd been ensconced for 23 years, had finally got to me, both physically and mentally. I was drained, drained from being fucked for all those years by guys who came and went, drained from all the nonsense and drama that had followed me, whether it be from friends or from clients, I was just done, and the 'kidnapping' and or 'rape' of Daz, had finally pushed me over the edge. It was time, I decided, for a complete re-think, a reinvention of sorts, and time to move on to new pastures, where earning a living would have to be a simpler process, and something more enjoyable than this.

Finale - Let's All Cum Together

My 'rebirth', or 'awakening', came during this crazy episode with Daz. The fact that I was unable to prove either way whether she'd been kidnapped and raped, bothered me immensely and led me to sit down and have a complete re-think about my life and where I was going. I was now 56 years old, I had been there, done that, seen it all, other than traveling all around the world, my life had been eventful, and I must say, self-satisfying too. Yes, I had been in situations I'd never dreamed would happen to me, and yes, I had taken a career path that some might say was self-destructive, but honestly, I had enjoyed 99% of what I'd done and I would go so far as to say that my career choice, E$corting in Orange County California, had been the best thing I could have possibly done. After all, I rarely had to worry about working 9-5 in an office, my clients had been, for the most part, rich guys, and my love of sex had been satisfied several times a day for more than 30 years, experiencing virtually everything a human body would want to do in bed, and out of bed, but with so many different guys, who, for the most part, had been a pleasure to fuck. There are so many of you out there who could never understand why I chose the sex industry to make my fortune, a fortune that never really materialized, but I have loved what I've done, from day one until now. Money has come and money has gone, and with better advice from so called friends, perhaps my financial situation would be in a better place today, unfortunately, due to some awful advice and dodgy investments, it's not. No matter what though, I have enjoyed what I've done and when I look back at my experiences, there's really not a lot I would change. Again, I don't expect anyone outside of this industry to understand what I am saying here, just take my word for it, it's been a fun time. I have met so many people in my life, some good and others not so good, but for the most part, some of those who I have embraced, especially some of my clients, have been wonderful friends and remain that way, even today. Life has taken me in many directions, but now, today, as I sit quietly contemplating my past, writing this memoir, life has suddenly change. I am in my mid to late 50's, knowing that my days as an E$cort are numbered. Indeed, I have no interest in sex right now, not that I don't want to have it now and again, but to have three or four guys fuck me every day, well, let's just say that my little kitty isn't quite up to it. I have some clients that remain with me, like loyal puppy dogs, but other than that, I don't advertise, unless Daz needs me for a threesome or for gentle relief when a client needs more than she can offer, which I am pleased to say, isn't that often. My time is now spent playing the stock market, a game for me, but a game that I have become really proficient at. I make great money, but then again, it's kind of boom time in that department and although I appreciate the money coming in every day, I do realize and understand that in this market, anyone could probably cash in and make a living. I will, however, take what I can get and I appreciate the opportunity to participate. I often go to one particular web site in the morning when I wake up, looking for daily investment tips, and to date, this same site has increased my wealth quite considerably over the past few months. My limited knowledge of stocks and shares has now become expanded and I am able to make good judgement calls on stocks that I'd previously never heard of. The fear of the great unknown has vanished and my risk-taking skills are far outweighing the benefits of my fears that haunted me in the past. Years ago, I would never have dreamed of trading stocks on a daily basis. Yes, the occasional tip would come my way through a client or two, and sometimes I would act on that tip and make a few bucks, perhaps lose a few bucks too. But now, things have really changed for me, becoming more decisive and ready to move on to new challenges, edging me closer to that dream, the dream of owning my own home and having 'fuck you' money to hand out to whomever I want, whenever I want.

    Moses dumped me, yes, while I was putting this book together, he unceremoniously dumped me. I was sitting at my sister's home in Oklahoma City, when my phone rang. Moses, I believed, was calling me to make sure I was doing OK. I'd been away a week and I hadn't heard from him, and that was unusual in our relationship. He still had no idea what I did for a living, but I was almost on the verge of telling him, only because I thought that the relationship had some kind of potential and if that was the case, coming clean was going to be best, especially if we were going to spend more time together. I answered the phone.

Moses said, "Hi, I think we need to take a break. Fuuuuuukkk!"

Honestly, that was all he said.

My response. "OK, if that's what you want"

I never heard from him again. I think he'd found someone younger and prettier, but I will probably never know. The best kisser I'd even met, was now history. God was definitely telling me something!

Sex is still available if I need it, but managing Daz and others like her has also become a priority. Not only a priority, but also a distraction, leading to arguments, sleepless nights and sessions that resemble counseling of the highest order. An example of this happened last week, when Hunter decided to call me, just as I was going into TJ Max to change some clothing I didn't like. I was sitting in my car when his call came through, thinking to myself, do I pick up or not? I picked up. The call, one of several he made to me each week since he and Daz became 'an item', lasted more than an hour, at which point, Hunter had not only talked my ears off, both of them, but had also confessed to me yet again, for the 25th time, that he was madly in love with Daz and wanted to marry her. Quite what all of this has to do with me, I fail to understand, but he seems to use me as his sounding board when he's feeling susceptible to her crazy behavior. The two of them are like fireworks with a short fuse, and one tiny match can set them both off with an explosive reaction that can rival any earthquake. Daz really loves Hunter, and the feeling seems to be mutual, and when Hunter needs confirmation of Daz's intent, he calls me and talks for hours on end, just to retrieve the confidence he'd seemingly lost five minutes before contacting me. It's such a crazy situation and it leads to nothing but grief for me, as I soon found out after putting the phone down to Hunter that afternoon. I exchanged my clothing and headed home, when entering through my garage door, I was simply attacked by Daz, who by then had been drinking yet again, and was in the foulest of moods.

"What the fuck are you doing B !!!" she shouted, with me having no idea what she was talking about. My initial reaction is always, take a step back, look straight into her eyes, assess if she's drunk or sober or somewhere in between, then make a quick plan on how to combat her aggression, knowing she always calms down in the end, even if it takes 5 minutes or 5 days.

On this occasion, it took an hour. She was pissed that I'd spoken to Hunter, having been told by him that I'd called to chat about her. I insisted I'd never ever called him to talk to him, ever, and that it was indeed he who always called me. Whatever her mood, Daz rarely listens and after some back and forth, asked to see my cell phone, where, after me passing it over to her, she proceeded to go through all my calls, confirming my side of the story of course. Daz then immediately, realizing she'd been in the wrong, transformed her personality into this cutesy, crying, self-absorbed, young teenaged girlie, kind of persona, where the only thing that matters is that I feel sorry for her, and that I accept instantly, the apology she isn't giving. Her apologies always come in the form of tears and self-pity, which, through time, I have learned to accept and to move on. It's just the way she is, and I get that, but it drives me insane, even though I love her to bits and as she quite rightly tells me, 'We were born to be together and we love each other more than any other two people on the planet' And it rarely ends there. I have two other ladies who work from my home and their drama is just as bad, if not worse than Daz's. With my 20 plus years of experience in this industry, they all rely on me for advice, help and for friendship when things go wrong. When things are going well, they take me for granted, again, something I have grown to accept over the years, knowing that I play a part in their lives, and that part is important, but really a 'bit' part, and a part they consume like alcohol, until things go badly wrong, and there I am, the bit part, ready and waiting to mop it all up and make it better. It's become my life now, and with that and the stocks that I buy and sell, my life has once again become full, in fact, fuller than it ever has been before. I am no saint, and of course, neither are they, but at the end of the day, we are all human, and human have good days and bad days, and I will be there for all of them through both.

From the day I began having sex, all those years ago, right up until today, I have loved every moment of every fuck I have ever had. Most of the sex I have had has been good, some not so good, but I have loved it nonetheless, if I hadn't then there's no way I could have ever entered this profession and been happy. I have also had great sex, momentous sex and mind-blowingly marvelous sex, which has far outweighed the good and not so good, encouraging me to keep going for all these years, knowing that my little pussy has been well-serviced and kept happy, and my bank account, even though it's had its ups and downs, has been mostly fluid and I have never had to rely on any husband to keep me in the style that I have become accustomed to. That style by the way, is very simple.

Changes always happen, and right now, while reminiscing in this book, I have realized that change is the one constant thing I have lived through since I was a child. Nothing, other than my parents and my siblings, has remained the same, although, as I've delved deep into my past in the pages of this book, I have realized that really everything is the same. I live in the same area I have always lived in, and my friends, the close one's at least, are the same as they've been for many years. I have always tried to be a nice and decent human being, and even though my adventures into the world of sex and debauchery may seem inconsistent with your views of decency, I can assure you, and I myself am comfortably assured, that my honesty and integrity remain intact, no matter what mud is slung in my direction. With Daz and the other ladies in my home, I have made new tracks that will enable me to conduct myself as more of a madame than an E$cort in the years to come. I am constantly organizing appointments, clothing, shopping trips and fun nights out, for all the ladies who surround me, giving me more of an 'executive' roll, and a roll that I feel I can become comfortable with as time marches on. I have been good at what I've done, from selling candies, to E$corting, and I know that whatever life throws at me in the future, I will be good at that too. My lifestyle is very simple. I don't need a lot to make me happy, and I know for sure that marriage, once something I might have contemplated, is just not for me. I am too independent, too set in my ways, and probably, at 57 years of age, too old, to meet anyone who would care to live with me full-time. I have mixed feelings on co-habitation anyway, and living a life alone, although never without company, is something I can handle, certainly from a mental standpoint. Physically? Who knows, but I have had enough sex to last three lifetimes, possibly four, and if I never had sex again? Well, I don't think I would care.

Being the 'Secret E$cort' in this book, has been fun, and I hope that I have been able to bring to life the trials and tribulation of not only my life and how difficult it can be to work in the sex industry, but also the lives of other ladies, all mentioned in this book, and just how hard they work, rest and play. This industry can age you well before your time, but thank goodness, it hasn't done that to me. I feel good that I can pick my moment to go into semi-retirement, if not full retirement, before retirement decides for me that time is up. My attitude will always be the same, live for each day, and my purpose, given to me from the God that I firmly believe in? Satisfaction to those who cannot attain peace in any other place.

All of the characters in this book have had their names change to protect their identities, but I can assure you that all of the stories told and the places we have visited, are accurate and true. I might, one day, consider writing another novel, outlining the seedier, yes, the seedier, side of this industry, but for now, I hope you have enjoyed my journey as much as I have. There's a massive issue with sex-trafficking all over this planet, and one of my intentions when commissioning this story, was to try not only to raise awareness to this issue, but also to raise funds for the charities and organizations who are trying to fight the problem around the globe. My own experiences of sex-trafficking have been few and far between, but that doesn't mean that it doesn't exist. It is rife, not only in the United States, but in many other countries around the world. Young girls sold for sex, against their will, and it needs to stop. I am not a politician, but I am a human being, and what happens to these young ladies after they are kidnapped and sold, is beyond all comprehension. With that in mind, I urge you, the reader, to consider donating either your time or your money to try to fight the wrongs that are sex-slavery. We live in a cruel world, but cruelty is often overshadowed by desires that are not necessarily dignified.

Sex-slavery is not only undignified, it's inhumane. Until the next time, I remain, The Secret E$cort

Epilogue

After completing my story, I wanted to just add some updates, additions that seemed to make sense from the standpoint of finishing stories that had already begun. Their completion I hope will bring clarity to what has already been said and provide you with an ongoing balanced look at how life goes on but yet, nothing changes.

Daz, as you now know, has always been a heavy drinker, and unfortunately, this hasn't changed in the past few months. No matter how hard I try to intervene in her life, it doesn't seem to matter and the drinking and fighting between her and Hunter, carries on regardless. Her DUI has now been upgraded to a 3-year suspended sentence, plus 100 hours of community service, which, after appeal, was reduced to 20 hours. If she fucks up again, it's prison time for sure. She and Hunter are still an item, although the subject of marriage, which is still on the cards, has not been approached for several months. They still fight like cat and dog, and regardless of where they are and what they are doing, their volatility as a couple, remains the only constant thing in their relationship. A few weeks ago, they were attending a party at Lucy's new home, which, by the way, is a massive 4000 sq ft mansion in Huntington Beach. They arrived on time, but before getting to the front door of Lucy's house, the got into a fist fight, all captured on the Ring camera system Lucy had installed a few weeks back. I have seen the footage, and it resembles the 'Rumble In The Jungle" when Ali beat Frasier. It began so innocently, but within moments, Daz can be seen 'laying' into Hunter, with several right hooks that even the great Ali would have been proud of. She pummeled Hunter, at least 5 times, several punches hitting him on his cheeks and nose. The damage, thank goodness, was minimal, before Hunter gained control of her and after pushing her to the ground, was able to calm her down, while sitting on top of her tits, and asking her quite calmly, to 'get a grip', which she eventually did. After that, according to Lucy, they were back again to being lovey-dovey, holding hands and madly in love with one another. This relationship has always baffled me, and probably always will. There's no point in going over ground I've already covered, but Daz is an accident waiting to happen, and in my humble opinion, if she makes it to her 40th birthday without being killed or killing herself, or at least without doing serious damage to her body, I will be absolutely amazed! She still makes great money, still has men lined up around the clock, and still fucks for free when tattoos turn her on. There's not too much I can add, other than, perhaps one day she will write her own book, and boy, will is have some great stories.

I took in another lady a couple of weeks back, after advertising on my usual web site. I received over 40 responses, all women looking to share my home and rent the only room I have left. Some of the applications were dismissed in seconds, but one in particular, which I received from a lady who goes by the name SpeedBunny6, stood out, along with the beautiful photographs she sent with her reply. I presumed we had hit the jackpot, when she told me she was making upwards of 200 grand a year, and that $1200 a month in rent to me wouldn't be an issue. Boy, was I to be proven wrong? We arranged an interview, she arrived, and at first, I believed it was someone who'd come to the wrong address and was knocking on the wrong front door. SpeedBunny6, was nothing like the pictures she'd sent to me. Her body was 20 years older and 200lbs heavier. I was shocked, and so were the rest of my crew. Surely this couldn't be the same woman in the pictures? Well, she was, and after chatting with her for a few minutes, believing everything she told me, I thought to myself, "There probably is a market for BBW woman, so why not give her a try?"

She moved in, and since that day, it's been a disaster, and now, I can't get rid of her. She's encamped!

She does drugs, has no money, is always miserable and men hate her. What on earth was I thinking when I decided to let her in? I don't know! I never learn, and now, with her fat ass parked on a bed in one of my rooms, her rent overdue, her mind, always as high as a kite, I just cannot get rid of this woman. It's as if she was sent to my house by the devil, just to haunt me. It's all about to come to a head now, and within the next few days, I hope to have her out of there and on her way to pastures new.

I have also increased my day trading portfolio, and I spend time buying and selling stocks and crypto each morning. I am doing fairly well with this hobby, and my bank balance is once again flourishing. I have another business that I would like to start. I see an opening for being a consultant to E$corts around the area, or perhaps around the country. These women are all cash flush, but don't know how to run their own affairs. I see a niche, educating all of them in the art of business, cleaning up their cash and making them all 'legal' entities. Something I have managed to do and perhaps can pass on to them, using the benefits of my prior experiences. But, with all of that in mind, and with my life as an E$cort really and truly at an end, who knows where my next paycheck will come from. Maybe in a year or two, more tales from my past will warrant another volume of The Secret E$cort, but until that day arrives, if indeed it ever does, I will leave you with a thought, and this is something I have always believed in. If men and women were meant to be monogamous, then why do so many of them seek other partners, either inside or out of their current relationships? If they want to cheat, let them, only let them cheat with us ladies who need the money. I can't understand why women, any woman, would fuck for nothing. It's out there ladies. There's a fortune to be made. Go spread your legs and reap the benefits of great sex and lots of cash. Trust me, you will never regret it!

© Alan Zoltie   October 2021